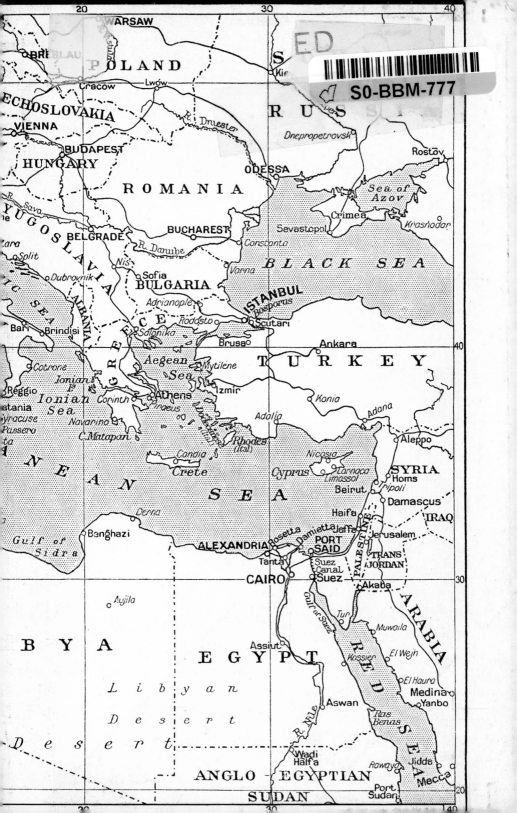

THE DANGEROUS SEA

THE MACMILLAN COMPANY
NEW YORK · BOSTON · CHICAGO · DALLAS
ATLANTA · SAN FRANCISCO

THE DANGEROUS SEA

The Mediterranean and its Future

By

GEORGE Edward SLOCOMBE

New York

THE MACMILLAN COMPANY

1937

PRINTED IN THE UNITED STATES OF AMERICA, BY THE
NATIONAL PROCESS COMPANY, INC., NEW YORK, N. Y.

CONTENTS

PART ONE: THE GATES OF THE SEA

CHAPTER   PAGE

I. The Mediterranean in History 9
II. Gibraltar 17
III. Tangier 26

PART TWO: THE SHORE OF EUROPE

I. Spain: the Fallen Empire 39
II. France in the Mediterranean 48
III. French Strategy: Oil and Men . . . 55
IV. French Air and Sea Power 62
V. Italy before 1914 71
VI. The Italy of Mussolini 79
VII. The Rise of the New Roman Empire . . 89
VIII. Albania: Italy's Puppet State . . . 104
IX. Jugoslavia and the Adriatic . . . 111
X. The Balkan Pact and the Little Entente . . 121
XI. Turkey, the U.S.S.R. and the Straits . . 132

PART THREE: THE SHORE OF AFRICA

I. Morocco 149
II. Algeria 160
III. Tunisia 167
IV. Libya Italiana 178
V. Egypt and the Sudan 185
VI. The Suez Canal 205

5

PART FOUR: THE SHORE OF ASIA

CHAPTER   PAGE

I. SYRIA 215

II. PALESTINE AND TRANS-JORDAN 221

III. THE ARAB RENAISSANCE 228

PART FIVE: PROBLEMS AND PERILS

I. THE CONQUEST OF ABYSSINIA 237

II. THE STRATEGIC ISLANDS 243

III. THE SPANISH CIVIL WAR 250

IV. BRITISH SEA POWER AND SECURITY 260

V. THE MEDITERRANEAN IN THE NEXT WAR . . 269

VI. THE CRADLE OF CIVILISATIONS—AND THEIR TOMB . 280

PART ONE

THE GATES OF THE SEA

CHAPTER I

THE MEDITERRANEAN IN HISTORY

[1]

BETWEEN thirty and forty thousand years ago the Mediterranean was a great tract of swamps and forests, lakes and prairies. The wild horse and the woolly mammoth and the bison ranged over it in herds. From his cave the Cro-Magnon man, six feet tall and big-brained and haunted by the artist's itch to be remembered of posterity, stalked them with cunning and appreciative eyes, slew them with spears of sharpened flint, clothed himself with their skins, nourished himself with their flesh, and commemorated this first of the Mediterranean conquests by making little figures of clay and eloquent drawings on the rock-face.

Twenty thousand years later the feathered Azilians left their vivid comments on contemporary life upon the walls of the Mas d'Azil cave. The bison and the mammoth had retreated into the fastnesses of the North. The Azilians hunted the diminishing herds of wild horse, the still plentiful but more suspicious herds of deer, with bows and arrows. They sewed their skins together with fine bone needles, fished in the lakes and rivers with hooks of bone and, as one of their cave drawings shows, smoked out bees' nests for their honey. Even before this time the pre-historic Mediterranean man had learned navigation. He floated on the windless lakes of his great domain in boats of basket-work covered with skins. He fished and hunted and sowed his seed in the propitious seasons of the moon; made sun-circles of great stones and mummies of his dead.

And then, between fifteen and twelve thousand years ago, the great earth barrier between the Pillars of Hercules gave way, and the waters of the Atlantic rushed through,

9

covering the swamps in which the woolly mammoth had roamed, and the pastures in which the wild horse had grazed. They spread steadily until they halted at the foothills of the Atlas and the Sierra Nevada, the spurs of the Alps and the Pyrenees, the flanks of the Apennines and the Dolomites, the great range of the Taurus. They made the tormented outline of modern Greece, the fantastic boot of Italy. They drowned a great hill country in the Aegean until only the red peaks of the submerged highlands rose out of the purple sea in a complex archipelago of small isles. They left intact the great submarine mountains of Corsica and Sardinia and Malta and Cyprus and Crete, to create problems of nationality and minority for future empires. And they delineated, for the next twenty and perhaps for the next fifty thousand years, the frontiers of the three great continents of Asia, Europe and Africa, which between them until comparatively recent times held all of the known and all the conjectured world.

The shores of this great inland sea, smiling, fertile and bountiful, were destined to become, during all the years of recorded history, the scene of the flowering and the decay of successive civilisations : the oldest of them so remote and so long buried by time that its outlines are only slowly coming to light in the inscriptions of a still undeciphered language on the Sumerian bricks and tiles ; and the youngest, that of Rome, so recent by comparison that its still-mighty monuments are as those of yesterday.

To the eastern borders of the Middle Sea came successive hordes of Semitic conquerors, wild and warlike hosts of nomads from Central and Western Asia, founding dynasty after dynasty in Egypt, empire after empire in Babylon and Nineveh. When Hammurabai reigned in Babylon the Semitic Phœnicians were already established in Tyre and Sidon and other great trading cities on the eastern coast of the Mediterranean. Their purple-sailed galleys had ranged the length and breadth of the inland sea. They had established colonies in Spain and Gaul, and on the coast of Africa had founded the city which was to be the seat of the empire of Carthage. Later they were to sail through the Pillars of Hercules northwards past the coast of Spain and France to the shores of Britain.

Long before the Greek captains or the Roman legionaries brought civilisation to the remote westerly shores of the inland sea, the Phœnicians traded dyes and spices and wines and cloth for Iberian copper and Cornish tin.

No grimmer evidence of the impermanence of empire and the finality of civilisation can be found than that furnished by the history of the Mediterranean. It has seen the great Ægean civilisation, at its zenith in Mycenæ and Troy, and in the Cnossos of the Minoan kings of Crete in the year 2500 B.C., overthrown and destroyed by the Aryan Greeks. It has seen the splendours of Egypt wax and wane and wax again; the Semitic conquerors of Asia Minor overthrown by other marauding Semites; a great Assyrian empire rise in Babylon, and its successors drive the Ethiopian invaders out of Egypt, to be attacked and defeated in their turn by the Medes and Persians; the age of Pericles dawn in Athens, and the empire of Alexander rise upon the ruins of the Greek republic. The empires founded upon its shores have extended as far westwards as the Atlantic Ocean, and as far eastwards as the Indian. Its quays have been loaded with the spoil of Africa and Asia. From its crowded harbours sailed the first ships that rounded Africa and ventured out wide into the waters that lave the shores of the New World. The influence of its two last and greatest civilisations is still powerful over the thoughts and actions of the white races, and their legacies of Roman law and Greek art and philosophy are still intact and treasured. Finally, it has witnessed the birth, the early struggles, the long triumph and the slow decay of two of the world's great religions. And for many centuries it was the stage on which the followers of Christ or Mahomet did battle, while time and the world seemed to stand still until the issue should be determined.

[2]

Until the twentieth century all the known naval battles of the world had been fought in or near Mediterranean waters. In 480 B.C. the great fleet of Xerxes the Persian was defeated by the Greeks in the bay of Salamis. In the following year, at Mycale, the remnants of it were destroyed. Five years later, in 474 B.C., the Etruscan fleet was overwhelmed by the Greeks of Sicily. The great struggle of the

Greek states for ascendancy which culminated in the Peloponnesian War (431 to 404 B.C.) was largely waged in an attempt to wrest naval supremacy from Athens. The fleets of Tyre and Sidon for long crippled the advance of Alexander of Macedon against the Persian hosts of Darius III. With the rivalry of Rome and Carthage, both essentially naval powers, the Mediterranean's scarcely interrupted history of naval warfare became crowded and tumultuous. Under the heights of Actium, in 31 B.C., between Octavian and Mark Antony, was fought the greatest naval battle of the old world. And in the same historic waters, in the Gulf of Lepanto in 1571, Don John of Austria, half-brother of Philip II of Spain, led the fleets of Christendom to victory in what was, until Trafalgar, the greatest sea fight in eighteen hundred years.

Loss of sea power in the Mediterranean brought to nothing Napoleon's dreams of an Empire in the East, as it was eventually to aid in the destruction of his Empire in the West. The victories of Nelson ended, for nearly a century, the long tale of rivalry and carnage in those fateful waters. After the battle of Navarino in 1827, when the Turkish fleet was destroyed by British and French warships, and the last vestige disappeared of a naval power once and for several hundred years supreme in the Mediterranean, no further engagement between ships of war took place until 1914, and then two antique German cruisers, the *Goeben* and the *Breslau*, gained a brief notoriety by challenging the Allied naval supremacy in the Middle Sea.

[3]

No stretch of water in the world compares with the Mediterranean in historic, in ethnographical and in human interest. Its horizons embraced the ancient world. Its dawns rise to-day equally over Arab and Greek, Jew and Egyptian, Italian and Slav, Spaniard, Turk, Frenchman and Moor. The humble men who live and labour on its shores, symbolised in the Provençal poet Mistral's character *Calendal*, approximate to an easily recognisable Mediterranean type, born out of a community of interests and occupations, many thousand years of intermingling of blood—Phœnician, Greek, Roman, Jew and Moor—a common diet, a common climate of sun and temperate wind, a common vista of vine-clad rocks and green or purple sea. It is the most personal of all the waters of the globe. Its secrets are darker, more ancient, more hidden. The Thames, the Tiber, the Seine, the Volga, the Rhine are creations of yesterday, capricious, unstable streams of water that pass out of the sight of men and are forgotten. The Mediterranean, in all its ten or fifteen thousand years of history, has remained constant, a tideless sea that mysteriously renews itself, a sea to all practical purposes as closed as it was in the times of the Romans, fixed, immutable, the many-coloured, enigmatical witness of the rise and fall of all the races of mankind whose blood mingles with our own.

[4]

From the earliest days it has drawn hungry invaders to its shores—the Goths and Vandals from the North, the Huns from the East, the Gauls and Franks and Norsemen. Alone the negro races of Africa, save for one brief Ethiopian descent on Egypt, have remained indifferent to its lure. Since the beginning of recorded time its waters have been ploughed by the oars of land-hungry, sun-hungry, gold-hungry seafarers, peoples like the Phœnicians incessantly in migration, piratical adventurerers like the Greeks and the Carthaginians. Until the last century the general drift of its commerce and migration was westwards. The straits of Gibraltar, through which the primitive mariner might win to the open Atlantic, were the inevitable objective of any bold and curious adventurer in Greek and Roman times. The rich, fertile, unsettled lands of Gaul and Iberia, the long, smiling coast of Africa from Carthage to Cape Spartel, offered wealth and plunder and escape to the crowded populations of the Eastern Mediterranean.

It is true that the movement of trade, the administrative channels, the imperial communications of the empires of Alexander and Augustus ran both eastwards and westwards. But during the long centuries of darkness which followed the fall of Rome and Byzantium, the centre of power in the Mediterranean again shifted to the Eastern waters. From Constantinople the Ottoman Empire overran Egypt, Persia, Arabia and North Africa as far as the Atlantic.

Tunis, the ancient Carthage, Algiers and Tangier became pashaliks of the Turkish despots. The closed sea became a sea of corsairs. Between the eleventh and the fifteenth centuries the Crusaders made repeated but vain efforts to stem the tide of aggression which ran more and more strongly from the East. But the powers of Christendom, disunited and feeble enough against the Saracens on land, were powerless against them at sea. The Knights of the Order of St. John of Jerusalem fell back steadily before the infidel. St. Jean d'Acre was abandoned; then Rhodes. Cyprus, a possession of the republic of Venice, remained in Christian hands only at the price of great concessions by the Venetians, a long and futile attempt to preserve by cowardice and bribery an island which was eventually to be defended heroically and heroically to fall.

In the reign of Suleiman the Magnificent the sea power of the Turk was unchallenged from the ports of Syria to the coasts of Spain. The Ottoman admirals and their confederates, the Moors of Africa, raided the coasts of Europe at will, defying the timorous Venetians in their own waters. The Emperor Charles V made a vain attempt to smoke the corsairs out of Tunis and Algiers. From the latter town he retired in confusion. In Tunis he succeeded in installing a Christian garrison in a fort which was to be captured during the reign of his son Philip. The island of Malta, on which the Knights of Jerusalem had retired at last, was long besieged and desperately defended. And not until late in the sixteenth century, after the Turks had brought their long and insolent supremacy in the Mediterranean to a triumphant climax by destroying the Venetian garrison in Cyprus, did the great naval armaments of the united Christian powers dare to challenge once for all the issue of sea power in those historic waters, and succeed in breaking the Ottoman stranglehold on the ancient Latin Sea.

[5]

Thenceforward the Mediterranean was Spain's, if she had cared or dared to grasp it. But the admirals of Philip II were increasingly preoccupied, after the glorious year of Lepanto, in protecting the great treasure fleets from the Indies, in convoying troopships to and merchant vessels from the Spanish Netherlands, and in resisting the growing aggressiveness of the sailors of Elizabeth. The preparations for the great expedition against England absorbed all Philip's mind, and most of his available gold, men and ships. The great sea which washed the shores of his dominions in Spain and Italy, which assured his communications with Genoa and Naples and Sicily, was outside the narrow field of his political and military imagination.

Philip II was by birth and instinct half Northern, and wholly Northern in his intense ambitions, his preoccupation with England and Elizabeth, and the revolt in the Netherlands. He had no large imperial ideas. He paid little attention to his great father's conquests and acquisitions in the New or the Old World. The grandiose titles of Emperor of the Indies and Dominator of Asia which he had inherited from Charles V he dismissed as mere contemporary verbiage. He deliberately sacrificed the fruit of his half-brother Don John's victories in the Mediterranean, as he would as cheerfully have sacrificed his father's immense legacy in the Indies, for the sake of that dream of spiritual and military domination in Northern Europe.

For long he had enjoyed the title, if not the substance, of sovereignty in the Low Countries. After the murder of the last Valois king, Henri III, he enjoyed the substance, if not the title, of sovereignty in France. The succession to the heretic Elizabeth of England seemed to the solitary recluse of the Escorial, who had already briefly enjoyed the prerogatives of kingship as consort to Mary Tudor, to be no more difficult than the suppression of a revolt of insolent burghers in Antwerp. The defeat of the Armada disillusioned him. And the destruction of the sea power of Spain on the barren coasts of Scotland and Ireland rendered the greatest military power of the Mediterranean impotent to sail peaceful shipping at her pleasure in waters which she had the strongest claim to command.

For two centuries the great sea knew the discipline of neither Christian nor infidel. The Turkish power waned, and with it the power of Venice. The corsairs of the African coast shook off their vassalage to the Sultans in Constantinople, and pursued a career of lawless brigandage, unchecked by any hand save that of the assassin who lurked in wait for every lord of Algiers or of Tunis. Not until the end of the eighteenth century was the rising sea power of the English freely exerted in those waters. And not until the advent of Napoleon did it establish a mastery which has remained unbroken until our own era.

CHAPTER II

GIBRALTAR

[1]

FOR nearly a century no attempt was made to claim the abandoned heritage of Spain in the Mediterranean. The successors of Elizabeth were reluctant to provoke new quarrels with the Catholic power, or had other and more dangerous business on their hands nearer home. Cromwell, the first of the economic imperialists, had he lived long enough, might have restored a Roman order in the piratical sea. His admirals Blake and Montague were sent on police expeditions against the Algerian pirates and the Spanish possessions in Italy. Plans were even discussed for the seizure and the holding of the bottle-neck of the great sea against all comers. Either side of the Straits seemed to the Protector's lieutenants a desirable post of vantage to command in the long struggle which they dimly envisaged. On the African shore lay the Arab harbour and Portuguese fort of Tangier. Facing it across the narrow waters rose the grim Spanish citadel of Gibraltar. Diplomacy might win the one, if military superiority could not triumph over the other. In September, 1657, General Monk, in a letter to Cromwell, urged the gentler tactic. A visit of the Portuguese ambassador, which the General rightly conjectured to be undertaken for the request of "some favour," provided the opportunity for bargaining.

"There is a castle in the Streights Mouth," wrote General Monk to the Protector, "which the Portugals have called Tangar . . . and which, if they would part with it withal, it would be very useful to us : and they make very little use of it unless it be for the getting of Blackamoors for which His Highness may give him leave to trade. An hundred men will keep the castle and half a dozen frigates there would

17

stop the whole trade in the Streights to such as shall be enemies to us."

In the previous year Cromwell himself had contemplated the possibility of dominating the northern shore of the Straits. In a letter written on April 28th, 1656, to Montague and Blake he asked, after enumerating the places at which the Spaniards might be attacked with profit, " Whether any other place be attemptable ; especially that of the town and castle of Gibraltar, which, if possessed and made tenable by us, would it not be both an advantage to our trade and an annoyance to the Spaniard ; and enable us, without keeping so great a fleet on that coast, with six nimble frigates lodged there to do the Spaniard more harm than by a fleet, and ease our charge ? "

By a remarkable coincidence the same thought had occurred at the same time to Montague, Cromwell's " General at Sea." In a letter written between April 20th and 29th to the Protector the admiral wrote : " I perceive much desire that Gibraltar should be taken. My thoughts as to that are, in short, these : That the likeliest way to get it is, by landing on the sand and quickly cutting it off between sea and sea, or so secure our men there as that they may hinder the intercourse of the Town with the Main ; frigates lying near, too, to assist them—and it is well known that Spain never victualleth any place for more than one month. This will want Four or Five thousand men, well formed and officered."

In the same year, according to Samuel Pepys, an attempt was actually authorised by Cromwell to sever the rock from the mainland. The diarist records in his *Naval Minutes* that either Sir Richard Haddock or Sir John Narborough once confided to him that " had not the ship which was sent by Oliver with spades and wheelbarrows been taken, he had certainly taken Gibraltar and made it an island."

But that attempt, if it was really made, came to nothing. Cromwell died, and with him, for a generation, the naval rivalry between Spain and England. Tangier came into English possession without a blow, as part of the dowry of Catherine of Braganza, and within a few years was surrendered to the Moors. Not until forty-six years after the death of Cromwell was the great effort to capture the citadel of the European shore made, and then, paradoxically enough, it was made at haphazard, not in any deliberation, but carelessly, and as the last-minute enterprise of commanders sent out on a far greater mission and fearing to return empty-handed.

[2]

The Rock which for two hundred and thirty-two years has served as a symbol of empire to the British people and to the world at large, was taken in July, 1704, as a minor trophy of the War of the Spanish Succession. The story is one of dramatic simplicity. To the claims of the grandson of Louis XIV, Philip V, to the throne of Spain, the Grand Alliance had opposed the candidature of a Habsburg prince, the Archduke Charles. England, as a member of the Grand Alliance, undertook the responsibility of landing the Habsburg pretender in Spain. In February of that year he was conveyed to Lisbon by Sir George Rooke with a fleet of twenty-three English ships of war and a land force of sixteen hundred English and Dutch soldiers and marines under Prince George of Hesse. Rooke then took his force through the Straits to Barcelona, which city was reputed to favour the Archduke. On May 16th the fleet anchored off Barcelona, and the marines were landed, only to find that the city was strongly defended by the partisans of the Bourbon king. The English admiral accordingly re-embarked his men, made an ineffectual effort to prevent a French fleet from Brest from joining the Toulon squadron, and retired before superior enemy forces upon Lisbon. In the meantime he was met and reinforced by a fleet of thirty-six English and Dutch vessels under Sir Cloudesley Shovell, and the two commanders held a council of war. The orders brought by Shovell from home offered them three alternative courses. They might make another attack on Barcelona. They might attempt the capture of Cadiz, a course strongly urged upon them by the impatient Habsburg. Or they might blockade the French fleet in Toulon and prevent it from attacking the Italian coast. All three courses were rejected as impracticable, and the council of war, almost in despair, decided on July 17th to essay the capture of Gibraltar.

On July 21st an English-Dutch force under Rear-Admiral Byng appeared off the rock, and was shortly joined by Admiral Rooke with the whole fleet. A summons to surrender was issued and indignantly refused by the Spanish governor. Thereupon the ships were brought up against the rock, marines were landed upon the sand, almost exactly as Cromwell's General at Sea had indicated half a century earlier, and the siege of Gibraltar began. It lasted two days, after which the little Spanish garrison of five hundred men surrendered and marched out with colours flying. The total casualties incurred by the conquerors were but sixty killed and two hundred wounded.

On August 13th the French fleet arrived and attempted to drive off the ships of the conquerors. After a fierce but indecisive engagement the French drew off, and the English squadron returned in triumph to the rock, celebrating their freedom from molestation, for victory it could scarcely be called, by firing harmless broadsides over the now dominated Straits.

[3]

The fortress which they had thus easily captured was in truth one to set fire to the imagination of British sailors and soldiers at the opening of the eighteenth century. It was, as it has remained, the most impressive of natural citadels in the world. Its grim bulk, its unique strategical position, dominating the shores both of Europe and of Africa, its fame in ancient times, its myths and legends, its strange non-European flora, fauna and fevers, its Barbary apes, its mysterious caverns, wells and fortifications, its traces of Roman, Arab and Visigoth, of the Arab conqueror Tarek-el-Zaid—who called it Jeb-el-Tarek, or Hill of Tarek, of which the name of Gibraltar is an obvious corruption— all invested the rock with a curious significance. It had since the earliest times been a symbol of power, both fortress and frontier. As Calpe, one of the Pillars of Hercules, it had marked the boundaries of the ancient world. Its capture by the Visigoths coincided with the fall of the Roman Empire. Its capture by the Arab invader prefigured the impending end of the Iberian empire of the Visigoths. Its re-conquest by the Christian kings, after a struggle which lasted a century and a half and knew ten sieges, ended the Moorish dominion in Spain. Its capture by the English crowned their long and successful naval rivalry with Spain, and set the seal, after two hundred and fifty years during which it had been deemed impregnable, on a policy of imperial enterprise and conquest to which the victors were henceforth committed.

Nevertheless the Spaniards did not soon reconcile themselves to the loss of their citadel. Little over a year after Rooke's victory a determined attempt was made to regain Gibraltar. The Marquis de Villadarias, with a strong force of French and Spaniards, besieged the rock in October, 1705. The siege lasted six months, and was raised in March, 1706, by the victory of an English-Dutch and Portuguese squadron, commanded by Admiral Leake, over the French fleet. Marlborough's victories brought the War of the Spanish Succession to an end, and when peace was made at Utrecht the English were confirmed in their possession of Gibraltar. The Treaty of Utrecht, signed on July 13th, 1713, transferred the rock, town and harbour of Gibraltar to England, leaving in Spanish hands the mainland separated from the fortress by but a few hundred yards of shallow water and sand. The inhabitants of the rock were guaranteed free exercise of the Roman Catholic religion, but Moors and Jews were denied rights of refuge thereon. Elaborate precautions were taken under the Treaty to prevent smuggling from Gibraltar into Spain, and the English conquerors even acquiesced in a clause which denied them jurisdiction over the import of goods into their new possession : a prohibition which seems never to have been abrogated, and to be the origin of the practical freedom from vexatious import duties enjoyed by all classes of goods, from Japanese silks to American petrol, imported into Gibraltar at the present day.

The Treaty of Utrecht did not end Spanish hopes of recovery of the stronghold. The ministers of Philip V, in the course of patient efforts to break up the Grand Alliance, endeavoured without success to persuade or coerce England to restore Gibraltar. In 1718 a formal offer was made for the purchase of the rock, and the English Foreign Secretary, Stanhope, a year later held out hopes that the restitution might be arranged. But neither Stanhope nor any other British minister dared face Parliament with such a proposal, and although George I promised Philip in 1721 to do what he could for Spain, nothing came of the negotiations. Popular sentiment in England, even although the price to be demanded was the tempting Spanish colony of Florida, remained unalterably hostile to any surrender of the rock upon which a century and a half later the British Empire was to be built.

In 1725, however, Spain abandoned diplomacy for force. The Habsburgs by this time were in brief if unnatural alliance with the Bourbons. Gibraltar was to be the reward for Spain's support of the Pragmatic Sanction and the Imperial Ostend Company with which the Austrian Netherlanders hoped to challenge the English and Dutch adventurers in the East Indies. In February, 1727, a considerable Spanish force, twenty thousand men in all, invested Gibraltar under the command of the Count de la Torres. The siege lasted four months and was then terminated by the peace negotiations which ended in the Treaty of Seville.

The fresh war between England and Spain in 1739, undertaken in despite of Walpole, brought the English a number of disasters, but the loss of Gibraltar was not among them. Not until the outbreak of the Seven Years War in 1756 was the rock again menaced. Then the British Admiral Byng, whose father had won the battle of Cape Passaro and had taken part in the original capture of Gibraltar, evaded battle with a superior French fleet, and forced to choose between the loss of Minorca and that of Gibraltar, preferred to sacrifice the former. Byng was court-martialled and shot, and his death inspired Voltaire to the famous witticism : " In England they kill one admiral to encourage the others." He had saved his fleet and with it Gibraltar, anticipating by a hundred and sixty years the decision to be taken by Jellicoe in the battle of Jutland. He did not foresee that in the following year Pitt would offer the great fortress in exchange for lost Minorca. Fortunately for England and for Pitt the offer was rejected, and Gibraltar survived as a British possession to encounter another attack.

It came in 1779, when Spain joined the rebellious American colonies in war against England. Gibraltar was blockaded, and towards the end of the year formally besieged. This, the last and the greatest of the attempts to retake the citadel, fully merits its place among the great sieges of history. It lasted over three years, until peace preliminaries were signed in February, 1783. The rock was attacked in great force and with all the skill known to the military engineers of that time. It was bombarded by floating batteries of heavy guns, the pride and wonder of the age. It withstood an artillery fire more violent and more sustained than any known to have been offered in siege warfare hitherto. It was heroically defended by the garrison of General Sir George Elliott. Besiegers and besieged fought with great valour and tenacity. The famous siege was ended by the naval victories of Rodney, and its end served to mark to the eyes of an admiring people both the rock's impregnability and their own victorious sea power.

[4]

During the century and a half which separate us from the treaty of 1788 Gibraltar has been unchallenged. It was expressly excluded from the negotiations which ended in that treaty. It has never been the subject of negotiation between Great Britain and a foreign power since that time. Nevertheless its future has been frequently enough discussed, and discussed without enthusiasm, in semi-official and official British circles during the past century. The voice of Cobden was raised in favour of its abandonment. Even after the acquisition by the British Government of a controlling interest in the Suez Canal, with the consequent enhancement of Gibraltar's strategical position at the other end of the Mediterranean, military and naval experts continued to cast doubt upon the importance, the impregnability and the utility of the fortress.

The development of aviation, with its creation of a host of new and for the most part incalculable factors in the field of naval warfare, and the enormous increase in the range of artillery, have revived and intensified the discussions of naval and military engineers concerning the strategic importance of Gibraltar. On the one hand, the range and accuracy of modern artillery make it possible for the fortress to command the entrance to the Mediterranean more thoroughly than has ever hitherto been possible. On the other the same factors bring the rock and its more accessible landward defences, its town and harbour and oil reserves, within shelling distance of battery positions of scarcely less great natural strength in Europe and Africa.

During the last war the rock was eagerly discussed by German naval experts. In March, 1917, the late Primo de Rivera, then Captain-General of the Spanish army, publicly suggested an exchange of Ceuta and Melilla for Gibraltar. In the same year Señor Maura made a speech demanding the cession of Tangier and Gibraltar as the price of Spanish neutrality. In 1918, Count Romañones, then Premier, offered Ceuta in exchange for the rock. In 1919, the former U.S. Ambassador to Constantinople, Henry Morgenthau, told his Government that Great Britain would grant the United States equal rights in Gibraltar if President Wilson would accept an American mandate for Constantinople, Armenia and Anatolia.

[5]

The rock is of little or no commercial importance. It imports all it consumes. It produces nothing. It is a picturesque port of call for tourist-cruisers. Its military and naval value is still subject to the test of time. Alone the next Mediterranean war can demonstrate the truth or falsity of its century-old legend of impregnability. Its chief significance is probably still one of prestige : the symbol of maritime power to an imperial nation, the security of whose world communications has scarcely yet been adequately challenged.

There is now, for all the doubts cast upon its utility in the years which immediately followed the World War, less likelihood than ever that it will ever be sold or bartered by Great Britain. The defences of the fortress have been considerably strengthened during the past two years. In British official circles it is not considered likely that hostile aircraft could make much impression upon its hidden batteries, or upon the elaborate shelters prepared for its entire civilian and military population in case of emergency. But one new factor has been created by the modern science of warfare to add to the conditions which determine the strength or weakness of Gibraltar. In the past, as has been seen, the rock has successfully resisted sieges, in part owing to its own great strength, in part owing to British naval supremacy in the surrounding waters. Naval supremacy and natural strength are henceforth not sufficient to prevail against a powerful adversary capable of arming and manning the coast of Africa. The security of Gibraltar, and with it British command of the Straits, will in future depend to a considerable degree upon our relations with the power which possesses the Moroccan fortress of Ceuta, and upon the continued neutrality of Tangier.

CHAPTER III

TANGIER

[1]

GIBRALTAR, Tangier and Ceuta form together an equilateral triangle of which the base rests in Africa and the apex in Europe. Tangier lies in the western angle of the base. To the traveller approaching it from the European shore the picturesque old town presents superficially much the same aspect that it possessed for the sailors of Cromwell. A cluster of white and blue Moorish villas rising in terraces upon a steep hill-side, a walled castle, a dozen slim minarets, and behind them a long range of wild hills. Only upon closer inspection is the extent of the modernisation of Tangier visible : the great tanks and advertisements of American and British oil companies, the new city of miniature skyscrapers along the shore, the modern quay, the great hotels in stucco and concrete. The officers and men of British steamers stare at the promising town regretfully, unconsciously echoing the acquisitive desire of General Monk ; more consciously, perhaps, repeating the command of Nelson : " Tangier must belong to a neutral power ; *if not, it must become English.*"

As we have noted in the preceding chapter, the city actually came into British possession five years after the famous letter written by Monk to the Protector. On the marriage of Charles II and Catherine of Braganza in 1662 it was included in the Portuguese princess's dowry. But in 1684 the Government decided that it was not worth the cost of maintenance, and restored it to the Moors, who had never accepted without armed protest the dominion of Portugal. Thus after being in Christian hands for over 200 years (it was originally captured by the Portuguese in 1471, was in Spanish possession from 1580 to 1656, and in

26

Portuguese from 1656 to 1662), Tangier became again one
of the chief cities of the Sultan and one of his principal
ports. Nevertheless, the footing thus early obtained by
European nations on Moroccan soil was not entirely lost.
The Christian garrison left the port ; the Christian traders
remained on sufferance. Two centuries before the term
" peaceful penetration " had acquired an ironic or a diplomatic significance in the mouths of statesmen the commercial exploitation of Morocco was in active progress.
Successive sultans, thinking to halt the advancing Christian
tide at the very gate of their dominions, designated Tangier
as the residence of Europe's ambassadors to their court.
The diplomatists remained in the port, under protection of
their country's ships and guns. But the traders quietly
advanced. And when the commercial occupation of the
Sultan's dominions had been in part accomplished, the
political occupation began. The soldiers and the diplomatists followed the traders. The Sherifian empire was
swallowed piecemeal stage after stage.

In the first zone, that of Tangier, capitulatory rights were
secured by France as long ago as 1767, by Spain in 1767 and
1799, and by Great Britain on December 9th, 1856. The
public health services in Tangier were handed over by the
Sultan in 1844, and in 1879 the European diplomats in the
city set up an International Sanitary Council, which body
three years later obtained control over the streets and
markets of the town, with power to levy rates. In 1903 this
council, already to all practical purposes a municipal
authority, was strengthened and extended, fourteen of its
members being nominated and the remaining twelve
elected from among the foreign residents.

Such was the growth of the special statute of Tangier.
From the beginning of this century, however, the history
of the international zone has been intimately involved with
that of the other zones in Morocco.

[2]

The modern history of Morocco, and with it the history
of modern Europe, begins in 1901. In that year Joseph
Chamberlain confided to the Kaiser his hopes for an Anglo-
German alliance. " The period of splendid isolation," he

said, "is over for England. Our desire is to discuss all questions of international policy, especially those of Morocco . . . with one or other of the great national groups. . . ." In that year the French began to take an active interest in the great Sherifian dominions bordering their Algerian territories. Three years later France had completed the first stage of her diplomatic conquest of Morocco, and had begun to undertake the diplomatic conquest of England, an enterprise in which she was ably abetted by the Kaiser and the Big Navy party in Germany.

Three separate agreements with Great Britain, Spain and Italy secured to France within a year the acquiescence of those Powers in her policy of expansion in North Africa, By the first of these conventions, signed on April 8th, 1904, the British Government gave the French a free hand in Morocco in exchange for a pledge not to interfere with the policy of Great Britain in Egypt. By the second agreement, signed with Spain on October 3rd, 1904, Morocco was divided into three distinct zones.

The first, that comprised by the city of Tangier and its immediate hinterland, an area of approximately 225 square miles, was to be internationalised as to its local administration, although the protection of its native population of Moors and Jews, and the collection of port and customs dues, remained nominally in the hands of the Sultan. The second zone, comprising the coastal region between Larache on the Atlantic and Melilla on the Mediterranean, and including the towns of Ceuta and Melilla already in Spanish occupation, was to be attributed to Spain, and under the convention France formally ceded to Spain the rights in this territory acquired under the previous agreement signed with Great Britain. The third zone, which included by far the greater part of Morocco, with almost all the Atlantic seaboard, the capital cities of Fez and Rabat, and the future ports of Agadir and Casablanca, was reserved to France.

This most active and fruitful year of imperial policy obtained for France the consent of yet another great power to her proposals for the division of Morocco. By a third diplomatic convention, signed between France and Italy on October 28th, 1904, the Italian Government formally recognised France's predominant interests in Morocco, and

was in return given by France a free hand in Libya—a
territory in which the Italians have since met with little but
disillusionment.

[3]

But at this stage Germany entered the scene. Von Bülow,
the German Chancellor, more interested in pursuing his
ancient feud with the French Foreign Minister, Delcassé,
than in making a serious bid for German expansion in North
Africa, inspired his Emperor to a personal intervention.
Wilhelm was reluctant. He was, he insisted to Edward VII
and to others, sincerely disinterested in Africa. At the
beginning of 1904 he forbade the despatch of a German warship to Morocco. But a year later he had veered round.
Bülow and von Kühlmann, the German chargé d'affaires in
Tangier, between them convinced him of the necessity of a
dramatic gesture. The Sultan was appealing for the aid of
other European powers against France's reformatory zeal
in Morocco.

In April, 1905, the Kaiser himself appeared at Tangier.
The passage had been stormy. The harbour had, as yet, no
quay. The ship rode uneasily at anchor in the roads. Von
Kühlmann, climbing with difficulty out of a small boat, and
drenched with salt water, urged an unwilling Emperor to go
ashore. An aide-de-camp was ordered to make the passage,
and returned in safety. The Kaiser reluctantly allowed
himself to be persuaded, and, landing without mishap, was
carried on a bucking horse (despite Bülow's urgent telegram
for a quiet one) up the steep streets to the whitewashed
palace in which the Sultan's uncle awaited him. There he
proclaimed that he had come to guarantee the integrity
of Morocco; while Bülow from Berlin announced that
Germany and all other Powers had equal rights with France
in Morocco.

The visit, nevertheless, was pure farce. It disgusted the
Emperor for ever with Africa. But it had the effect of
cementing the growing Anglo-French *rapprochement*. A
year later, at Algeciras, the fruits of the Kaiser's sabre-
rattling at Tangier were seen. The fate of Morocco
remained vague, but that of the relations between Germany
and her Western neighbours was settled beyond any doubt
for a generation to come.

The Conference of Algeciras, demanded by the Sultan largely at the instigation of Germany, assembled in 1906 ostensibly in order to discuss the reforms pronounced necessary by France in the Sultan's dominions, but actually to define the rival ambitions of European powers in North Africa. The countries represented in the conference were Great Britain, France, Spain, Italy, Germany, Russia, Austria-Hungary, Sweden, Belgium, Portugal and the United States. On April 7th, 1906, the Governments concerned signed a convention known as the Act of Algeciras, which, although its provisions respecting Morocco at large were later to be considerably revised, had the merit of establishing the basis for the present international statute of Tangier.

At this conference France had been obliged to submit to the other powers her proposals for the reorganisation of the Sultan's finances, customs and taxes, and thus formally to concede the German argument of equal rights in Morocco. But in fact, and thanks to British support at the Conference, France was confirmed in the possession of her existing privileges and interests in the country. She obtained the right to negotiate directly with the Sultan in various important matters like the reorganisation of the police force and the prevention of arms smuggling, and she obtained the major interest in the newly-created State Bank, which, with her control of the police, gave her paramount influence in all Morocco save in that part already ceded to Spain.

[4]

Two years later another Moroccan crisis arose. Civil war broke out between the Sultan and his brother. The French sent troops to protect their commercial interests, notably at Casablanca. Germany protested against this military intervention on the ground that her own economic interests were thereby prejudiced, but was induced to agree to a joint Declaration, signed on February 9th, 1909, recognising France's special political interests in Morocco and her right to intervene to restore order. Two years later, in 1911, again in the interests of order, a fresh military intervention was judged necessary by France, and the Sultan's ancient capital of Fez was occupied. This time Germany thought it politic to reassert her own rights of intervention. On July 1st, 1911, the cruiser *Panther* arrived off the little Moroccan port of Agadir, on the Atlantic seaboard, ostensibly to protect German mining interests, and the famous Agadir crisis was launched.

The Agadir incident ended the last of the three phases of the European penetration into Morocco. With the aid of British support France made good her claim to a complete protectorate over the Sultan's dominions. Germany was bought off by the cession of the Cameroons and the Ubanghi. Spain had already been conciliated. Italy, then entirely occupied with the difficult enforcement of her own protectorate over Tripolitana, offered no objections to a similar French enterprise in an even more turbulent region of North Africa. The Sultan finally capitulated in the Treaty of Fez, which was signed on March 30th, 1912, and formally recognised the French protectorate over Morocco, except for the Spanish zone ceded in 1904, which cession was now formally confirmed.

[5]

The Treaty of Fez, which constitutes the charter of France's rights in Morocco, and is the basis of her present administration of that vast territory, incidentally reaffirms the special international character of Tangier. The details of the international régime to be applied to the Tangier area were left for subsequent discussion, and, owing to the interruption of the war years, were not actually discussed until 1923. In that year an international conference assembled in Paris to consider the future of Tangier. To it, however, Italy was not invited : M. Poincaré, then French Premier, objecting that Italy had renounced all further interest in Moroccan affairs in the Franco-Italian pact of 1904. This studied omission proved later to be of some consequence in the light of the subsequent intensification and increased aggressiveness of Italian imperialism under Mussolini.

At the Paris conference three distinct policies were urged respectively by Great Britain, France and Germany. The first-named demanded the permanent neutrality of Tangier and its administration by an international consortium of Powers. France, in the name of the Sultan, reaffirmed the

Sultan's sovereignty over the port. Spain, on the ground that Tangier was geographically within the Spanish zone, demanded its incorporation in her own administrative area. The result of the discussions was a compromise between all three demands. The Tangier Convention, signed on December 18th, 1923, and ratified on May 14th of the following year, established the status of Tangier for a period of twelve years from the latter date. The principle of Tangier's permanent neutrality first enunciated by Nelson was solemnly reaffirmed. The administration of the city and its zone was relegated to a Legislative Assembly, part native, but in the majority European, under the presidency of the Sultan's Mendub, or representative ; a Committee of Control, composed of the consuls of the signatory Powers, and having the powers of a second chamber ; and an international mixed court of four judges, two British, one Spanish and one French. A French administrator-general was appointed for the zone.

The native police force of Tangier, officered by Europeans, was placed at his disposal. Finally, the city was declared a free port, all nations having economic equality therein.

This administrative structure, so precise in its general aspects, soon proved loose and vague enough in application. Spain grumbled that the French nationality of the administrator, the retention by France of the control of foreign policy and the collection of port dues by Sherifian (that is to say French) officials appointed by Rabat, destroyed the pretension that Tangier had been effectually internationalised. Italy refused to recognise the whole system. The United States equally rejected it. Foreign residents in Tangier, and particularly the British, complained bitterly of the character of the Mixed Court, of the lack of a competent Court of Appeal (at present appeals are heard by the same judges who tried the cases), of the regulation that juries must be composed entirely of persons of the same nationality as the accused, and of the frequency with which skilled litigants can drag out a case for three years and then prove inability to satisfy a judgment debt. The Riff war, with its wholesale contraband in arms through Tangier to the insurrectionary region, and the public passage of French and Spanish troops through the international zone, effectively disposed of the theory of Tangier's neutrality. And Spaniards accused Frenchmen of conniving at the smuggling of arms to the Riff leaders.

In 1928 France attempted to give satisfaction both to Spain and Italy. The Spanish Government was induced to waive its demand for the incorporation of the international area in its own zone. A Spanish officer was appointed inspector-general of police, with especial duties of surveillance in regard to security and neutrality. Italy, which in the previous year, repeating the Kaiser's gesture in 1905, had sent a naval squadron to Tangier under the command of the Prince of Udine, and had publicly stated that the visit was to be interpreted as a " reminder that the Italian Government maintains its policy of non-recognition of the existing status, and will accept no settlement that has been arrived at without its consultation and co-operation," was now offered membership of the international committee of control, and after some months of discussion her consul in Tangier took his seat on that committee.

[6]

When the end of the twelve-year period of control approached it was generally anticipated that a fresh attempt would be made to secure the revision of the Statute of 1924. That period expired on May 14th, 1936, and since none of the contracting Powers had given notice of its intention to demand revision, the Statute was automatically renewed for another period of twelve years. The reason for Italy's abstention has now become clear. In November, 1935, when the time arrived for renewing or revising the régime of Tangier, Mussolini was fully engaged with the preparations for war in Abyssinia. And it is generally understood that Italian acquiescence in the existing administrative system in the international zone formed part of the general exchange of concessions which led to the signature of the Mussolini-Laval agreement in Rome earlier in 1935.

At present, therefore, the Statute of 1924 is still in force, and will remain in force, subject to minor adjustments between the Powers, until 1948. The most urgent adjustments to be made are in respect of the finances of the international zone. Tangier complains bitterly of the burden of statutory charges imposed as its contribution towards the service of the Moroccan loans of 1904 and 1910, and also of the Tangier-Fez railway bonds—the latter contribution amounting to 1,700,000 francs a year, although only nine miles of the railway lie within the international zone. The town pays a high rate of interest on the port loans, and it suffers from the high cost of the collection of customs duties, which is now undertaken by officials of the French and administered from the Sherifian capital of Rabat. There is little direct trade between Tangier and the other Moroccan zones. The result is that the Budget of Tangier, except during the years of prosperity after the war, has been in deficit. Hitherto this annual deficit, amounting to about 3,000,000 francs, has been made up by France and Spain, under protest. And herein lies one source of menace to the international status of Tangier.

The international zone derives its charter from the concession granted by the Sultan's Government in 1923. The convention signed in that year transferred to the Tangier zone the rights and obligations accruing to it from the deed of the port concession signed two years earlier. If these obligations are not fulfilled, the Sultan's Government, which in the last resort means France, reserves the right of intervention to protect its own interests. Thus under Article 40 of the Convention of 1923 :

> " The Zone will assume in their entirety the obligations devolving on the Sherifian Government under the conditions of the concession. The annuities of the capital guaranteed by the Sherifian Government shall be met by the Zone as a first charge on the Customs receipts and the profits on the working of the port and on the port lands. . . . In default of the fulfilment by the Administration of Tangier of the obligations referred to in the preceding paragraphs, *the Sherifian Government will resume the sole financial control of the concession.*"

Since at present France is the sole guarantor of the port loans, she has only to withdraw her subsidy to precipitate the emergency in which the Sultan's Government would be

empowered to intervene. Another anomaly of the administration of the international zone is that in certain questions
its international character is severely limited. Since the
majority of the population of Tangier (just over 60,000
inhabitants : 40,000 of them being Moors, 10,000 Jews and
10,000 Europeans, only 700 of whom are British) is either
Moorish or Jewish, and Moors and Jews in Tangier remain
the subjects of the Sultan, the control of native affairs is in
practice entirely in the hands of the French, and by virtue
of the French protectorate over Morocco, foreign relations
are also reserved to France.

The neutrality of the zone is also subject to limitations.
When the Convention of 1923 was being negotiated the
French and Spanish Governments were engaged in war with
the Riff chieftain Abdel Krim, and they specified in the
Convention that subject to previous notice being given to
the Administrator-General of Tangier (a Frenchman),
French and Spanish troops should be permitted to embark
or disembark in the port of Tangier, and should have access
to their respective zones in Morocco through the international territory. The facilities then provided for are still
available, and this loophole in the international charter of
Tangier might be used by either Power to violate the
neutrality of the zone.

During the Fascist and Monarchist insurrection in Spain
in July, 1936, the neutrality of Tangier was again threatened.
Spanish Government warships bombarded the rebels in
Ceuta from the roadstead of Tangier, and were in turn
bombed by rebel aeroplanes. Fighting took place between
Spanish loyalists and insurrectionaries on the limits of the
international zone, and in some instances actually within it.

In the last resort the neutrality of Tangier depends, of
course, not upon the international treaties guaranteeing it,
but upon :

(*a*) unchallenged British naval control of the Straits of
Gibraltar, and

(*b*) continued friendly co-operation between Great
Britain, France and Spain.

In the event of a Mediterranean war in which Great
Britain were involved, with or without the assistance of
France and Spain, or even in the unlikely event that one or

both of these Powers would be opposed to her, the valuable strategical port of Tangier would cease to be neutral and international over night, and would fall like a ripe apple into the outstretched hand of the naval power strong enough to grasp it.

PART TWO

THE SHORE OF EUROPE

CHAPTER I

SPAIN: THE FALLEN EMPIRE

[1]

FOUR hundred years ago Spain was the greatest naval and military power in the world. She provided the Emperor Charles V with the iron soldiers who overawed Germany and the Netherlands, subdued the factious princes of Italy, and took prisoner on the field of Pavia the arrogant Francis I of France. Her conquistadors won for the same great monarch the incredibly rich kingdoms of Mexico and Peru, and established Spanish colonies in Lima, Santiago, Caracas and a score of other towns on the shores of South America. Her admirals, her sailors, her sumptuous galleys, built in the royal shipyards at Barcelona from Galician oak and Asturian iron, carried the Emperor on his expedition against Algiers, fought back the Turkish corsairs to the eastern waters of the Mediterranean, checked Sultan Suleiman the Magnificent's great admiral, Barbarossa, at Prevesa, and finally, under the celebrated Don John of Austria, and in league with the Venetians and the Genoese, won at Lepanto the greatest naval battle fought in the world since Actium, thereby laying the axe at the root of the Moslem empire in Europe, and destroying for ever the legend of Turkish invincibility at sea.

The sixteenth century saw Spain reach the zenith of her world power, and saw also the beginning of her decline. The victory of Lepanto was never repeated. The next great battle in which the Spanish fleets were engaged, the battle of the Armada, ended the brief but glorious naval career of Spain. The seventeenth century brought no new naval laurels to gild the tarnished and crumbling panoply of a Power which had once dominated the ancient and the new worlds. The British capture of Gibraltar, at the beginning of the eighteenth century, marked at once the disappearance of Spain from the ranks of the naval powers now re-entering the Mediterranean lists, and the onset of the naval decline of France. Late in the nineteenth century Spain did indeed issue one belated challenge to Anglo-Saxon domination in the western ocean. But since the Spanish-American War no further attempt has been made by the Spaniards to contest the ruling of their own strange destiny. They entered the twentieth century with the singular privilege of having no armed quarrel, dynastic, political, racial or economic, with any other nation under the sun. They remained neutral throughout the World War. And except for the brief interlude of the war in the Riff, which temporarily clouded their modern colonial history, they had succeeded in living on terms of peace and amity with all their neighbours during the most critical and controversial period in world relations since the age of Napoleon.

Geographically and economically Spain had always seemed destined to play an important and even a dominant rôle in the great sea which forms her natural frontier on the east and south of the Iberian peninsula. She lay south of the Pyrenees and north of Africa, and so long as the great rock of Gibraltar remained under her sceptre the guardianship of the narrow strait which until the last century was the only gate of the Mediterranean devolved naturally upon her. Behind her stood Christian Europe ; before her, across the narrow sea, the hosts of Islam. She held Italy and the Netherlands in vassalage, and the Americas in fee. Portugal was for a century and more united under her crown, and from her double vantage ground overlooking two seas she could have controlled, had she but desired ardently enough, and patiently enough pursued her desire, the great trade routes to the East Indies between Northern Europe and the Cape of Good Hope which Portuguese adventurers had first charted, and the older traffic through the straits of Gibraltar to the coast of Southern France, Italy and the Levant.

Her natural advantages were immense. The greater part of her coast was endowed with good natural harbours and washed by a tideless and on the whole equable sea. She had, until they had become exhausted by extravagant use, immense resources in timber forests, copper and iron mines. Her shipbuilders were the best in the world. To man her stoutly-built navies she could draw upon the fishermen of the Catalan and Basque coasts, in addition to the splendid sailors of Genoa and Naples and Sicily, that great race of Mediterranean seamen whose ancestors first sailed beyond the confines of the known world in barques out of Tyre and Sidon. To arm them she had the services of the finest bronze-founders, armourers and swordsmiths in the world. Her fighting-men were celebrated and feared in two continents. Her great ships were floating arsenals and floating fortresses, each fleet carrying an army of warriors experienced in battle by sea as by land. They fought in coats of steel, anticipating by four hundred years the naval battles of the modern world in which the ships are of steel, and the men unarmed. Yet they were driven off the seas, defeated not by professional fighting-men but by merchants and fishermen in small wooden ships who outsailed and outshot them.

[2]

The causes of the naval and commercial decline of Spain are not within the scope of this work, and there is no need to examine them. We are here concerned not with causes but with effects. The consequences of that decline are obvious in the field of Mediterranean strategy. The power which by virtue of its past, its geographical position, its harbours and its proximity to Africa is potentially capable of playing a dominant rôle in the Mediterranean is fortunately committed to a policy of practically permanent neutrality. It is neutralised at once by its strategical position and by its poverty. The great coast which would become formidable in the hands of a rich, highly organised, populous and aggressive state, is impotent for offence in the hands of a nation small in numbers, deficient in industrial organisation, poor and unambitious.

The great Spanish cities lie within easy bombing distance of France and Italy. The great Spanish ports could be rendered untenable by modern warships. The guerilla warfare which harassed the infantry of Napoleon would prove as ineffectual against the aeroplanes, tanks and armoured cars of a modern invader as the bows and arrows and elephant-guns of the Abyssinian tribesmen have proved against the gas and bombs and tanks of the Italians. The fact is that modern warfare is purely industrial. Courage, numbers, skill and strategy prove in the end inferior to scientific organisation, wealth and industrial efficiency. The history of Europe during the past century and a half has been largely the history of the progress of the industrial states. The superior industrial organisation of England and Prussia triumphed in the end over Napoleon. The superior industrial organisation of Prussia vanquished Austria in 1866 and France in 1871. In 1905 the modern industrial efficiency of Japan defeated the superior man-power of the great backward agricultural state of Russia. In 1918 the wealth and industrial power of America turned the evenly balanced scales of the European struggle into a victory for the Allies.

Spain in 1936 is in the position of the Ottoman Empire in 1914. She holds by virtue of tradition and geography a channel of great strategical importance which she is impotent to defend *unaided* against a powerful and determined aggressor. It is extremely unlikely that, without the aid of Germany, Turkey would have ventured to defend the Dardanelles against the naval power of the Allies. It is even more unlikely that Spain would succeed in overcoming, without the aid of France or Great Britain, a determined aggression against her territories in Europe or Africa. Her non-aggressive foreign policy is at once the reflection of a national fatalism almost Oriental in its passivity, and of Spain's deficiencies in wealth, population, industrial organisation, and all the other factors which determine the imperialistic policy and expansionist policy of nations. With a surface area of 196,607 square miles (including the Canary and Balearic Islands) she barely supports a population of 23 millions, whereas Italy is forced to feed almost twice the number on an area of but 119,710 square miles.

[3]

Nevertheless there have been periods during the present century when Spain threatened to revolt against the rôle of passive neutrality forced upon her by her military and industrial inferiority, her political backwardness. The acquisition in 1904 of a sphere of influence in the northern region of Morocco re-awakened her long-dormant imperial ambitions. Her attention was again fixed upon that old and painful problem of Gibraltar. Anglo-German naval rivalry, which caused the strengthening of the British fleet in the North Sea and a consequent weakening of British Mediterranean forces, seemed to provide Spain with an opportunity to reassert her interests in fortifying the Straits of Gibraltar. Ceuta, on the African coast, was hers. With Gibraltar in Spanish hands the gates of the Mediterranean could be closed against a belligerent. In the name of her own claim to permanent neutrality in European disputes Spain again raised the question of the cession of Gibraltar.

On March 26th, 1917, when the Allied cause seemed to have reached low water, the future dictator of Spain, General Primo de Rivera, made a speech before the Spanish-American Academy in Madrid publicly advocating the cession of Ceuta and Melilla in exchange for Gibraltar. A month later, on April 29th, 1917, Señor Maura made a more positive demand for both Gibraltar and Tangier, as vital to the maintenance of Spanish neutrality. Just after the Great War, on December 23rd, 1918, the Spanish Premier, Count Romañones, raised the question of exchanging Ceuta for Gibraltar. During the Peace Conference the matter seems actually to have reached the point of official consideration by both Governments. In 1922 and 1923 the naval and military experts of Great Britain were once again fiercely divided on the importance and strategic utility of Gibraltar, and it was argued in Parliament that since the defence of the rock largely depended upon the attitude of Spain, it might as well be ceded to her.

Meanwhile some Spanish statesmen had conceived the idea of neutralising the power of Gibraltar by making a tunnel under the Straits between Spain and Africa. The idea was first bruited during the World War, and was eagerly discussed by German naval experts as a potential threat to British domination of the Straits. By 1929, when Primo de Rivera was firmly in the dictatorial saddle, and dreamed of sharing with Mussolini the overlordship of the Mediterranean, the scheme had reached the prospecting stage. A commission was appointed, and soundings were begun. It was hinted that the construction of a tunnel would force Great Britain to restore the rock to its natural owners. But early in the following year Primo de Rivera was overthrown, and with the advent of the Republic in 1931, interest in the costly enterprise flagged.

During the past five years Spanish opinion has cooled towards the dictatorships of Italy and Germany, and turned in friendship to the democracies of France and Britain. British naval power in the Mediterranean has again become a source of strength and protection to Spain. And Gibraltar, which was ever a thorn in the side of the Bourbon kings, is now viewed with equanimity by the Spanish republicans. The agitation for the tunnel is no longer a manœuvre to force the cession of the rock, but a movement of purely economic inspiration designed to provide work for Spain's idle industries and cheap communications with the still unexploited resources of Spanish Morocco. The phase of active neutrality insisted upon by the Spanish Conservatives during the World War and the immediate post-war years is over, and Spain has resumed the policy of passive neutrality incumbent upon a State which is so easily attacked, and with such difficulty defended.

[4]

The triumph of the Popular Front in the elections of February, 1936, however, and the marked Communist sympathies of the largest body of voters represented in that Front, provoked suggestive speculations as to the effects of a revolutionary Spain on the balance of power in the Mediterranean. After the triumph of the Left parties in February, 1936, relations with Moscow significantly improved. Diplomatic missions were exchanged. Public interest in the Soviet Union grew considerably. The Spanish Socialists who took refuge in Russia after the sanguinary repression of the insurrection in the Asturias in October, 1934, returned with glowing tales of Bolshevik progress in social measures. There was an eager demand in Spain for works on the U.S.S.R. The pre-election reconciliation between the Socialist, Communist and Anarcho-Syndicalist sections of the working-class, hitherto mutually hostile, was cordially approved if not actually initiated by agents of the Communist International in Moscow. All the extreme Left parties in Spain were united in the desire to transform the conquest of a parliamentary majority into an effective conquest of economic power, however widely they might differ as to the character of the revolutionary régime they wished to institute.

The outbreak of a Fascist and military insurrection in July, five months after the victory of the Popular Front, crystallised the definitely proletarian and Syndicalist tendencies of the majority. The consequences of the attempted *coup de force* of Generals Franco and Mola are not yet clear. The Monarchist and Fascist reaction in the country is still powerful and may yet be victorious. The only alternative to the native military dictatorship which was the objective of the July insurrection seems to be a dictatorship of the extreme Left, led by Socialists, Communists and Syndicalists. The fulfilment of Lenin's prophecy that Spain would be the next country to follow in Russia's revolutionary path is therefore perceptibly nearer at hand. If a Marxist state should be established in that country, an interesting situation would arise in the Mediterranean.

Already a Bolshevik fleet dominates the Black Sea, which is merely the prolongation of Mediterranean waters beyond the Ægean and the narrows of the Dardanelles. Since 1923, when the Lausanne Treaty obliged the Turks to renounce the fortification of the Dardanelles, the Red fleet has been merely the peace-time master of its own waters. A superior naval force might at any time have bottled it up in that sea without interference from land defences on the shores of the Straits. Now, however, that Turkey has obtained the right to fortify the Straits, and the warships of the U.S.S.R. are permitted under the Montreux agreement to move freely in and out of the Black Sea, the Soviet Navy becomes a force to be reckoned with in the Eastern Mediterranean. The guns of its Turkish allies will, in the near future, be available to ward off a hostile fleet. The Red squadrons acquire the real freedom of their own waters, and with it the power of movement in the neighbouring waters of the Mediterranean. Thus at the moment that a Red navy demands to be reckoned with at one end of the Middle Sea, the prospect has to be entertained of an attempt to create a second Red fleet at the other.

[5]

The Spanish coastal defences comprise fortresses at the following points : Ferrol, Cadiz, Cartagena, Mahon in the Balearic Islands, and Ceuta on the coast of Spanish Morocco. A naval wireless telegraphic station, working the Telefunken system, is established at San Fernando, outside Cadiz, and other radio stations exist at the naval dockyards of Cartagena and Ferrol.

Before the outbreak of the civil war in Spain the Government's naval forces consisted of the vessels shown on the opposite page.

Name.	Launched.	Displacement in tons.	H.P.	Speed in knots.	Armament.	Torpedo tubes.
2 BATTLESHIPS						
Jaime I . .	1914	15,700	15,500	19·5	8 12-in.	—
España . .	1913	"	"	"	20 4-in.	
8 CRUISERS						
Baleares (building) .		10,000		33	8 8-in.	—
Canarias .		10,000		"	" 6-in.	4
Republica .	1920	5,500	25,000	25·5	9 6-in.	"
Blas de Lezo .	1922	4,725	45,000	29	6 6-in.	"
Mendez Nunez .	1923	"	"	"	"	"
Libertad .	1925	7,850	80,000	33	8 6-in.	12
Almirante Cervera .	"	"	"	"	"	"
Miguel de Cervantes .	1928	"	"	"	4 4-in.	"

In addition: 14 large and 3 smaller destroyers, all of modern construction, 18 modern torpedo boats, 7 gunboats and 15 submarines.

The strength of the Navy before the outbreak of civil war in 1936 was approximately 11,600 officers and men.

CHAPTER II

FRANCE IN THE MEDITERRANEAN

[I]

AFTER Great Britain, France is the Power most immediately and vitally concerned in the freedom of the Mediterranean. Great Britain's interests in that sea are imperial and economic. Her own metropolis is far from those dangerous waters. Apart from her possessions and protectorates in the Mediterranean area—Gibraltar, Malta, Cyprus, Egypt, Palestine—her direct national interests in that sea, and in its peaceful trading and communications, are subordinate to the security of a world empire. France, on the other hand, has a great natural frontier on the Mediterranean. She is the greatest of the littoral states. Her coast from the earliest days of the Phœnicians has been a centre of Mediterranean commerce and colonisation. For hundreds of years Roman civilisation, Roman law, Roman military science and Roman architecture marched northwards into Gaul along the valleys of the Rhone. Ultimately Christianity entered ancient France through her southern frontiers.

The effects of that century-long invasion are found everywhere in France, moulding her life, history, manners, language and thought. More authentic traces of ancient Rome can be identified in the French nation than the Italian. The whole history of the French Revolution, its rise and decline, and the military dictatorship which grew out of it, might have been lifted unchanged from Roman times. Nothing in Italian history, mediæval or modern, can parallel that vast repetition of an antique drama. The so-called Fascist revolution of our own times is, in comparison, a mere spectacle enacted in a village barn.

Yet vital as was that great window on the Latin world

to her subsequent development, it is not until comparatively recent years that France has developed her Mediterranean seaboard. Under the monarchy, as under the republic, the political tendencies of France, her urge to expansion and conquest, lay northwards and eastwards, rather than towards the south. It was not until the conquest of Algeria in 1830, and the successive French occupations of Tunisia and Morocco, that France began to expand outwards from her Mediterranean frontier. And not until this century, when she laid the foundations of an Eastern empire in Indo-China, and acquired a mandate over Syria, that the East-West communications of the Mediterranean assumed strategic importance in her eyes.

The historic reasons for this long indifference to Mediterranean expansion are of interest. One lay in the remoteness of the political centre of France. Another in the absorption of the early French kings in the long struggle first with the Dukes of Normandy, then with the Norman kings of England. The battle for the unity of the French kingdom was fought in the centre and in the north-east. Then came the long rivalry between the Valois kings and the house of Austria. The French monarchs were content to acknowledge the naval mastery of the Turk in the Mediterranean so long as it effectually diverted Spanish arms from their own unprotected coasts. François I, Henri II, Charles IX and Henri III even made treaties of alliance with the hereditary enemy of Christendom. Until the reign of Henri IV the authority of the monarch was too weakly exerted in Southern France to permit of the raising of royal armies or fleets in so unsubordinate a region. It was a territory alternately swept by civil and foreign wars. Legions of marauding warriors from Spain or Italy ravaged it. A great army of Charles V starved to death on its barren hills and sun-scorched plains. During the religious wars of the sixteenth century its cities were frequently laid waste, burnt and put to the sword. Its fishermen were carried away as captives to Algiers and Tunis. Its coast was alternately possessed by the Moors and raided by them.

The sixteenth century, the great age of maritime discovery, found the French ports of the Mediterranean

absorbed in internal political dissensions, with their eyes
turned inland instead of towards the sea. The French
adventurers sailed northwards to Canada and the great
cod-banks of the frozen seas, and westwards to the smiling
coasts of Florida, but they sailed from La Rochelle, Bordeaux, Cherbourg and Brest, from the Atlantic and not
from the Mediterranean harbours. Not until the reign of
Louis XIV was an attempt made to create a fleet of war-
galleys in the ancient Latin sea, and not until his great
engineer Vauban built forts at Marseilles and Toulon did
the Mediterranean become a field for French naval enterprise. But the first attempt at imperial adventure in the
Mediterranean region was left for Napoleon. The history
of French Mediterranean ambitions begins with the
Corsican Bonaparte, who was, appropriately enough, a
child of that tumultuous sea. He took the first French
army that sailed out of southern ports on conquest bound
since the Crusades. He was successful in Egypt but beaten
in Syria, and driven out of both by British sea power.

[2]

An Italian's ambition first drew France eastwards across
those waters. An Italian's ambition, over a century later,
challenged French prestige in that disputed sea. During
ten critical years of the post-war period, between 1922 and
1932, French dislike and suspicion of Mussolini brought
war in the Mediterranean dangerously within the field of
possibility. In the pre-Fascist era there were no serious
grounds of enmity between the two nations. Forty years
earlier, as we shall see, Bismarck had cleverly exploited
the Italian irritation at the French occupation of Tunis.

But the fires of that old quarrel had died down. There
is no historic Franco-Italian rivalry in the sense in which
Anglo-French rivalry had existed for centuries, or in which
Franco-German rivalry has existed since 1870. There are
no frontiers in dispute between the two countries, no border
populations (despite occasional talk of Fascist claims to
Nice and Savoy) claimed by the one and denied by the other.
In the economic field there is no life-and-death struggle
between the two countries, no fierce competition for
markets, raw materials or economic spheres of interest.

Italian and French rivalry in the Balkans, which will be examined later in this work, has been rather the consequence of political ambitions than of economic pressure. Italian industry is still largely dependent upon other countries for its raw materials. It is not yet highly developed enough to compete advantageously with the industries of France. And until the world depression was felt by the French, Italy's chief export—agricultural labour—was absorbed by France to the advantage of both countries.

The real conflict between France and Italy was one of doctrine and prestige. The French were hostile to the principles of Fascism, were critical of Mussolini's achievements at home, and suspicious of his activities abroad. He was suspected of desiring to overthrow the Versailles system, except in so far as it sanctioned the return of the Italian provinces of the Austrian Empire to Italy. He was accused of intriguing with Roumania and Bulgaria, of threatening Greece and Jugoslavia, of conspiring with defeated and discontented Hungary and Germany. The result was a growing tension in the diplomatic relations between the two countries, a mutually hostile press, and a marked cordiality displayed by the French towards the Italian exiles and refugees.

In the international sphere this antagonism was chiefly reflected in the controversy over the limitation of naval armaments. France is the fourth naval power in the world, immediately after Great Britain, the United States and Japan. Italy, which has the next largest navy, has claimed since the Washington Conference in 1922 to be conceded the right to build up to the naval tonnage conceded to France, and is only willing to accept the limitation of her armaments provided this right is acknowledged. France has repeatedly offered to meet this demand by accepting parity with Italy in the Mediterranean, which until the conquest of Abyssinia was the only sea in which Italy could reasonably claim to be interested. Full naval parity, it is claimed by the French, would mean in effect a considerable inferiority for France's fleet in the Mediterranean, since her widely scattered imperial interests and her long Atlantic seaboard oblige her to keep only a part of her naval forces in that sea. It was upon this issue of

Franco-Italian naval parity that the attempt to achieve a Five Power Cruiser Pact broke down in 1927.

For long, however, it had been evident that prestige, and not the urgent necessities of national defence, secretly dictated Mussolini's demand for parity with France. It was acknowledged that Italy had not the financial resources to enable her to build up to French tonnage. No serious claim to parity was put forward by the non-Fascist Governments in Italy after the war. It was the advent of Mussolini which created the naval problem, kept it alive and bitter, and prejudiced the negotiations for naval disarmament from 1927 onwards. Franco-Italian jealousies in the Mediterranean, typified in the question of naval parity and the nationality of the Italian settlers in Tunis, poisoned all the attempts made to promote international co-operation between 1923 and 1932. They seemed to rear an insuperable obstacle to any reconciliation between Rome and Paris. They brought to nothing the many suggestions made by French Prime Ministers to make a personal visit to Rome in order to end the long feud.

The late Aristide Briand was often urged to seek a direct encounter with Mussolini, often pondered the matter but delayed and procrastinated until it was too late. Poincaré wrote personal letters to M. André Tardieu, urging him in 1930 and again in 1931 to mend the widening breach which he had himself in part created. But M. Tardieu, although a man of courage and vision, and unprejudiced by the Liberal and Socialist bias against Mussolini, failed to seize the opportunity, or hoped perhaps that a better occasion would be offered. When it came—and the triumph of Hitler and the *revanchard* spirit in Germany showed that it could not long be delayed—it was seized by M. Pierre Laval, and the Rome Pact of January, 1935, was the triumphant result.

[3]

Fully two years before that event, however, signs of an imminent Franco-Italian reconciliation were not wanting. The Italian dictator's plan for a Four-Power consortium in 1933 was nothing less than a covert attempt to gain France's friendship—and that of Germany—on Italian terms. In

the summer of 1934 the late Louis Barthou, then French
Foreign Minister, was invited by Mussolini to visit Rome at
the end of the series of diplomatic journeys he was planning
to Poland, Czechoslovakia, Roumania and Jugoslavia. It was
the first invitation launched by the Italian Premier to any
French Foreign Minister since the beginning of the Fascist
dictatorship.   M. Barthou was pressed to accept it by the
French Ambassador in Rome, M. de Chambrun.   Prudently,
however, he declined on the ground that diplomatic
preparation for such a meeting had not yet been made.
Conversations thereupon began between the Quai d'Orsay
and the Italian Ambassador in Paris, and between the
French Ambassador and the Palazzo Chigi in Rome,
regarding the questions at issue between the two countries.
The thorny problem of naval parity was, for the moment,
and by tacit consent, waived, and the full attention of the
negotiators was concentrated on :

1. The delimitation of the frontiers between the Italian
   colony of Libya (Tripolitana and Cyrenaica) and the
   French possessions in Northern Africa ; and
2. The future status of the large Italian population in
   French Tunisia.

Considerable progress was made during 1934 with the
basis of a settlement of these old disputes, and although
the assassination of M. Barthou and France's ally King
Alexander of Jugoslavia at Marseilles in October, 1934,
raised fresh storm-clouds on the Franco-Italian horizon,
both Powers soon realised their essential community of
interests in the face of the greater danger threatening
them from Central Europe.

In the beginning of the following year M. Laval, then
Premier and Foreign Minister of France, visited Rome, and
on behalf of his Government signed a Pact of Friendship
with Italy which among other things pledged Franco-
Italian support for the independence of Austria, promised
Italian respect for France's mandate over Syria and protectorate over Tunisia, readjusted in Italy's favour the
frontier between Libya and Tunisia, and promised French
recognition of Italy's economic interests in the hinterland of Eritrea—a concession which has been generally

interpreted in Italy and elsewhere as implying M. Laval's *carte blanche* for Mussolini's designs on Abyssinia.

The first and most important result of the Pact of Rome was the transfer of the main weight of the Italian frontier forces from the French Alps to the Brenner, and a corresponding transfer of French troops from the Italian frontier to the marches of the East. It gave France a breathing-space in which to prepare for the struggle with a rearmed Germany, and incidentally—although this result was not fully foreseen at the time, even if M. Laval had a hint in January, 1935, of Mussolini's preoccupations in the Eastern Mediterranean—it freed the Italian General Staff for the organisation of the colonial expedition against the Negus.

Subsequent events have left unchanged the territorial military dispositions arising out of the Rome agreement.

The Italo-Abyssinian War, however, with its concomitant of League sanctions and reluctantly accorded French support for Great Britain's naval action in the Mediterranean, has reopened the whole question of Franco-Italian relations in that sea, and has forced France to reconsider the Mediterranean problem in terms of war strategy.

CHAPTER III

FRENCH STRATEGY: OIL AND MEN

[1]

FOR France the Mediterranean, like the Rhine, has become a potential source of danger. Since the end of the war and the destruction of Germany's Grand Fleet at Scapa Flow, the French naval forces in the Mediterranean have been superior in quality and quantity to the Atlantic fleet. It seems likely that in the future they will be considerably reinforced. The crisis of 1936 has forced France to the realisation that great as may become the military pressure on her eastern frontiers, the Mediterranean holds the key to two of her vital supplies in time of war. These supplies are:

1. Oil.
2. Man-power.

It will be shown that in the event of war France's supply of oil depends upon the security of the East–West route in the Mediterranean; and of man-power upon the freedom of the North–South routes between France and Africa.

Since the Versailles Treaty the oil problem has not ceased to preoccupy the minds of French statesmen and strategists. France's needs in oil have steadily risen since the war. Until the last year or two her production of petrol-driven automobiles was the greatest in Europe and second in the world only to that of the United States. Her navy and her mercantile marine employ very large quantities of heavy oil. The efficacy of her submarine arm—the form of naval protection upon which France chiefly relies to compensate for her deficiencies in battleships and heavy cruisers—depends entirely upon large reserves of oil fuel stored in convenient bases. Since the evacuation of the

Rhineland and the steady diminution of the term of military service very considerable progress has been made with the mechanisation of the French Army. It is now largely a mobile force, and therefore dependent for its mobility and its striking power on enormous numbers of fast motor transport.

French peace-time consumption of petroleum and its derivatives has now reached a total of over 4 million metric tons annually. With the exception of about 80,000 metric tons a year furnished by the wells at Pechelbronn, in Alsace, oil-boring in France has not materially affected the situation. The ever-growing demand is met in part by imports from America; in part by oil from Irak, furnished in accordance with the San Remo agreement, which reserved to France 23·75 per cent of the annual yield of Mosul oil; in part by imports from the Dutch East Indies and from Roumania.

In 1934, the latest year for which statistics are available, the total quantity of unrefined petroleum imported was 4,321,000 metric tons, derived from the following sources :

Irak	.	.	.	.	.	45 per cent
United States	.	.	.	.	24·5 ,, ,,
Other American countries	.	.	22 ,, ,,
Dutch East Indies	.	.	.	5·5 ,, ,,
Roumania	.	.	.	.	.. 3 ,, ,,

In addition to which the French Navy has from time to time purchased large quantities of motor fuel from the U.S.S.R. which have been applied to the building up of vast reserves at the French naval bases at Toulon, Brest, Bizerta and Dakar.

Thus of the total peace-time consumption of oil in France, it will be seen that 46·5 per cent of the supply crosses the Atlantic, and in time of war would be subject to the still incalculable consequences of the recent Neutrality Act passed by the United States Congress. Of the remaining 53·5 per cent, the greater proportion relies for its safe transport on the security of French communications in the Mediterranean. The oil from Irak is pumped into French tankers at Tripoli in Syria, after a considerable journey overland by pipe-line, with all its incidental risks from aggression by air, land and sea. It requires no great effort of the imagination to appreciate the anxiety of the French Defence Staffs to assure themselves of supplies of fuel which would not in war-time be at the mercy of a hostile Mediterranean power.

[2]

The French High Command is now believed to be considering the development of two other sources of oil fuel which would not be exposed to the same dangers in time of war. The first is the still untapped and only partially prospected oilfields of French Morocco. By a *dahir* or decree of the Sherifian Government, dated May 2nd, 1935, a State monopoly was declared over all the deposits already prospected on the left bank of the River Moulouya, and a credit of 10 million francs was opened for further boring operations in that region. Five months later a second *dahir* extended State control over the right bank of the river. The oil-bearing region now controlled by the French Government, through the Government of the Sultan, covers an area of about 120 square miles, and is believed to be exceedingly rich. During the next few years it is probable that energetic efforts will be made to exploit this oilfield, in order to render France independent equally of American supplies and of oil directly menaced by a Mediterranean blockade. It is argued that if that sea were closed to her by the naval or air operations of another power, France would still be able in comparative security to bring oil from Casablanca, on the Atlantic coast of Morocco, to one of her own Atlantic ports.

The other source of fuel for internal combustion engines now being actively developed by the French war staffs is spirit directly distilled from wood. Some years ago a French engineer invented a simple apparatus called a gasogene, by which motor spirit could be manufactured directly from wood or wood charcoal. Thirty pounds' weight of wood is estimated to yield one gallon of motor spirit, and the cost is trifling in comparison with that of petrol. The ingenuity of the invention, however, lies in the fact that both distilling apparatus and raw material may be carried by the fuel-driven vehicle. A country like

France, with almost inexhaustible forests, has thus the means of motive power at the side of every road. It is not feared that the adoption of this easy fuel-making on a large scale would lead to the deforestation of the country, since within ten years of the war the ravages committed by both the invader and the invaded in the forest areas of France had been made good.

Marshal Pétain, who was twice Minister of War in recent French Cabinets, revealed in an article published in the *Revue Hebdomadaire* on April 25th, 1936, that between 1927 and 1934 the War Ministry had spent 45 million francs on experiments on the development of gasogenes. He urges the new French Government to facilitate the employment of gasogene-driven vehicles among the civilian population by offering premiums to manufacturers, since the initial cost of transforming or of purchasing a wood-gas motor is not immediately recoverable in the economy of the gas over ordinary petrol.

He stated that of the 30 million cubic metres of timber yielded annually by the French forests, 11 millions are not consumed. This surplus, it had been estimated, would yield the equivalent of 500,000 metric tons of motor spirit, sufficient for the average needs of 70,000 heavy lorries a year.

For some years past the French Government has remedied its own deficiencies in petrol, and at the same time achieved the creation of an immense reserve of high-grade fuel for aeroplanes, by releasing large quantities of industrial alcohol for admixture with petrol in low-grade fuels for commercial transport. In time of war, however, this additional source of motor fuel would not be available, since all the surplus alcohol distilled would be absorbed by the State munition plants. The value of the new wood-gas invention is that it requires neither industrial plant, refinery, pipe-line, nor oil-tanker to provide motive-power for the great fleets of heavy lorries now running on French roads, and is immediately serviceable for war-time purposes.

[3]

The danger of a blockade on the southern coast of France has also revived French interest in the old project of a canal between the Atlantic Ocean and the Mediterranean.

At present, it is obvious, the Atlantic and the Mediterranean naval forces of France are isolated from each other by the Iberian peninsula and the Straits of Gibraltar. Mines, submarines, aircraft and the possession of either Gibraltar or Tangier by a hostile power could separately or collectively prevent one fleet from going to the aid of the other. France has to fight a naval war on two fronts, and hitherto it has been impossible to move ships from one front to the other without the protection of British sea power, the master of Gibraltar. A submarine can be taken to pieces and transported overland, as the Germans successfully demonstrated during the war. The movement of a battleship from one sea to another was thought impossible until the Panama Canal was built, and an American battle-squadron crossed the Andes by an elaborate arrangement of locks and water-levels. French engineers built the Suez Canal, and made the first plans for the Panama. They are now turning their attention to the possibility of defying geography and history at once, eliminating the land barriers of the Pyrenees and the Iberian peninsula, and the sea passage of the Bay of Biscay and the Straits of Gibraltar, by linking their two seas in a canal—le Canal des Deux Mers.

The notion is nearly four centuries old. It was first bruited five years before the reign of François I. Half a century later it was proposed to Henri IV by the Cardinal de Joyeuse, who desired to unite the coasts of Gironde and Languedoc. But not until the reign of Louis XIV was an attempt made to realise the ambitious project. With the support of Louis XIV's great Minister Colbert, an engineer named Pierre Paul Riquet, celebrated in his generation, constructed a channel known as the Canal du Midi. When it was opened for traffic in 1681 it had a depth of six feet and more than a hundred locks. It had cost over 160 millions of francs in modern values and had ruined both the estates of Languedoc and the engineer Riquet. The canal is still navigable for the greater part of its length, but before it can become serviceable for ocean-going traffic it must be enormously widened and deepened.

On several occasions during the past century projects for the linking up of the two coasts of France have been discussed. The latest scheme, which was examined as recently as 1932, received encouragement from M. Gaston Doumergue, the former President of the Republic, and of M. Albert Lebrun, his successor in office.

The Canal des Deux Mers, which it is proposed to construct along the course of the old Canal du Midi, would be 120 miles long. It would have a width of 250 metres and a depth of between 15 and 20 metres, a capacity which would permit of the passage of vessels of the largest tonnage and would create a sea channel of the greatest importance between the Atlantic and the Mediterranean by way of Bordeaux, La Réole, Agen, Toulouse and Narbonne. The enterprise is estimated to cost 12,000 million francs, and to require five years of labour. It would employ 200,000 workers, and would thereby considerably reduce the number of unemployed now drawing State or municipal relief. The capital sum involved is considerable, but not prohibitive when compared with the deficit of 21,000 million francs incurred by the French railways during the past thirteen years, the responsibility for which has been assumed by the State.

If the canal were built France would have less cause to argue that naval parity with Italy imposed upon her a virtual inferiority in the Mediterranean. With the possibility of reinforcing at will her naval forces in that sea or in the Atlantic, and the foreign-controlled bottle-neck of Gibraltar eliminated by a sea passage owned and protected by the French, the danger of having her Mediterranean ports blockaded and her Mediterranean squadron overpowered without hope of deliverance would be considerably mitigated.

[4]

The third danger to France in the rise of a power eager to challenge the naval *status quo* in the Mediterranean is in the threat to her communications with North and Central Africa : the potential sources of the man-power required to complete the deficiencies in the French Army caused by the low birth-rate of the war years.

The total population of the French dependencies and possessions in Africa is roughly 34,700,000, composed as follows :

Algeria . . .	7,000,000 (in round figures)	
Morocco . . .	5,000,000	
Tunisia . . .	2,300,000	
French Congo . .	3,200,000	
Madagascar . .	3,700,000	
French West Africa and		
Sahara . . .	13,500,000	

When the World War broke out Morocco was still largely unsubdued. It was rather a source of anxiety to the French Government than a source of material aid. During the last twenty years, however, the statesmanship of the late Marshal Lyautey and other French soldier-administrators in Morocco has extended and consolidated French authority in the Sultan's domains. The population of Morocco is not large, but it includes a million adult Arab males of good fighting stock, and in an emergency might contribute a valuable contingent to the French defence force. Algeria has a population of about 7 millions, of whom nearly 1 million are Europeans. In Algeria, unlike Morocco and Tunisia, which are still nominally protectorates, the natives are under the obligation of serving three years with the colours and can be called up as reservists in case of mobilisation. Nominally these troops are recruited for service only in North Africa, or on colonial expeditions, but they are attached to the Metropolitan Army and not to the Colonial Army and in an emergency may be sent anywhere at the orders of the French Ministry of War.

CHAPTER IV

FRENCH AIR AND SEA POWER

[1]

FRENCH air power has known strange vicissitudes since 1918. At the end of the World War it was definitely inferior in material and personnel to the military aviation of Great Britain. It was scarcely superior to that of Germany, which had nevertheless incurred heavy losses in the summer of 1918, and was soon to be sacrificed entirely on the altar of Versailles. During the years 1923–1930 the French air force was the most powerful in Europe, and probably in the world. By 1932, however, it had again fallen to a position of inferiority. Its machines were out of date. Its fighting planes were slower than those of Russia, of the United States and of Italy, and those secretly being built in Germany in anticipation of the imminent day when Hitler would publicly denounce the disarmament clauses of the Treaty of Versailles. The German menace proved a salutary shock to France. During the past two years strenuous efforts have been made to recover lost ground, with the result that in the summer of 1936 French military aviation was again claimed to be in advance, both in quality and in numbers, of the air fleets of Germany, Italy, Great Britain and the U.S.S.R. It has, temporarily at least, recovered its paramount position in Europe. And one of the last measures passed by the French Senate before the summer session ended in August was a Bill providing for the expenditure of £7,350,000 annually for the next five years for the renewal of material and personnel for the air force.

The machines of the French pursuit squadrons fly at maximum speeds varying according to the type from 225 to 250 miles an hour. The Bristol Bulldog and the Hawker

Fury machines of the British air force have a speed of
140 and 218 miles an hour respectively. The Italian Fiat
CR-30 achieves 206 miles an hour at a height of 6000 feet.
The Italian Fiat CR-32 a speed of 222 miles an hour at the
same height. The German Heinkel He-51 flies at 194 miles
an hour at 4000 feet. The Aradio Ar-65 has a speed of
200 miles an hour at the same height. The new fast
fighting planes of the Soviet Union, it is claimed in France,
have not yet got beyond the experimental stage. The only
country in the world which is said to possess a pursuit
plane which rivals in speed the French Dewoitine D.510,
a series of which type has just been ordered by the French
Air Ministry, is the United States, whose new Northrop
fighter has a speed of 250 miles an hour.

French pursuit planes are armed with light guns and
armoured machine-gun towers, and have an advantage in
speed over the fastest German bomber of 75 to 100 miles
an hour. The French scouting plane of the Les Mureaux
115 and 117 type acknowledge only one superior in
Europe—the German Heinkel He-70, a modified form of
which is already considered to be the fastest commercial
plane in the world. The most interesting development in
French military aviation since the war is the invention of
the light aeroplane gun known as Type 23, which fires
through the hub of the propeller, and is claimed to be the
only gun of its kind in the world. Recently the French
Air Ministry's decision to furnish the Soviet Government
with the plans and a working model of this gun aroused
considerable opposition in Conservative quarters.

The Marcel Bloch-200 machines of the French bombing
squadrons are from 12 to 18 miles an hour faster than the
German Junkers Ju-52, and are more heavily protected.
As the result of engine improvement, they are expected
shortly to reach a cruising speed of 150 miles an hour at a
height of 12,000 to 13,000 feet. Considerably greater
speeds have, however, been achieved by the new Marcel
Bloch-210. The Fairey Hendon bombers of Great Britain
fly at 150 miles an hour, and the Handley Page Heyfords
at 142 miles. Both have a cruising range of 600 miles.

Faster than the British bombers, but less speedy than the
newest French Marcel Bloch-210 and Potez-54 types, are

the three-engine Italian bombers of the Savoia-Marchetti
S.81 series, which reach a maximum speed of 175 miles an
hour.

The enormous improvement in the French air force is
attributed less to ceaseless experimentation with new and
sensational models than to the rapidity of construction of
new planes in series. Thanks to the equipment of French
aircraft factories for the mass production of aeroplane
engines, the replacement of all out-of-date machines is
proceeding daily, and by the end of 1936 an entirely new
fleet of first-line machines will have been created.

The most remarkable achievement of French aviation
since the war has been the development of the long-distance
air services from France to Indo-China and to South
America. The latter service, in particular, has been
singularly successful and has demonstrated the speed, ceiling
and dependability of the modern French plane.

[2]

French naval policy has, if anything, been rather helped
than hindered by the negotiations, successful or abortive,
initiated since the end of the World War for the limitation
of naval armaments. The Washington Naval Treaty left
France in a position of superiority in capital ships with
regard to the rest of continental Europe, and until 1932,
three years after Germany had alarmed French naval
opinion and excited the experts by laying down her sensational pocket-battleship *Deutschland*, France did not add
to her existing vessels in this category, all of pre-war
construction. During the twelve years which followed the
war she was thus freed from the financial burden of the
capital ship programme and enabled to reduce her naval
Budget below its pre-war level and to concentrate on the
type of protective vessels—light cruisers and submarines—
most suited to her needs.

The policy of successive French Governments with
regard to naval disarmament has not varied. It was
candidly described in the memorandum which the Government of M. André Tardieu submitted in 1929 to the Naval
Conference held in London in that year. In this memorandum the French Government reiterated its conviction

that the land, sea and air forces of a country were inter-
dependent, and that one could not be limited without
affecting the efficacy of the other. It insisted that the
tonnage of the French Navy must correspond with the
national and imperial needs of a country fronting three
seas, with a seaboard of more than 30,000 kilometres, a
colonial empire with an area of 11 million square kilometres,
populated by 60 million inhabitants, and a trade amounting
to 32,000 million francs.

The French Government then made, for the first time
in public, a proposal which had for some years been agitating
in private the Ministers and naval experts of France and
other continental powers. This proposal was thus worded :

> " Remembering the beneficial effects produced by
> the Pacific Treaty on the conclusion of the Washington
> Naval agreements, the French Government considers
> that in a narrower field, but one in which most of the
> European fleets are concerned, some progress might
> be achieved. Its communications through the Mediter-
> ranean are of an importance for the British Empire
> which the French Government by no means dis-
> regards. They are equally vital for France. Might
> not an agreement of mutual guarantee and non-
> aggression be negotiated between the Mediterranean
> naval powers, to which those not represented in
> London would be associated, and first and foremost a
> power like Spain, on the importance of whose naval
> interests in the Mediterranean emphasis need hardly
> be laid ? "

The notion of a Mediterranean Locarno thus first
outlined by France was lost in the mutual recriminations
which accompanied the French and Italian withdrawal
from the conference. During the next five years it was
never resurrected, and when, in 1936, a partial Mediterranean pact of guarantee came into existence, it was
limited to the sanctionist States among the Mediterranean
powers, and was directed against Italy, who seized the
pretext of a hostile combination thus afforded her to refuse
her signature to the 1936 London Naval Treaty.

The French delegation left London in 1929 with the

main planks of its naval disarmament policy intact—i.e. no quantitative disarmament, complete flexibility in regard to construction and transfers of tonnage from one category to another, and full publicity and advance notice for building programmes. These principles, for which the French have repeatedly fought in meeting after meeting of the Disarmament Conference, are incorporated in the London Treaty of 1936, and although the French delegation's desire to see a reduction in the maximum tonnage prescribed for capital ships was not satisfied, the limitation of the permissible tonnage of submarines to 2000 tons, and the other provisions of the Treaty, conform very closely to French needs.

[3]

In 1924 the Navy Commission of the Chamber of Deputies drafted a Bill which for the first time outlined a constitution for the French Fleet. This constitution, or *Statut Naval* as it was called, laid down the following as the essential components of the naval arm of France :

BATTLE FLEET

1. *Capital ships :* A total tonnage of 175,000 tons (as prescribed by the Washington Treaty, but since exceeded).
2. *Capital ships (aircraft-carriers) :* A total tonnage of 60,000 tons (as provided by the same Treaty).
3. *Light surface ships* (each under 10,000 tons) :
   Cruisers
   Destroyers } A total of 360,000 tons.
   Torpedo-boats
4. *Submarines :* A total of 96,000 tons.

NON-COMBATANT SHIPS

1 repair ship.
2 minelayers.
2 submarine depot ships.
2 aircraft transports.
2 net-layers.
Scouts, coal and petrol transports, instruction ships, service vessels, hydrographic vessels and fishing guardships.

The Naval Statute further laid down the following periods for the life of ships :

Capital ships	.	.	.	.	. 20 years
Cruisers	.	.	.	.	. 17 ,,
Destroyers	.	.	.	.	. 15 ,,
Submarines	.	.	.	.	. 12 ,,

It will be noticed that a number of battleships and cruisers in the tables on pages 68–70, showing the strength of the French Fleet on January 1st, 1936, are considerably over the prescribed age-limit.

Name.	Launched.	Displacement in tons.	H.P.	Speed in knots.	Armament.	Torpedo-tubes.
BATTLESHIPS						
9 Built :						
Lorraine	1916	22,189	29,000	20	8 13·4-in. 14 5·4-in. 8 3·9-in. AA	4
Provence	"	"	"	"	10 13·4-in.	4
Bretagne	1915	"	"	"	14 15·4-in. 8 3-in. AA	"
Courbet	1913	"	28,000	"	12 12-in. 22 5·4-in. 4 3-in. AA	
Jean Bart	"	"	"	"		
Paris	1914	"	"	"		4
Condorcet	1911	17,597	22,500	19·25	4 12-in. 12 9·4-in. 14 3-in. (3 AA)	
Diderot	"	"	"	"		
Voltaire	"	"	"	"		2
3 Building :						
Dunkerque	—	26,500	—	—	8 13-in., 16 5·1-in.	—
Strasbourg	—	"	—	—		—
1 Battleship	—	35,000	—	—	8 15-in. (maximum)	—

1 Projected :

		35,000			8 15-in. (maximum)	
1 Battleship	—	35,000	—	—	8 15-in. (maximum)	—

17 Built :

CRUISERS

La Galissonnière	1935	7,600	84,000	31	9 6-in., 8 3·5-in. AA	4
Algérie	1934	10,000	,,	,,	8 8-in., 12 3·9-in. / 8 smaller guns	6
Dupleix	1932	,,	90,000	32	8 8-in., 8 3·5-in. AA / 6 smaller guns	6
Colbert	1931	,,	,,	,,	8 8-in., 8 3·5-in. AA / 8 smaller guns	6
Foch	,,	,,	,,	,,		
Suffren	1930	,	,,	33·3	8 8-in., 8 3-in. AA / 8 smaller guns	6
Duquesne	1928	,,	120,000	33·2	8 8-in., 8 3-in. AA / 8 smaller guns	6
Tourville	,,	,,	,,	,,		
Duguay-Trouin	1926	7,249	110,000	33·1	8 6·1-in., 4 3-in. AA	12
Lamotte-Picquet	1927	,,	,,	,,		
Primauguet	,,	,,	,,	,,		
Emile Bertin	1934	5,886	102,000	34	9 6-in., 3 3·5-in. AA / 4 smaller guns	6
Strasbourg	1914	4,723	32,500	26	7 5·9-in., 2 3-in. AA	4
Waldeck Rousseau	1910	12,617	37,600	24·4	14 7·6-in., 10 3-in. (2 AA), 10 smaller	

Name.	Launched.	Displacement in tons.	H.P.	Speed in knots.	Armament.	Torpedo-tubes.
CRUISERS—17 Built—*continued* :						
Ernest Renan .	1909	12,234	37,600	24·4	4 7·6-in., 12 6·5-in. / 6 3-in. (2 AA) / 8 smaller guns	2
Jules Michelet .	1908	11,072	30,000	22·8	4 7·6-in., 12 6·5-in. / 2 3-in. AA	2
Jeanne d'Arc (training) .	1931	6,496	32,000	26	8 6·1-in., 4 3-in. AA / 2 smaller guns	2
5 Building :						
Jean de Vienne .	—	7,600	84,000	31	9 6-in., 8 3·5-in. AA	4
Marseillaise .	—	,,	,,	,,	,,	,,
Gloire .	—	,,	,,	,,	,,	,,
Montcalm .	—	,,	,,	,,	,,	,,
Georges Leygues .	—	,,	,,	,,	,,	,,

In addition :

32 smaller cruisers of an average displacement of 2,432 tons built and building.
1 cruiser minelayer.
2 minelayers.
1 armoured coast defence vessel.
2 aircraft-carriers.
71 flotilla leaders and destroyers built, 17 building.
3 torpedo-boats.
82 submarines built, 8 building, 2 projected.

The total strength of the French Navy in 1935 was approximately 4,000 officers and 54,000 men.

CHAPTER V

ITALY BEFORE 1914

[1]

FOR close upon three thousand years Italy has been the focus of Mediterranean traffic. The Phœnician and Greek settlements in Sicily, and the Greek towns in Southern Italy, were natural stages on the great westward sea-route to the Phœnician colonies on both shores of the Straits of Gibraltar. The long, narrow peninsula almost divides the Mediterranean into two, and from its shores the Romans easily dominated both waters. During the long period of Roman power Italy became the political, as it had already become the commercial, centre of Mediterranean activity. Even after the fall of Rome and during the dark centuries of the barbarian inroads the Italian coastal cities retained their lucrative commercial relations with the East. The merchandise of the Levant, of Persia and of the Indies was sea-borne to the ports of Northern Italy, and thence carried overland through the passes of the Alps to the empire of Charlemagne and the German cities of the North. So long as the Mediterranean remained the great trade route of the world, Italy sat profitably astride it. Its relations with the East reached their climax in the Crusades, a period in which the earlier migratory movements of the Greeks and Slavs and Huns and Tartars were repeated by the Christian chivalry of the West. The Venetians alternately challenged and conciliated the naval supremacy of the Ottoman empire in the eastern waters of the Middle Sea, while their rivals of Genoa and Pisa disputed with the Moorish corsairs of Africa the command of its western waters. For several centuries the merchants, bankers and mariners of Venice, Genoa and Florence held the eastern and the western worlds in fee.

While the great sea in which they held so strategical a

position remained the only great avenue of world trade, the cities and states of mediæval and Renaissance Italy knew an unexampled prosperity. Their power was checked but not destroyed by the increasing incursions of the Turks into the Western Mediterranean, and in their own domain the activities of Slav pirates on the Dalmatian coast were successfully overcome. Not until the discovery of the Cape route to India by the Portuguese was the commercial supremacy of the Italian maritime states threatened. And not until the discovery of the New World, and the consequent rivalry of Spanish and English adventurers in American waters, did Italy enter upon its long period of decline.

The construction of the Suez Canal, and the subsequent resumption by the Mediterranean of its ancient monopoly of sea- and land-borne traffic to the East, found Italy too weak, too rent by internal disputes, too backward industrially and politically to profit by the great opportunity. When the Canal opened in 1869 Italy had been but nine years a kingdom, and was not until the following year to be re-established in its ancient capital of Rome. Nearly half a century later, at the end of the World War, she had scarcely made good her claim to the status of Great Power. Her economic organisation was primitive ; her industries but little advanced, and almost entirely dependent upon other countries for their raw material. Of her two half-hearted attempts to rival the colonial enterprises of France, Germany and Great Britain, and to win for herself a new empire in the Eastern Mediterranean, one, the war with Menelik of Abyssinia, had ended in disaster ; and the other, the war with the Turks in Tripoli, had proved indecisive, and had only left the Italians in possession of a desert of doubtful possibilities. Her two possessions on the Red Sea, Eritrea and Somaliland, had resulted from the slow expansion of trading-posts, and had been gained without opposition from France and Great Britain, the one fully occupied with her diplomatic conquests in the westward end of the North African coast ; the other equally intent upon consolidating her protectorate over Egypt and the Sudan.

Moreover, Italy in the half-century of her national existence before the Treaty of Versailles had had neither capital nor colonists to waste upon doubtful schemes of settlement in North Africa. Her capital was fully engaged in the development of her scanty mineral and industrial resources. Her surplus population was profitably exported to the new cities of North and South America, where unskilled labour rejoiced in high wages. Her statesmen were in the majority scornful of colonial enterprises. Signor Nitti, one of her most brilliant economists, once contemptuously referred to the twin Italian colonies of Tripolitana and Cyrenaica, more generally known as Libya Italiana, as a mere " box of sand." Her real ambitions in the colonial sphere lay in the ancient, long-settled, tumultuous cities of the Levant, in Smyrna and Asia Minor. But Germany and Austria, her partners in the Triple Alliance, who had already expressed concern at the Italian campaign against Turkey in Africa, were unalterably hostile to any Italian designs on Turkish possessions in Asia. In 1898 the Kaiser had made his spectacular entry into Damascus, followed by an even more dramatic declaration of his friendship for the 300 million Moslems in the world. In 1902 the policy of the Easterners in the entourage of the Kaiser had resulted in the projection of the Berlin–Baghdad railway. Italy found the road to Asia closed, as she had already found it partly closed in Africa.

The fundamental weakness of the Triple Alliance, soon to be dramatically demonstrated by Italy's intervention in the World War on the side of France and Great Britain, was already manifest in 1912. Italy could never satisfy her ambitions in the Eastern Mediterranean so long as she remained bound to the chariot wheels of powers already secretly committed to a policy of *Drang nach Osten*. Her hopes of realising these dreams led her to desert her pre-war allies. Her disillusionment in 1919, when the victorious Western powers refused to enrich Italy at the expense of the already sadly depleted empire of the Turk, and therein dishonoured the pledges made to Italy in the secret London Treaty of 1915, led almost directly to the rise of Fascism in Italy. And the dictatorship of Mussolini culminated, after years of secret hesitation, intrigue and counter-intrigue, in the drastic imperialist adventure of 1935–1936 : the expedition against and rapid conquest of Abyssinia.

[2]

Until Mussolini suspended the critical and the reasoning faculty of the Italians, colonial expansion had never been popular in modern Italy. The cynical attitude of Signor Nitti and other Liberal statesmen towards Libya was strengthened by the support of a large body of radical and democratic opinion, which already mercilessly condemned the exploitation of native peoples conducted by other capitalist powers. Among unofficial sections of the nation, peasants and working men, it was more than justified by bitter memories of the Italian military disasters in the war against the Emperor Menelik.

It is of ironic interest now to recall that the first Italian settlement in Eritrea, on the Red Sea, which dates from 1869, was formally encouraged by Great Britain. British support was equally given for the leasing from the Sultan of Zanzibar in 1892 of a strip of territory on the Benadir coast which later became Italian Somaliland. The Italians even gave the British Government aid in the expedition against the Mahdi, but a subsequent invitation to assume with Great Britain joint control of Egyptian affairs was declined. The Italian port of Massowa lay in the low, swampy and fever-ridden region of the coast, and early attempts by the settlers to push inland to higher and healthier areas aroused the bitter opposition of the Ras or ruler of the province of Tigre. A force of Italian soldiers which penetrated into the interior as far as Dogali was surprised and overcome, and about 500 of them were massacred. Subsequently the Italian Government aided the Ras Menelik to seize the throne of Abyssinia, and in return for their aid the new Emperor secured the Italians in their possession of Eritrea and signed with them at Ucciali in 1889 a treaty of friendship.

The Italian text of the Treaty of Ucciali seemed to establish an Italian protectorate over Abyssinia. Under it Menelik undertook " to avail himself of the Government of the King of Italy in all matters whereon he may have to treat with other Governments." Under the Amharic text of this treaty, however, it was merely stated that the Emperor " *may* avail himself of the Government of the

King of Italy " in such matters. When therefore in 1893 the Italians, fortified by their version of the document, continued their advance into the Tigre province of now united Abyssinia, Menelik denounced the Treaty of Ucciali and was supported in this action by France and Russia.

The Italian advance continued, and thereby aided Menelik to consolidate his divided empire. In self-defence, the rival tribal chieftains rallied to the standard of the Emperor. In March, 1896, an Italian force of 14,500 men was utterly defeated by an army of 100,000 Abyssinians at Adowa. The Italians left 6000 dead on the field and a large number of captives in enemy hands. They were driven back to their port of Massowa and forced to sign a treaty at Addis Ababa in 1896 accepting the annulment of the Treaty of Ucciali and recognising the absolute independence of Abyssinia. The adventure had cost Italy thousands of lives, a heavy loss of prestige in Europe and Africa, and a sum of money estimated at £20,000,000. The court-martial ordered subsequently to fix responsibility for the disaster at Adowa was held in secret, and the causes of the defeat are still mysterious. Most Italian writers agree, however, in censuring the commander of the force, General Baratieri, who although already heavily criticised for incompetence, and superseded in the command, rushed headlong against a superior force in an impregnable position, and involved his country and his army in his own disgrace.

[3]

The next great Italian military adventure in Africa was undertaken on a more considerable scale, and although even more costly in blood and treasure, ended in the acquisition of a territory of great extent, if of insignificant colonial possibilities. Since the beginning of the twentieth century Italy had claimed a virtual protectorate over the decaying Ottoman Empire's possessions in North Africa. In 1903 she had obtained French recognition of her interests in Libya (i.e. Cyrenaica and Tripoli), in return for a similar recognition of French interests in Morocco. In 1911, startled by the increase of German influence in Turkey, and learning that the Turks were proposing to fortify the fine harbour of Tobruk, in Tripolitana, Italy suddenly presented the Sultan with a demand for the Turkish evacuation of Tripoli within twenty-four hours. The ostensible reason for this ultimatum was the long series of vexations and constraints suffered by Italian subjects in Tripoli. The real reason was the opportunity offered Italy by the growing embarrassments of Turkey in the Balkans, embarrassments which in the following year were to end in open war.

The Italian ultimatum was rejected, and on September 20th, 1911, before the great European powers could recover from their surprise and intervene, Italy declared war on the Sultan.

The eagerness displayed by Italy to secure territory on the African shores of the Mediterranean was not unnatural. She had been impotent to prevent the occupation of Tunisia by France, although her own nationals outnumbered French citizens in Tunis by three to one. She had seen Great Britain establish herself in Egypt, and Spain in Northern Morocco. She had seen the French tricolour advance westwards to Casablanca and Agadir on the Atlantic coasts of the Sultan's dominions, and the French sphere of influence extend from the Republic's great province of Algeria southwards to Timbuctoo and the Sahara and eastwards to the fringe of the Libyan desert.

She had suffered the military and political reverses in Abyssinia already described. She had seen her partners in the Triple Alliance practise without scruple and without opposition a policy of imperialism over south-eastern Europe and Turkish Asia—Austria seizing Bosnia and Herzegovina and dominating the Adriatic; Germany planning the Baghdad railway and laying predatory hands on the crumbling dominions of the Turk. And nothing remained to her, of all the great empire of the Mediterranean which had owed allegiance to Rome and Roman law, but a few coastal settlements on the edge of the ancient wheat-producing region of Libya which had once, although long since invaded by the sands of the desert, boasted of being the granary of Rome.

Thus the events of the year XIV of Fascism found themselves anticipated by the events of the year 1911. The war against the Moslem Sultan in Tripoli was begun as suddenly

and as systematically as the more recent war against the
Christian Emperor in Ethiopia. Military operations, undertaken by an Italian army entirely reorganised since the
disasters of 1896, were supported by naval operations
undertaken by an Italian fleet recently renovated and
reinforced. The Tripolitan ports of Tripoli, Tobruk,
Derna, Bengasi and Homs were captured one after the
other. A force of 10,000 men was landed at Bucamez,
near the Tunisian frontier, and occupied the town of
Zuara. Another force landed at Bu Sceifa and captured
Misurata. These towns gave Italy effective possession of the
country. The rest of Tripolitana was mere desert, haunted
by Arab nomads.

In December, 1911, the Italians won their first real
engagement with the Turks, that of Ain Zara. In the
following March they won another pitched battle at Bengas.
Twice the Turks rallied against them at Zanzur. In the
second battle fought at this place, in September, 1912,
aeroplanes co-operated with the Italian army for the first
time in the history of warfare, and the intelligence they
gave the Italian commander, General Ragni, of Turk and
Arab concentrations, enabled him to achieve a decisive
victory over the troops of the Sultan.

Meanwhile the Italian Navy had effectively blockaded
the coast of Arabia. Destroyers had entered the straits of
the Dardanelles, bombarded the forts at the mouth of the
straits and escaped without loss. Three Italian cruisers
sank seven Turkish destroyers off Konfudah. In the
Ægean the Italians were equally triumphant. They
captured the island of Rhodes and overcame a Turkish
garrison of 2000 men. They seized and occupied, almost
without resistance, the islands of the Dodecanese—Lindos,
Stampalia, Icaria, Patmos, Leros, Calymnus, Cos, Nisyros,
Episcopi, Syme, Khalki and other smaller isles—in possession
of which they were to be confirmed at the close of the
World War.

The end of the war in Tripoli was precipitated by the
outbreak of the Balkan war against Turkey. The Turks
hastily made peace with Italy, surrendered Tripoli and
Cyrenaica and paid a small indemnity in order to liberate
their arms for the struggle nearer home. The second

Italian war of conquest in Africa had lasted just over a year and had planted the Italian flag on the only considerable strip of African territory which had not yet been claimed by the Great Powers. It cost Italy roughly £20,000,000 —an amount equal to the cost of the disastrous war with Menelik—and brought her a land area of about 350,000 square miles, on only one-fifth of which the soil was cultivable.

[4]

The Tripolitan War revealed to Italy, beyond any doubt, the illusory character of her alliance with Austria and Germany. Early in its history a demonstration by an Italian naval force under the Duke of the Abruzzi off Prevesa on the Albanian coast had brought a spirited protest by Count Ærenthal, the Austrian Foreign Minister, as a result of which the Adriatic was practically closed to the Italian Fleet. Later, objections had been raised to the presence of Italian warships off Salonica, and in the straits of the Dardanelles, and Austria had threatened to denounce her treaty of friendship with Italy. Thus, three years before the collapse of the Triple Alliance, the conflict between Italy's Mediterranean ambitions and those of her allies had already exposed the hollowness of their friendship.

Italy went out of the Alliance, as she had gone into it, over a Mediterranean question. She had entered it as a result of the French occupation of Tunis and the agitation aroused by Mazzini's fears that the Mediterranean would become " a French lake." A British railway in Tunis had been bought by the Italians, with the consent of the Bey of Tunis. The French had retaliated by seizing Tabarca and Bizerta, and forcing the Bey to accept a French protectorate over his country. The result was a violent anti-French agitation in Italy, riots in Rome, the advent of the Francophobe Premier Crispi and the signature of the Triple Alliance with Austria and Germany. The alliance thus born in Tunis received its death-blow in Tripoli. Its existence was artificially prolonged for two years until the outbreak of the World War. Its birth and death may significantly be synchronised with two phases of the European conquest of Africa.

CHAPTER VI

THE ITALY OF MUSSOLINI

[1]

THE history of the Italy of Mussolini dates not from the day of the March on Rome, at the end of 1922, but from November 15th, 1914, when the most aggressive and revolutionary of the Italian pacifists executed the first of a long series of dramatic *volte-faces*, and defied his fellow-Socialists by publishing the first number of his interventionist newspaper *Il Popolo d'Italia*, with for its battle-cries the epigram of Napoleon : " Revolution is an idea which has found bayonets," and another of the rebel Blanqui : " Whoever has a weapon has bread."

This unexpected, although not entirely uncontrived, support for the War party was largely responsible for the violent campaign which drove Italy into denunciation of the Triple Alliance with Germany and Austria, and into public intervention on the side of the Allied Powers in May, 1915. Italy had been a more or less willing partner in the alliance between the Central Empires since May 20th, 1882, when Bismarck, profiting by the Italian outcry over the French activities in Tunis, arranged for a visit of King Humbert and his consort to Vienna, and induced the Italian sovereign to make his peace with the Austrian Emperor. The alliance was renewed, each time on terms more favourable to Italy, on a number of occasions between 1882 and 1912. The original alliance between the Central Empires contained the following principal clauses :

1. Should, contrary to the hopes and against the sincere wishes of the two High Contracting Parties, one of the two Emperors be attacked from the side of

Russia, the High Contracting Parties are bound to support one another with their entire forces, and accordingly only to conclude peace jointly and in agreement with one another.

2. Should one of the High Contracting Parties be attacked by another Power, the other High Contracting Party hereby binds himself not only to assist the assailant against his High Ally, but at least to preserve benevolent neutrality towards his High Contractant.

If, nevertheless, in such case the attacking Power should be supported from the side of Russia, whether in the form of active co-operation, or of military measures which threatened the attacked, then the obligation of mutual support with the entire forces stipulated in Article I of this Treaty at once comes into force in this case also, and the war will then also be carried on jointly by the two High Contractants until the joint conclusion of Peace.

On May 20th, 1882, Italy adhered to this engagement, in separate instruments signed with Germany and Austria. During the following thirty years the alliance underwent certain minor modifications, and on December 12th, 1912, when the outbreak of war in the Balkans threatened to provoke a general conflagration in Europe, a single treaty was signed between the three powers, of which the following (according to the Austrian White Paper issued in May, 1915) were the vital clauses :

Article III.—In case one or two of the High Contracting Parties, without direct provocation on their part, should be attacked by one or more Great Powers not signatory of the present Treaty and should become involved in a war with them, the *casus fœderis* would arise simultaneously for all the High Contracting Parties.

Article IV.—In case a Great Power not signatory of the present Treaty should threaten the state security of one of the High Contracting Parties, and in case the threatened party should thereby be compelled to declare war against that Great Power, the two other contracting parties engage themselves to maintain

benevolent neutrality towards their Ally. Each of
them reserves his right, in this case, to take part in the
war if it thinks fit in order to make common cause with
its Ally.

    .   .   .   .   .

    Article VII.—Austria-Hungary and Italy, who have
solely in view the maintenance, as far as possible, of the
territorial *status quo* in the East, engage themselves to
use their influence to prevent all territorial changes
which might be disadvantageous to the one or the
other of the Powers signatory of the present Treaty.
To this end they will give reciprocally all information
calculated to enlighten each other concerning their
own intentions and those of other Powers. Should,
however, the case arise that, in the course of events,
the maintenance of the *status quo* in the territory of the
Balkans or of the Ottoman coasts and islands in the
Adriatic or the Ægean seas becomes impossible, and
that either in consequence of the action of a third
Power or for any other reason Austria-Hungary or
Italy should be obliged to change the *status quo* for
their part by a temporary or permanent occupation,
such occupation would only take place after previous
agreement between the two Powers, which would have
to be based upon the principle of a reciprocal compensation for all territorial or other advantages that
either of them might acquire over and above the
existing *status quo,* and would have to satisfy the
interests and rightful claims of both parties.

The clause last enumerated had, in fact, formed a
secret annexe to the general treaty between the three
powers for some years before its formal incorporation in
the Treaty of 1912. It was successfully invoked by Austria
during the Italian war with Tripoli, in order to prevent
Italy from attacking the European possessions of the Turk.
And it was to be successfully invoked, two years later, after
the outbreak of the Great War, as a pretext for Italy's
denunciation of the Triple Alliance. Italy held that the
Austrian aggression against Serbia was a flagrant breach of
Article VII of the treaty, and demanded compensation for

this wilful violation in the form of cession to herself of the Italian provinces under Austrian rule. Germany, on behalf of her ally, promised that at the end of the war a part of the Italian Tyrol, the western bank of the Isonzo, and the Albanian town of Valona should be ceded to Italy, and that Trieste should be made a free city. But Baron Sonnino, on behalf of the Italian Government, rejected the offer, and Italy promptly struck a more advantageous bargain with the Allies. In return for extensive and complicated cessions of as yet unconquered territory, and an immediate loan of 50 millions sterling raised in London, she declared war on the Central Powers.

[2]

The secret treaty signed between the representatives of Italy, France, Great Britain and Russia in London, on April 26th, 1915, defined the conditions of Italy's intervention in the World War. It is a document of more than academic importance. It throws a brilliant light on the historic ambitions of Italy in Europe and Asia. It explains as no other diplomatic convention has done before or since, the extent and character of Italy's policy in the Mediterranean. It gives us the measure of the Italians' profound disappointment with the results of the Versailles peace negotiations. It enables us to appreciate the grounds for the national disillusionment which provided Gabriele d'Annunzio and Benito Mussolini with such fertile soil for the seeds of Fascism in 1920–1922. It indicates the boundaries of the new *terra irredenta*, outside Italy's enlarged frontiers, whose incorporation within the new Roman Empire may well become the ultimate objective of Mussolini.

The significant clauses of this historic London Treaty were the following :

Article 4.—Under the Treaty of Peace, Italy shall obtain the Trentino, Cisalpine Tyrol with its geographical and natural frontier (the Brenner) as well as Trieste, the counties of Gorizia and Gradisca, all Istria as far as the Quarnero and including Volosca and the Istrian islands of Cherso and Lussin, as well

as the small islands of Plavnik, Unie Candiole, Palaz-
zuole, San Pietro di Nembi, Asinello, Gruica and the
neighbouring islets.

Article 5.—Italy shall also be given the province of
Dalmatia within its present administrative boundaries,
including to the north Lisarica and Tribania ; to the
south as far as a line starting from Cape Planka on the
coast and following eastwards the crests of the heights
forming the watershed, in such a way as to leave within
Italian territory all the valleys and streams flowing
towards Sebenico, such as the Cicola, Kerka, Butisnica
and their tributaries.

She shall also obtain all the islands situate to the
north and west of Dalmatia, from Premuda, Selve,
Ulbo, Scherda, Maon, Pago and Patadura to the north,
up to Meleda to the south, including Sant' Andrea,
Busi, Lissa, Lesina, Tercola, Curzola, Cazza and
Lagosta, as well as the neighbouring rocks and islets
and Pelagosa, with the exception of Greater and
Lesser Zirona, Bua, Solta and Brazza. . . .

(The remaining coast of the Adriatic, not already
or eventually in Italian possession, was to be neutralised, with the exception of the coast of Italy's ally
Montenegro. The port of Fiume, with other towns
subsequently claimed by Italy, was under this Treaty
promised to Croatia.)

Article 6.—Italy shall receive full sovereignty over
Valona, the island of Saseno and surrounding territory
of sufficient extent to assure defence of these points.

Article 7.—Should Italy obtain the Trentino and
Istria . . . together with Dalmatia and the Adriatic
islands . . . and if the central portion of Albania be
reserved for the establishment of a small autonomous
neutralised state, Italy shall not oppose the division
of northern and southern Albania between Montenegro,
Serbia and Greece should France, Great Britain and
Russia so desire.

Italy shall be charged with the representation of the
State of Albania in its relations with foreign powers. . . .

Article 8.—Italy shall receive entire sovereignty over
the Dodecanese Islands which she is at present occupying.

Article 9.—Generally speaking, France, Great Britain and Russia recognise that Italy is interested in the maintenance of the balance of power in the Mediterranean, and that, in the event of the total or partial partition of Turkey in Asia, she ought to obtain a just share of the Mediterranean region adjacent to the province of Adalia, where Italy has already acquired rights and interests which formed the subject of an Italo-British convention. The zone which shall eventually be allotted to Italy shall be delimited at the proper time, due account being taken of the existing interests of France and Great Britain.

The interests of Italy shall also be taken into consideration in the event of the territorial integrity of the Turkish Empire being maintained and of alterations being made in the zones of interest of the Powers.

If France, Great Britain and Russia occupy any territories in Turkey in Asia during the course of the war, the Mediterranean region bordering on the province of Adalia within the limits indicated above shall be reserved to Italy, who shall be entitled to occupy it.

Article 10.—All rights and privileges in Libya at present belonging to the Sultan by virtue of the Treaty of Lausanne are transferred to Italy.

·　　·　　·　　·　　·　　·

Article 13.—In the event of France and Great Britain increasing their colonial territories in Africa at the expense of Germany, those two Powers agree in principle that Italy may claim some equitable compensation, particularly as regards the settlement in her favour of the questions relative to the frontiers of the Italian colonies of Eritrea, Somaliland and Libya and the neighbouring colonies belonging to France and Great Britain.

[3]

The consent of Russia to the foregoing territorial concessions to Italy had been obtained with difficulty during the secret negotiations which preceded the signature of the Pact of London. Subsequent discussions between France and Great Britain, and between France, Great Britain and Italy, respecting the eventual partition of the Ottoman Empire were held without Russia's participation. The Sykes-Picot agreement of May 16th, 1916, which delimited the future zones of British and French influence in Turkish Arabia, was never approved by the Tsar's Government or its successors. Nor was the agreement signed between the three Western allies at St. Jean de Maurienne on April 17th of the following year. This agreement, concluded by the Premiers of the three countries in an effort to revive Italy's waning interest in the war, confirmed the promises made to Italy under Article 9 of the Treaty of London, and in return for Italy's acquiescence in the French and British partition of Syria and Mesopotamia recognised Italy's interests in Anatolian Turkey, and particularly in the zone of Smyrna and Adalia.

The agreement of St. Jean de Maurienne, signed by Italy with the prudent reserve that it was subject to Russian approval (never subsequently received), contained the following clauses :

1. The Italian Government gives its assent to the provisions of Articles 1 and 2 of the Franco-British agreements of May, 1916 (Sykes-Picot). For their part, the French and British Governments recognise the rights of Italy . . . in the zones indicated on the attached map.

2. Italy undertakes to make Smyrna a free port as far as concerns the commerce of France, her colonies and protectorates, and of the British Empire and its dependencies. Italy will enjoy the rights and privileges mutually guaranteed to each other by France and Great Britain in the ports of Alexandretta, Caiffa and St. Jean d'Acre (Akka). . . . Mersina will be a free port for the trade of Italy, her colonies and protectorates. . . . Italian products will be given free passage through Mersina and on the railway which crosses the vilayet of Adana. No discrimination will be made against Italian goods on any railway or port along the coast of Cilicia. . . .

7. The provisions contained in the (Sykes-Picot) agreements concerning the peninsula of Arabia and the Red Sea will be considered to apply equally to Italy, as if this power were mentioned therein and were one of the contracting parties thereto.

8. It is understood that in the event of its proving impossible at the end of the war to obtain for one or more of the powers mentioned the totality of the advantages envisaged in the agreements respecting the attribution of portions of the Ottoman Empire, *the maintenance of the balance of power in the Mediterranean* shall be equitably taken into consideration, in conformity with Article 9 of the Pact of London.

[4]

Such were the alluring objectives for which Italy engaged in the Great War on the side of the Allies. When the war ended it found the peoples of the British Empire in virtual possession of ex-enemy territories 770,000 square miles in extent, with a population of 6 millions. It found France —for all the popular French belief that she acquired no colonial possessions as a result of the war—with more than 300,000 square miles of new territory outside Europe, and 2,500,000 fresh citizens of her colonial empire. The Ottoman dependencies were indeed to be partitioned, and under the thin guise of League of Nations mandates France and Great Britain were to receive large areas for economic exploitation. But Italy, if she was rewarded for her contribution to the Allied cause by the attribution of all the Italian-speaking lands formerly under the sceptre of the Austrian Emperor, was denied that equitable part in the Mediterranean equilibrium for which she had persistently pleaded.

Under the Treaties of Versailles, St. Germain and the Trianon, Italy was confirmed in her sovereignty over the redeemed territories into which her troops had marched at the collapse of the Austrian Empire. She was given possession of the Trentino, Cisalpine Tyrol (with a largely German-speaking population) as far as the Brenner, and a part of Dalmatia. Fiume, which was not demanded by Italy in the secret agreement of 1915, was given to Jugoslavia, and was the subject of a famous freebooting exploit by D'Annunzio. Italy was left in possession of the Dodecanese Islands, which she had occupied since the war in Tripoli in 1912, but her other claims in the Eastern Mediterranean and the Ægean were ignored.

France and Great Britain had taken advantage of the Soviet Government's repudiation of the secret treaties to withdraw their own pledges to the Italians. The territories in Anatolian Turkey long coveted by Italy—the zones of Smyrna and Adalia—were given instead to Greece. The new and aggressive state of Jugoslavia succeeded to the rôle of Italy's hereditary enemy Austria on the farther shores of the Adriatic. A semi-protectorate over Albania was, indeed, disdainfully offered to Italy. But the tiny territory of her old political and dynastic ally Montenegro was swallowed up in the new kingdom of the Serbs, Croats and Slovenes.

Thus the Peace Conference of 1919 left Italy unsatisfied in Europe, and empty-handed in Asia. In Africa she was, after several years of agitation, to receive a belated satisfaction. The private conversations held in 1926 between Sir Austen Chamberlain, then British Foreign Secretary, and Mussolini on Sir Warden Chilcott's yacht *Dolphin*, in harbour at Leghorn, resulted in a minor British concession to Italian claims in Jubaland. A territory of about 33,500 square miles in area, lying between Italian Somaliland and Kenya, and containing a population of 100,000, was ceded to Italy. At the same time a slight rectification of the frontiers of Southern Libya was made in her favour.

In the Mediterranean, however, the balance of power remained heavily weighted on the side of Great Britain and France. Italy, for all her strategical position and imperial traditions, was still a second-class power in the historic waters in which for nearly a thousand years the Roman eagles had been supreme. Across the Alps she faced an unfriendly France. Across the Adriatic she was menaced by the growing military power of Jugoslavia. In the Eastern Mediterranean Greece had been ejected by the renascent Turkey of Mustapha Kemal from the foothold in Asia promised to the Italians, but the new Turkish Republic proved even more hostile to Italy than the Turkey of the Sultans. And across the Mediterranean the shores of Africa offered the Italian imperialists no more promising enterprise than the thin settlement on the edge of the Libyan desert. Except for that much-criticised " box of sand," all Northern Africa had already been parcelled out among Italy's rivals. Such was the melancholy view of the ancient Latin Sea which presented itself to the inheritors of ancient Rome in the first years of Fascism.

CHAPTER VII

THE RISE OF THE NEW ROMAN EMPIRE

[1]

ON May 9th, 1936, two days after the advance body of Italian troops entered the Negus of Abyssinia's abandoned capital of Addis Ababa, Mussolini announced to the world from the balcony of the Palazzo Venezia the creation of an Italian Empire. He had been preparing for this consummation since the day he was called to power. Fourteen years had gone by since Victor Emmanuel summoned the leader of a turbulent minority from his newspaper office in Milan, and placed the dictatorial toga on his shoulders. Belatedly, and after many slights and embarrassments, the King of Italy was now to receive his reward from the magniloquent Cæsar whom he had created. Upon the brows of the long-obscured monarch of the Prussia of the South, the modern Bismarck placed the imperial crown.

Mussolini cannot be reproached with one failing: the racial impatience of the Latins. Eight years earlier, on May 7th, 1928, an American admirer, the late General Sherrill, asked him if the rumour was justified that he was contemplating the proclamation of an Italian Empire. "How can you proclaim an empire," replied the Duce disdainfully, " before you possess an empire? It would be an eminently foolish move on our part." (General Charles H. Sherrill : *Bismarck and Mussolini*, Boston, 1931.)

Nevertheless he was already obsessed with the notion of resurrecting the greatness of Rome. His career in office had been a logical and consistent pursuit of the imperial chimera. His public acts and speeches, his archæological excavations, his draining of Lake Nemi to recover the galleys of Caligula, his reconstruction of the Via Imperia in Rome, his frequent evocations of the Roman Empire, his spectacular visit on the battleship *Cavour* to Tripoli in April, 1926, when he was greeted on landing with the title of " Cæsar ! " and posters reprinted his speech under the heading " Ave Cæsar ! "—had all prepared the Italian nation for the imperial destiny which was the cherished dream of its leader. His public utterances echoed the imperial refrain :

" Fascism will transmit to posterity its heritage of Power and Will."

" Imperialism is at the base of the life of every people which desires economic and spiritual expansion."

" We must have the courage to say that Italy cannot remain for ever penned up in one sea, even if it is the Adriatic."

" All Italians of my generation understand the lack of territory. It is not surprising, therefore, that our spirit is frequently excited as it turns towards imperialistic aspirations. This is an expression of immanent historic reality, *because people who are progressing have their rights against people who are declining.* These rights are marked with letters of fire in the pages of our destiny."

" Invasion of sovereign rights has been in progress for centuries. Where is the nation to-day which during its history has not invaded the sovereign rights of others ? Take the United States. How did you push your frontiers back ? "

" Italy is an immense legion which marches under the Fascist symbols towards a greater future. Nobody can stop her. Nobody will stop her."

" Despite scientific effort, Italy cannot nourish her people. *We must expand or explode.*"

[2]

The process of expansion began long before the war. It was economic, and on the whole peaceful. Millions of Italian labourers emigrated to the United States and to the Argentine. Their savings returned in part to Italy to swell the national income. After the war, when the United

States Government severely restricted immigration, an outlet was found for part of Italy's surplus population in the depleted agricultural regions of South-western France. This proved but an illusory remedy, however, for the French Government discouraged seasonal migration, and insisted that the several hundred thousand of Italian colonists who had acquired small holdings in France should become naturalised French citizens. Moreover, a certain number of the immigrants in France were actually political refugees, with no desire to return to Italy under the Fascist régime. The result was that Italy, desiring to lose neither her subjects to France nor their considerable contribution to the national income, imposed in her turn restrictions upon emigration abroad. As far as France is concerned, the economic crisis, which has been acute since 1931, has proved an effective barrier to all further imports of foreign labour.

The population of Italy is at present between 44 and 45 millions. It increases on an average by 446,000 persons a year. The Duce's much-vaunted reclamation of the Pontine Marshes, of coast lands in Tuscany and Sardinia and the Campagna, has not succeeded in providing occupation for more than 100,000 people. The annual surplus of population remains, therefore, as a permanent source of anxiety to Italy's rulers, and the strongest of all incentives to large-scale colonisation in undeveloped countries.

One other factor exists to urge Italy along the path of imperial adventure : her lack of raw materials. She has no important mineral resources—neither iron, coal nor petroleum. She imports annually 11 million tons of coal, a million and a half tons of petrol and petroleum spirit, 2 million tons of petroleum, 2 million tons of cotton and a million and a half tons of wood. All her steam coal is imported from Wales. Although she has enormously increased her hydro-electric plants, and her production of hydro-electric power is equivalent to the yield of not less than 12 million tons of coal a year, her expanded industries still require the import of as much hard coal as before the war.

All the raw materials urgently needed by Italy are believed by prospectors to exist in more or less accessible deposits in Abyssinia. Coal, iron, gold and platinum have been reported. Mr. F. W. Rickett, the British financier, has stated that large deposits of petroleum have been located in the country. Wheat, coffee, cotton and sisal can be grown with ease in the fertile valleys of Central Abyssinia. Several years before the Italian conquest, Japanese agents began negotiations for a large cotton-growing concession in the north, between Lake Tana and Eritrea. The country is particularly suitable for the cultivation of vegetable fibre, required in ever larger quantities for the Italian hat-making and other industries. Moreover, the climate of the Abyssinian highlands is temperate, and infinitely more favourable to white men than the malarial humidity of the coast of Tripolitana and Cyrenaica. Cultivation is practised under far easier conditions in Abyssinia than in Southern Italy.

Finally, the two conditions essential to colonisation in the mind of the Fascist apologists are realised by Abyssinia —an under-populated, undeveloped, potentially rich territory, and a declining or backward race. " People who are progressing," according to Mussolini, " have their rights against people who are declining."

The cynical logic of that assertion has been fully justified in the acquisition of the first great dependency of the new Roman Empire.

[3]

Mussolini's first essay in imperialism was made as long ago as 1923. It was undertaken against Greece, then the object of the bitterest Italian recriminations as the power that had unjustly inherited Italy's promised legacy of lands and concessions in Smyrna and Adalia. Its pretext was afforded by an incident on the Greek-Albanian frontier. An Italian general and four members of his staff were surprised and murdered on August 24th, 1923, by Albanian bandits near Janina. Mussolini had been in power a little over nine months and was bursting with impatience to show his mettle. Without waiting to learn whether the Italians had been assassinated on Greek or on Albanian soil, he sent an ultimatum to Greece demanding an official apology, a Greek memorial service for the dead, honours for the Italian flag, an immediate inquiry into the affair, capital sentences on the assassins, an indemnity of 50 million lire, to be paid within five days, military honours for the victims and a reply within twenty-four hours. Greece accepted five of these demands and asked for a compromise on the amount of the indemnity. Mussolini interpreted this as a rejection of his ultimatum. Ignoring the Council of Ambassadors, which had hastily assembled in Paris, he mobilised his fleet and on August 31st his battleships bombarded the undefended Greek island of Corfu, in which the single and antique fort was occupied not by a military garrison but by refugees from Smyrna. After an hour's bombardment, which killed twenty persons and wounded eighty others, many of them children, the Italians landed and occupied the unresisting island in the name of Mussolini.

There was an international outcry. Greece appealed to the League of Nations. Mussolini publicly proclaimed his indifference to Geneva. " Italian public opinion," he said in a signed cable published in the *New York Herald*, " does not like the League of Nations, for a very good reason. We respect its aims, but I completely deny its authority to intervene in a matter affecting Italian honour. The present affair does not come under the League Covenant, as there is no danger of war." A day or two later, on September 4th, when the League had been reminded by Lord Robert (now Viscount) Cecil and other influential partisans of its undoubted obligations under the Covenant, and clamour was heard for economic and even naval sanctions against Italy, Mussolini said in an official statement : " In case the Council of the League of Nations shall declare itself competent, the question whether to remain in or to resign from the League of Nations will arise in Italy. I have already voted for the second solution."

The threat sufficed to cow League opposition. The competency of Geneva was adroitly transferred to the Council of Ambassadors in Paris, which found a formula to save the faces of all concerned. The Greek indemnity was paid. The island of Corfu was evacuated. A month later the mission of inquiry, composed of British, French and Japanese military experts, reported that Greece was innocent of any complicity in the murder of the Italian officers.

There was a sequel to the Corfu incident which passed unnoticed in the Press at the time, but which is of interest in view of the British naval activities in the Mediterranean during the Italo-Abyssinian war thirteen years later. It was described by V. Demetrio in his critical study of Fascist foreign policy (*La Politica estera di Mussolini*, Milan, 1925) and is quoted in *Sawdust Cæsar*, the well-documented indictment of the Duce published in 1936 by the American writer George Seldes. Signor Demetrio wrote : " The first anniversary of the occupation of Corfu was celebrated by Great Britain, not by Fascist Italy. It was exactly twelve months after the ephemeral occupation by the Italians that the British Admiralty organised grand manœuvres in the Ionian Sea, and it was on this occasion that the British Government obtained from the Greek Government permission to land heavy artillery in Corfu for the purpose of participating in a mock war. A similar permission had never before been asked for or granted. That was Great Britain's reply to Mussolini."

[4]

From the first the Mediterranean question has dominated Fascist imperial policy. The first challenge to Mussolini's Italy as a great European power, during the first decade of Fascism, was almost hourly anticipated from France. Italy resented French criticism of the Fascist régime, envied France her possessions in Africa, her mandates in Syria, and contested her domination (through the French diplomatic and financial protectorate over Jugoslavia and Roumania) of the Balkans. Italy obstinately refused to accept anything less than complete naval parity with France, a restriction which would place France at a grave disadvantage in the Mediterranean, which is only one of the seas through which her imperial communications pass, whereas it is Italy's unique field of naval activity.

Franco-Italian political and naval rivalry steadily increased until January, 1932, the date of Hitler's advent to supreme power in Germany. Then an unmistakable *détente* set in, With the Nazi threat to the independence of Austria. Mussolini was faced with the formidable danger of a great Pan-German State extending from the North Sea to the Alps. The military danger at the very gates of Italy seemed to him more imminent than the theoretical French naval threat to Italy in the Mediterranean. The land danger lay no longer in the 303 miles of frontier between France and Italy in the maritime Alps, but in the German-speaking Tyrol and the Brenner Pass.

The Four-Power Pact, inspired by Mussolini and signed by the representatives of Great Britain, France, Italy and Germany in Rome on June 7th, 1933, was an attempt by the Fascist dictator to neutralise the threat from Nazi Germany. It provoked so much hostility among the smaller powers, and particularly among the States of the Little Entente, that it speedily proved worthless and was tacitly abandoned. Mussolini then tried the policy of conciliation in regard to Germany. He announced the close identity of character between the Fascist and Nazi régimes. He invited Hitler to Venice, and the meeting between the two dictators was awaited with anxiety in France and the Balkans, and with curiosity in the rest of the world. But the encounter ended in sheer fiasco. A complete incompatibility of ideas and temperament was mutually discovered. Mussolini went back to Rome bitterly hostile to Hitler and now convinced that he had to deal not only with a fanatic but with a dangerous fanatic, intent on nothing less than the unification of the 100 million German-speaking or German-thinking persons in Europe.

The Nazi agitation in Austria confirmed him in his new policy towards Germany. The assassination of his friend Chancellor Dollfuss, by Austrian Nazis in July, 1934, provided him with the pretext and the opportunity for dramatic action. He mobilised 50,000 men on the Brenner frontier as a challenge to Germany, and publicly assumed responsibility for maintaining the independence of Austria. Six months later, in January, 1935, he signed the Pact of Rome with M. Pierre Laval, then Premier and Foreign Minister of France, by which he gave a new and dramatic reorientation to Fascist foreign policy, obtained, in return for concessions in Tunisia, the surrender of the French island of Doumetrah in the Red Sea, and laid the basis of the schemes for Italian imperialist expansion in the Eastern Mediterranean which were to result before the end of that year in the attack on Abyssinia, and sixteen months later in the creation of the Italian Empire.

[5]

The Pact of Rome removed France from the position of chief rival to Italy in the Mediterranean. The war with Abyssinia transferred that rôle to Great Britain. It has not been difficult for Italians to discover sound historic reasons for resentment against the dominant part hitherto played by a Northern European power in waters traditionally associated with the power and splendour of Rome. On January 4th, 1936, one of the principal lieutenants of Mussolini, Signor Luigi Federzoni, a Fascist from the earliest days, and now President of the Italian Senate, gave public expression to a significant series of reflections on Italy's foreign policy.

Signor Federzoni made his speech at the opening session of the Milan Institute of International Affairs, and devoted almost the whole of it to the Mediterranean problem. He described in detail the rise of British naval power in that sea during the past three centuries. The modern Mediterranean problem, he declared, dates actually from 1704, the date of the British capture of Gibraltar. The World War successfully removed the fear of German competition in those waters. The Russian Revolution ended the danger of Russian naval rivalry. Since 1918, according to Signor Federzoni, Great Britain has steadily consolidated her mastery of the Mediterranean by developing her mandates and communications in the territories of the former Ottoman Empire. So long as Italy remained torn by internal dissensions and paralysed by the corruption of her parliamentary régime, there was no challenge to British dominion. Italy possessed, indeed, such strategical transversal lines in the Mediterranean as those of Sicily–Tripoli and Dodecanese–Tobruk, but in the pre-Fascist era little if any importance was attached by the British imperialists to such advantages. They were not considered to constitute any serious menace to the East–West traffic lines of the British Empire.

Since the regeneration of Italy under Fascist leadership, declared the President of the Senate, the balance of power in the ancient Latin Sea has been dramatically altered. Great Britain is now forced to change the proportions established by tradition in the naval forces maintained by the Great Powers in these waters. "That explains," he added, " why England took umbrage at the activity of Italy, above all when the prospects of an understanding between France and Italy, general as well as in the Mediterranean, brought to an end a long and acute period of conflict between the two Latin nations." Signor Federzoni concluded his study of international relations with the declaration that " *in the Mediterranean, New Italy is a political reality that cannot be abolished.* Nobody can pretend that a nation of 44 million souls can renounce its own expansion and its own future."

[6]

Within a few months of the delivery of this candid and suggestive oration, it became clear that the Italian Government had decided upon an important policy in regard to the Mediterranean. It was proposed not only to reorganise and strengthen the Italian Navy, but also to gain absolute control over the south-eastern waters of that sea, and the highway to the East. As soon as the military operations in Abyssinia were successfully completed, an extensive naval programme would be undertaken, the air arm of the fleet would be enormously increased, and new naval bases and landing-grounds would be built in Italy and Africa.

On January 1st, 1936, according to official British statistics, the fleet of Italy comprised the vessels shown on pages 98–100.

[7]

The Treaty of Washington assigned to Italy, in capital ship tonnage, a replacement figure of 175,000 tons. Her existing ships, prior to the signature of the London Naval Treaty in 1930, had a standard displacement of only 86,532 tons, and at any time between 1927 and 1930 Italy was therefore entitled to begin the construction of capital ships. Under the London Treaty she continued to enjoy the right of laying down capital ships, at any time up to 1936, to a total displacement of 70,000 tons. It is significant, however, that Italy did not avail herself of the privilege until 1934, when the improvement of Franco-Italian relations and the simultaneous tension between Italy and

Name.	Date laid down.	Date of completion.	Displacement in tons.	H.P.	Speed in knots.	Armament.	Torpedo tubes.
BATTLESHIPS							
4 Built:							
Andrea Doria	1912	1916	21,555	34,000	21·0	{ 13 12-in., 16 6 in.; 13 3-in., 6 3-in. AA; 2 smaller guns	2
Caio Duilio	,,	1915	,,	31,000	21		
Conte di Cavour	1910	1915	21,604 (since transformed)	31,000	22	{ 13 12-in., 18 4·7-in.; 13 3-in., 6 3-in. AA; 2 smaller guns	2
Giulio Cesare	,,	1914	21,818 (since transformed)	31,000	,,		
2 Building:							
Vittorio Veneto	1934	—	35,000	125,000	33	{ 9 15-in., 12 6-in.; 12 3·5-in. AA	?
Littorio	,,	—	,,	,,	,,		
CRUISERS							
28 Built:							
M. Attendolo	1931	1935	5,857	110,000	37	{ 8 6-in., 6 3·9-in. AA; 16 smaller guns	4
Montecuccoli	,,	,,	,,	,,	,,		
E. Filiberto	1932	,,	6,791	,,	36·5		
Gorizia	1930	1931	10,000	100,000	32	{ 8 8-in., 16 3·9-in. AA; 6 smaller guns	—
Pola	1931	1932	,,	,,	,,		
Zara	1929	1931	,,	,,	,,		
Fiume	,,	,,	,,	,,	,,		

						Armament	
San Marco .	1907	1911	9,350	23,030	23·7	{ 4 10-in., 8 7·5-in. 16 3-in.	2
B. Coleoni	1928	1931	5,069	95,000	37	8 6-in., 6 3·9-in. AA 8 smaller guns	4
G. della Bande Nere	,,	1930	,,	,,	,,		
A. di Giussano	,,	,,	,,	,,	,,		
A. da Bardiano	,,	,,	,,	,,	,,		
Diaz .	,,	,,	5,008	,,	,,	8 6-in., 6 3·9-in. AA 8 smaller guns	4
Cadorna .	,,	,,	,,	,,	,,		
Trento .	1925	1929	10,000	150,000	35	8 8-in., 16 3·9-in. AA 8 smaller guns	8
Trieste .	,,	,,	,,	,,	,,		
Bolzano .	1930	1933	,,	,,	,,		
Quarto .	1909	1912	2,904	29,215	28·6	{ 6 4·7-in., 4 3-in. 2 smaller guns	2
Libia .	1911	1913	3,700	11,530	22	8 4·7-in., 3 3-in. AA	—
Ancona } ex-	1912	1915	3,838	30,000	27·5	7 5·9-in., 3 3-in. AA	2
Brindisi } enemy	1911	1914	2,756	24,619	27	9 3·9-in., 1 3-in. AA	4
Venezia } ships	,,	,,	,,	,,	,,		
Bari .	1912	1915	3,248	28,000	27·5	8 5·9-in., 3 3-in. AA	2
Taranto .	1910	1914	3,184	25,000	27	7 5·9-in., 2 3-in. AA	4
San Giorgio .	1905	1910	9,232	19,595	23·2	{ 4 10-in., 8 7·5-in. 6 3-in. AA	2

Name.	Date laid down.	Date of completion.	Displacement in tons.	H.P.	Speed in knots.	Armament.	Torpedo tubes.
CRUISERS—28 Built—*continued* :							
Pisa	1905	1909	8,760	20,808	23·4	{ 4 10-in., 8 7·5-in. 12 3-in., 6 3-in. AA	2
F. Ferruccio	1899	1905	6,299	13,635	19	{ 1 10-in., 2 8-in. 4 6-in., 8 3-in.	—
3 Building :							
E. di Savoia	1932	—	6,791	110,000	36·5	{ 8 6-in., 6 3·9-in. AA 16 smaller guns	4
Giuseppe Garibaldi	1933	—	7,874	100,000	35		
Luigi di Savoia }						{ 8 6-in., 6 3·9-in. AA 16 smaller guns	4
Duca degli Abruzzi }	,,	—	,,	,,	,,		

AIRCRAFT-CARRIERS
Built, 1   Building, Nil

FLOTILLA LEADERS AND DESTROYERS
Built, 96   Building, 8

TORPEDO-BOATS
Built, 2   Building, Nil

SUBMARINES
Built, 64   Building, 13

In addition : 26 sloops, 42 coastal motorboats, 6 gunboats, 2 river gunboats and 48 minesweepers.

Germany seemed to eliminate France from the rôle of
naval rival to Italy in the Mediterranean. In that year
Mussolini ordered the construction of two 35,000-ton
battle-cruisers, the *Vittorio Veneto* and the *Littorio*, each
to possess an armament of nine 15-inch guns, and a speed
of 33 knots.

At the beginning of the Italo-Abyssinian War, and the
consequent tension between Italy and Great Britain in the
Mediterranean, the Italian Government ordered the construction of these two new vessels to be speeded up. The
Littorio and the *Vittorio Veneto* are now almost completed
and will, it is announced, be launched early in 1937. Each
of them is 1100 tons larger than the British battleship
Rodney, the largest battleship yet launched. They will
have a speed approaching 33 knots, whereas the *Rodney's*
maximum is 23. Their range of action is stated to be a
radius of no less than 15,000 miles. They are armed with
nine new and highly efficient 15-inch guns as against the
Rodney's nine 16-inch guns, and, like the *Rodney*, with
twelve 6-inch guns. The anti-aircraft batteries of these
new battleships are, however, greatly superior to those of
the British ship. They comprise twelve 3·5-inch and twenty
machine-guns. Each vessel will carry four seaplanes.

In armour and anti-submarine protection as well as anti-
aircraft defences the two new battleships are the most
modern creation of naval science. Admiral Cavagnari, the
Italian Deputy Minister of Marine, claims for them that
" they represent to-day, and for a long period to come, the
most powerful ships in the world." The only British
warship which can be compared with them in speed and
fighting power is the battle-cruiser *Hood* of 42,100 tons,
which was laid down in 1916 and completed in 1920. The
Hood has a speed of 31 knots and is armed with eight
15-inch and twelve 5·5-inch guns, being therefore slightly
inferior in both speed and gun-power to the new Italian
ships.

Of the four Italian battleships already completed, two,
the *Conte di Cavour* and the *Giulio Cesare*, are now undergoing a radical rebuilding process. When they were
launched at the beginning of the World War they were
twin vessels of between 21,000 and 22,000 tons, with

machinery of 31,000 h.p., a speed of 22 knots and a principal armament of thirteen 12-inch and eighteen 4·7-inch guns. They have now been completely transformed. New machinery of 75,000 h.p. will raise their speed to 27 knots. They are being armed with new batteries of ten 13-inch and twelve 4·7-inch guns, and a large number of anti-aircraft guns. When these two ships are completed the other two old Italian battleships will be similarly rebuilt, and before the end of 1937 Italy expects to possess a battle squadron of six vessels with speed between 27 and 30 knots —the fastest first-line squadron in the world.

Italy's ambitious naval programme also includes, as will be seen from the details of the Italian Fleet already given, the building of three new cruisers with speeds varying between 35 and 36½ knots. These new vessels will be completed before the end of 1936, and will increase Italy's fleet of fast modern cruisers to nineteen. A number of new 1850-ton destroyers are also being built, and the total strength of this arm of the navy will shortly reach 104. The submarine flotilla, which has been more than doubled since the war, is to be increased to bring its first-line strength up to 100 vessels. A large increase in the aircraft assigned to the navy is also to be made. Even more significant, perhaps, is the decision to build and fortify new bases and aircraft stations in Sicily and Sardinia, on the shores of Europe, and in Libya and Eritrea, on the shores of Africa.

For the first time in nearly twenty centuries, since the days of the power of the Roman Empire, a Government in Rome is making a concerted bid for the domination of Central and Eastern Mediterranean waters. Italy's ports in Southern Sardinia and Sicily are only between 110 and 125 miles from the coast of Africa. Italy's geographical situation makes it possible for a great combination of naval and aerial forces to control the Mediterranean at its narrowest part. The existence of the British naval base at Malta, 65 miles from Sicily, is not considered by Italian strategists an insuperable obstacle to their plans, for the island could, in their opinion, be rendered useless to its present occupants by heavy air offensives. The French naval bases at Tunis and Bizerta are equally within an hour's flight from Italian aerodromes, and could, in the event of

France opposing Italy's ambitions in these waters, be rendered untenable.

Italy's present resources in submarines and aeroplanes, the enormous increase it is proposed to make in these aggressive weapons, and the great strength of her army (on May 27th, 1936, Mussolini claimed that Italy was able to mobilise thirty-seven classes of reservists, which would give her an army of 8 millions) are believed by the Fascist imperialists to give her the power to exploit her geographical and strategical advantages. The concentration of over fifty submarines carried out in the narrow passage between Sicily and Africa early in 1936, together with a simultaneous concentration of over 400 aircraft in Sicily and Sardinia, was ordered as a significant demonstration of Italian preparedness to dispute the mastery of this channel.

Thus for the first time since Napoleonic days, a great European State contests with Great Britain the supremacy of Mediterranean waters. For the first time since the opening of the Suez Canal revived the ancient East–West traffic in the Mediterranean and made that sea the chief channel of communications for the British Empire, a nation seated almost astride the sea-way to the East throws out unmistakable hints of its power to stop all sea-borne traffic between Gibraltar and Suez.

CHAPTER VIII

ALBANIA: ITALY'S PUPPET STATE

[1]

FORTY miles from the Italian coast across the Straits of Otranto lies Albania. The smallest kingdom in Europe, and known to its inhabitants under the old name of Shqipria, it is a mountainous territory little more than 10,000 square miles in extent, with a population of just over a million, two-thirds of whom are Moslems. It entered modern history by becoming the scene, in 1912 and 1913, of the rehearsal of the drama which precipitated the World War. Until 1912 it was Turkish. It owed its independence partly to the revolt of its people against the rule of the Turkish pashas, partly to the jealousies of the Great Powers, reluctant to add to the territory of newly liberated Serbia, yet fearful to leave it to share the fate of Bosnia and Herzegovina.

For two years it was governed in theory by an International Commission, but Serbian troops occupied the strategic heights within its southern frontier, and the Austrians supplied the Albanians with arms in the hope that a Serb-Albanian war would justify Austrian intervention. In October, 1913, Austria issued a hard ultimatum to Serbia demanding her immediate withdrawal in terms which anticipated the second ultimatum which led, ten months later, to the outbreak of war. Serbia, failing to receive the support from Russia which was unhappily forthcoming on the later occasion, surrendered to force. A few months later the German prince, William of Wied, came on the scene and was the nominal ruler of Albania for six months, only to flee the country when the Great War broke out.

The secret London agreements of 1915 divided Northern and Southern Albania between Serbia, Montenegro and

Greece, gave Valona to Italy, neutralised the port of Durazzo, and left in semi-independence only a small region in the middle of the kingdom. In June, 1917, however, an Italian army occupied part of Albania and its commander, General Ferrero, repudiated the secret partition of the country already consented to by his Government and pronounced Albania independent. When the war ended the Albanians themselves took a hand in the game, expelled both the Serbs and the Italians from their territory and reasserted their independence.

The new State became a member of the League of Nations in 1920. Five years later it declared itself a republic under the presidency of Ahmed Beg Zogu, the hereditary chieftain of the Mati clan of Moslems, who had been head of the Government from 1920 to 1924, and after his expulsion in that year and flight to Italy, returned in 1925 with Italian aid and overthrew the revolutionary Government of Monsignor Fan Noli. In 1928 a Constituent Assembly of the country changed the republic into a monarchy, with Ahmed Beg Zogu as king under the title of Zog I.

In the meantime, however, Italy had returned to the attack. Her troops had been driven into the sea in 1920. By 1925 her engineers, financiers, concession-hunters and military experts had succeeded in establishing themselves in the little kingdom. In that year the National Bank of Albania was created with a nominal capital of 12½ million gold francs. Fifty-five per cent of the capital was to be subscribed by Italian bankers; 45 per cent by Albania. In the end Italy subscribed practically the whole of the Albanian share, and the remainder was furnished by an international group in which the Credito Italiano was predominant. The Bank has a monopoly of paper and metal currency in Albania, and has since wielded supreme financial power in Albania.

In the same year, 1925, Italy granted a loan to Albania of 50 million gold francs. The loan was administered by the S.I.V.A., an Italian company for the development of Albania. It was guaranteed by the Albanian customs receipts, and by the Albanian state monopolies of salt, matches, cigarette papers and playing cards.

This systematic financial and economic penetration was accompanied by a tightening of Italy's political control over the country. Italy had already been given special powers of protectorate by the Conference of Ambassadors. A resolution of this body signed on November 9th, 1921, and communicated to the League of Nations a year later, stated that " if Albania found herself unable to maintain her territorial integrity, she should be at liberty to ask the Council of the League for foreign assistance." In that case, the resolution continued, the Governments of Great Britain, France, Italy and Japan " should instruct their representatives on the Council that the restoration of the territorial frontiers of Albania be confided to Italy." On November 27th, 1926, a treaty of friendship, arbitration and guarantee was signed at Tirana, the capital, between Albania and Italy, in which Italy seized the opportunity to proclaim the special rights in Albania which accrued to her as the result of the decision, some years earlier, of the Conference of Ambassadors. News of the signature provoked an outburst of indignation in Jugoslavia, whose Prime Minister, M. Ninchich, resigned in protest. In other countries, notably in France, the treaty was interpreted as a declaration by Italy of a semi-protectorate over Albania, and as an earnest of Mussolini's intention to assume in future the rôle in the Balkans exercised in pre-war days by the Government of the Tsar.

The principal clauses of the Treaty of Tirana were the following :

1. Italy and Albania recognise that any disturbance directed against the political, juridical and territorial *status quo* of Albania is opposed to their reciprocal interest.

2. To safeguard the above-mentioned interest, the High Contracting Parties undertake to give their mutual support and cordial collaboration ; they likewise undertake not to conclude with other Powers political or military agreements prejudicial to the interests of the other Party as defined in the present Pact.

3. The High Contracting Parties undertake to

submit to a special procedure of conciliation and of
arbitration questions which may arise between them
and which cannot be settled through regular diplomatic
channels. . . .

4. The present Pact shall remain in force for five
years, and may be denounced or renewed one year
before its expiry.

A year later, on November 22nd, 1927, eleven days
after the signature of a treaty of alliance between France
and Jugoslavia, the Treaty of Tirana was reaffirmed and
supplemented by a formal military alliance, signed by the
Italian and the Albanian Governments, and valid for
twenty years. Under this second treaty each party pledged
itself to support the other " with all its military, financial
and other resources·'" in case of a war not provoked by it.
An annexe to the treaty provided that in such case an
Italian general should become Commander-in-Chief in
Albania.

[2]

Italy had now publicly assumed the rôle of exclusive
guardian and protector of the Moslem kingdom. Her
activities in the country were considerably enlarged.
Italian councillors, technical experts, financiers and revenue
officials filled all the offices of State. An Italian military
mission was sent to Tirana to reorganise the Albanian
Army. Military roads were built. Defensive works along
the Greek and Jugoslav frontiers, and in the port of Durazzo,
were undertaken by Italian engineers. Albania became an
economic dependency of Italy. Relations between Albania
and foreign powers henceforth became a subject which
primarily interested the Italian Government.

The reasons for Mussolini's growing interest in Albania
are both political and economic. Strategically, Albania lies
at the gate of the Balkans. Through its territory an
Italian army may march in security to attack the frontiers
of Greece or Jugoslavia. It is also at the gates to the
Adriatic. Under the protection of its friendly coast
Italian cruisers and submarines can dominate that inland
sea, can close it to the ships of a hostile power, can blockade
the coast of Jugoslavia.

In his autobiography Mussolini speaks of Albania in almost lyrical terms :

" . . . This noble land, which is but twelve hours distant from Bari, and which had always absorbed an influx of our civilisation, this land in which some sparks of modern civil life had gleamed only because of the influence we exercised there. . . .

" We had been at Valona with sanitary missions since 1908, and since 1914 we had had military there. There we had built the city, the hospital, the magnificent roads which were a refuge for the Serbian army routed in 1916. In Albania we had sacrificed millions of *lire* and had devoted thousands of soldiers to maintain her in efficiency and to give the little state a future and a well-ordered existence."

The economic reasons are equally obvious. Albania is rich in timber, salt, bitumen and in undeveloped minerals, among them valuable deposits of petroleum. There is a third and more curious reason. Albania is a Moslem state, and Mussolini has always shared with the ex-Kaiser Wilhelm II a strange preoccupation with Islam. At the outset of his dictatorship, in November, 1922, in outlining the foreign policy of the Fascist Government in the Chamber of Deputies, he made this significant declaration :

" The situation in the Balkans *and in Islam* merits attentive watchfulness. Let us not forget that there are 44,000 Mussulmans in Roumania, 600,000 in Bulgaria, 400,000 [the number should be 600,000] in Albania, and a million and a half in Jugoslavia—an entire world that the Crescent's victory [in Asia Minor over the Greeks] has exalted."

More than one foreign observer in Rome has noted the increasing interest shown by the Italian dictator in Moslem affairs. The American writer Carleton Beals, in his work *Rome or Death*, states that " particularly is Fascist policy interested in a *rapprochement* with the peoples of the Orient, Far and Near. The Fascisti desire that Italy dominate the Mediterranean with the co-operation of the Mussulman world, for the sake of dispossessing France and

England; besides, Italy's geographical position actually suggests her as a mediator between the Occident and the portals of the Orient."

[3]

Nevertheless Italian domination was not easily achieved over a nation so fiercely independent as the Albanians. The resentment of Jugoslavia, which saw in the colonisation of her small neighbour State the prelude to military operations against herself, was shared by the hardy mountaineers of the threatened State. Popular revolts were organised against the Italian usurper. The country's revenues fell. The payment of interest on the Italian loan was refused. Public indignation at the continued subjection of the country to Italy became so manifest that in 1931, when the Treaty of Tirana was due for renewal, King Zog refused his signature. The gold stream from Italy promptly stopped.

Later in that year, when the impossibility of paying State salaries without financial help from outside broke down the King's resistance, Italy offered a fresh bribe in the form of a ten-year credit of 100 million gold francs, to be paid at the rate of 10 millions a year. The treaty was tacitly renewed, but relations between the two countries were not thereby improved. Albania refused payment of the arrears of interest owing, which now equalled the original credits. In 1932 Italy retaliated by cutting off supplies, and by withdrawing the chief of her military mission in Tirana. In 1933 a revolutionary movement directed against Italy broke out in Southern Albania, headed by a number of patriotic Albanians. It was savagely suppressed, but it had the effect of stiffening the King's resistance to Italy.

Two years later, at the beginning of 1935, animosity to Italy inspired another revolt against the royal authority—this time by the King's close friend and personal aide-de-camp Muharram Bajraktari, who fled into Jugoslavia to escape arrest.

A significant recrudescence of Italian activity in Albania began in the spring of 1936, when the Mediterranean crisis engendered by the Italo-Abyssinian War was at its most grave.

King Zog, who in the previous year had seemed anxious to make another effort to shake off the yoke of his self-appointed protectors, was conciliated by a fresh outpouring of Italian gold. A new financial and economic agreement was signed with Italy on March 19th, 1936, by which the Italian Treasury advanced 40 million gold francs for works of defence. The National Bank of Albania, already dominated by Italian capital, was supplemented by a new bank of industry under the title of *Crédit Foncier*. And in return for the large credits extended to Albania, the largest of the Government monopolies, that of tobacco, which is the main source of the country's revenue, has been surrendered to Italy.

The oilfields of Albania have also passed under Italian control, and the result of these further concessions by King Zog is that effectively all the finance, customs revenues, export and import trade of the country are now in Italian hands. Albania has become an Italian colony, like Eritrea. And its chief port, Durazzo, threatens to become another Massowa, the jumping-off place for the next Italian imperial adventure.

Of the new credit of 40 million gold francs, 4 millions are being applied to the fortification and extension of the harbour of Durazzo. Further sums are destined to be spent on the land frontiers of Albania, particularly on the Jugoslav border. A new contingent of Italian administrators, military and naval officers, engineers and prospectors has arrived in Tirana since the signature of the accord of March 19th.

Even more important perhaps is the agreement's re-affirmation of the terms of the Tirana Treaty of 1926, under which Italy undertook to defend the existing régime in Albania against any measure which threatened the political or juridical *status quo*—a vague undertaking which might serve to cover any military or naval action by Italy within the Albanian borders. There are said to be other and unpublished articles of the agreement which go farther than this ; but hitherto the secret of these clauses, if they exist, has been well guarded.

CHAPTER IX

JUGOSLAVIA AND THE ADRIATIC

[1]

IN his exultant proclamation of the Italian conquest of Ethiopia, uttered from the balcony of the Palazzo Venezia on the night of May 9th, 1936, Mussolini used words which were subsequently deleted from the official Italian report of his speech. He referred to the new colony of Abyssinia as " the *nucleus* of the new Roman Empire."

The import of this declaration was unmistakable to those who heard it, and among the most interested auditors were the diplomatic representatives of Turkey, Greece and Jugoslavia. Mussolini subsequently made an effort to allay the suspicions of his neighbours by declaring, in an interview published in the *Daily Telegraph* on May 27th, 1936, that the end of sanctions " would mark the entry of Italy into the ranks of the satisfied States." Nevertheless he evaded the direct question of the interviewer, who had asked if it was to be understood that with the acquisition of Abyssinia " the Roman Empire was now complete." And this evasion, following upon the original indiscretion of May 9th, has confirmed many fearful States in the immediate orbit of Fascist ambitions in their suspicion that Italian imperialism has but entered upon its first phase.

Two great powers, France and Germany, deny to Mussolini fulfilment of any ambition he might once have entertained of reviving the ancient Roman Empire north of the Alps. There thus remain to the rebuilder of Rome only two possible fields of expansion in Europe : the great basin of the Danube in its winding course to the Black Sea ; and that mountainous Balkan region between the

Adriatic and the Ægean, in which modern Europe has found the pretext of all its wars. Over Austria and Hungary, two States within the Danube basin, the invisible empire of Rome has already been established. Over Albania, the gate of the Balkans, as has been seen, an Italian protectorate has been imposed. Nevertheless the road to Italy's penetration of the Balkan peninsula is still obstinately blocked, and the obstacle, now as at the beginning of the Fascist era, is Italy's nearest eastern neighbour, Jugoslavia.

The Jugoslavs have succeeded to the pre-1918 rôle of the Austrians as the historic enemy of Italy. More than once during the past seventeen years Italian-Jugoslav enmity has come dangerously near to war. It broke out violently at the Peace Conference over the possession of Fiume. It has since continued, in forms more or less violent, over the question of the coast of Dalmatia, which the Peace Conference—in denial of the rights claimed by the Italians under the secret agreements of 1915—attributed largely to Jugoslavia. It remains the most dangerous of all the existing threats to peace in Southern Europe.

[2]

The Italians have a sentimental as well as a political interest in the eastern shore of the Adriatic. Under the Roman Empire the Adriatic was a Roman sea. Its eastern shores formed part of the old kingdom of Illyria, which the Roman legions overran and subdued in 168 B.C., and which subsequently gave several emperors to Rome, among them being Diocletian who was born in Spalato and returned there to die. In A.D. 1000, when the great Doge Pietro Orseolo attacked and destroyed the Dalmatian pirates' strongholds on the islands of Curzola and Lagosta, began a long period of Venetian domination on the Dalmatian coast. The Lion of Saint Mark, the emblem of the Venetian Republic, was perpetuated in many images of stone and bronze in the Dalmatian cities. And even in the days of decline, for nearly four centuries, from 1420 until the arrival of Napoleon in 1797, Venice still exacted allegiance from the city-states of the Eastern Adriatic.

The Austro-Hungarian Empire had no sooner collapsed in 1918 than Italy, already occupying Albania farther to the south, essayed to gain a foothold in the Northern Adriatic. In 1919 Italian naval forces occupied Northern Dalmatia and several of the islands off the coast. A year later bands of D'Annunzio's *arditi*, in emulation of their leader's exploit in Fiume, attempted to capture Trau and Spalato. In November, 1920, the Liberal Government of Giolitti created better relations between the two countries by a policy of reciprocal concessions. By the Treaty of Rapallo, Italy recognised Jugoslavia's sovereignty over Fiume and the whole of Dalmatia except for the town of Zara and its environs, which was ceded by Jugoslavia as an Italian *enclave*.

Two years later, however, the smouldering embers of enmity were revived by the triumph of Mussolini. The Adriatic question was reopened. A pro-Dalmatian League was formed in Italy. Processions of students carried Dalmatian flags under the windows of the Jugoslav legation, and were encouraged by the spectacle of Mussolini himself waving a handkerchief in the Dalmatian colours. Stones were thrown. The Fascist press took up the cause of the Croat autonomists, and these, although secretly anti-Italian, accepted Italian support in order to exacerbate the Serb imperialists in Belgrade. In Jugoslavia the campaign of provocation was met with equal provocation. Demonstrations took place outside the Italian legation. Italians were attacked in the streets. The stone lions in Trau and other Dalmatian cities, the symbol of the past authority of an Italian State, were destroyed or mutilated.

The long feud reached its tragic climax in October, 1934, when King Alexander of Jugoslavia was assassinated in the streets of Marseilles by Croat autonomists, and one of their reputed accomplices, the leader of the band, Ante Pavelitch, fled to Italy and found safety in an Italian prison ; from which, in spite of French and Jugoslav protests, he was two years later released.

[3]

Italy's claim to Dalmatia is founded on even less ethnic ground than her claim to, and successful acquisition of, the German-speaking Tyrol. There is only a small Italian-speaking population in the province, and that exclusively commercial in character, and confined to the coastal towns.

The overwhelming majority of the inhabitants are Slav by race. Her real motives in desiring possession of the Dalmatian coast, it may be guessed, are reasons of State, strategical and defensive. Italy, in spite of her long coast-line, has few harbours. She stares across the Adriatic— " that bitter sea," as Mussolini once called it—with envious eyes at the many harbours and islands of Dalmatia. So long as that coast and its many potential submarine bases remain in the hands of another and a hostile power, Italy fears for her own security. She reminds herself that Jugoslavia is the third military power in Central Europe, with a standing army only inferior in striking force to that of Germany and Poland. Jugoslavia is, moreover, the ally of France, who was until recently Italy's rival in the Mediterranean, and of Roumania and Czechoslovakia. With her partners in the Little Entente she can claim the resources and the prestige of a Great Power. The Little Entente has already won one victory against Mussolini—the destruction of the Four-Power *bloc*. It is, collectively and individually, a vigilant and hostile critic of Fascist foreign policy. It stands behind Jugoslavia's stubborn resistance to the eastward march of Mussolini's new Roman Empire.

Nevertheless Jugoslavia is anything but a stable political entity. She inherited many of the racial antagonisms which caused the epithet " ramshackle " to be applied by a British Prime Minister to her predecessor, the Austro-Hungarian Empire. The history of the kingdom of the Serbs, Croats and Slovenes during the seventeen years which have succeeded its creation out of Serbia, Montenegro and the Slav provinces formerly under the rule of the Habsburgs, has been one of intolerance, terror, savage repression, military dictatorship, assassination, police brutality, parliamentary corruption and intrigue.

Yet the fundamental incompatibility of the two warring factions of the kingdom, the Serbs and the Croats, is not so much racial as cultural. They are both branches of the Slav tree. They speak the same tongue. A thousand years ago they were kinsmen. In the interval, however, they have been subject to distinct and rival political systems, modes of life, customs and religions. The Croat branch was in-fluenced during many centuries by Central and Western

Europe, acquired the Catholic religion, a Western culture, was in touch with the slow growth of democracy, and the revolt of ideas of freedom against the autocratic system of government. The Serb branch, after its first heroic resistance against the Turk, was sunk for centuries in the slough of decaying Islam. When it re-emerged, it appeared, like many men liberated from slavery, with all the vices of the oppressor. It exalted the military discipline to which it owed its freedom. It was harsh, brutal, intolerant, contemptuous of the rights of minorities, indifferent to the culture which once, during the days of obscure struggle, had been eagerly imbibed at friendly founts in the West.

The results of this incompatibility of two of the three nations federated in the Jugoslav kingdom were manifest soon after the Peace Conference. The Serbs, most numerous and most aggressive of the three, cynically rejected the principle of federation, and assumed the privileges of a conqueror instead of the rights of a partner. They regarded the aggrandisement of the territories of Serbia from the 34,000 square miles of pre-war days to the 94,000 square miles allocated by the Peace Conference, and the increase in their country's population from 4 to 14 millions, as the spoils of war, the reward for their sacrifices and sufferings at the hands of Austria. They ignored their pledges of equal rights and provincial autonomy to their new partners in the Southern Slav federation. They repudiated the promise of provincial assemblies to Croatia, Slovenia, Bosnia and Herzegovina. They brutally crushed the attempts of the 4 or 5 million Croats to attain equal citizenship and representation in the kingdom. They menaced, intimidated, imprisoned and tortured the leaders of the Croat Opposition. They suppressed the Croat autonomist and other popular parties. They permitted the murder of the Croat leader Stephen Raditch in broad daylight during a session of the Belgrade Parliament. And Serb Liberal politicians who urged measures of greater tolerance to the racial minorities were exposed to insults, threats and on occasion the revolver of the assassin.

[4]

In 1931 the Pan-Serb policy of absorption and assimilation by force culminated in the new Constitution promulgated by the late King Alexander in 1931. Under this Constitution all political parties were abolished save one—the so-called Jugoslav Party. Regional representation was practically ended under the new electoral system. The government of the country was vested in a military dictatorship headed by the King. The non-Serb provinces were governed by Serb officers appointed directly by the Sovereign. The national unity which had been impossible in the days of parliamentary government, however fictitious, was imposed on the country in the name of the monarch.

Alexander's real purpose, it is claimed, and probably with justice, was eventually the reconciliation of the warring factions of his subjects. His successor, the Regent Prince Paul, has endeavoured to pursue the same objective, at the same time, however, relaxing the rigours of the royal dictatorship. But it is doubtful whether the late King could have succeeded in his mission. His real authority in the country was vested in the army. His real power subsisted only so long as he identified his aims and actions with those of the Pan-Serbs and the General Staff. If he had leaned too heavily in favour of conciliating the Croats, he ran the danger of as bitter opposition from the Serbs as that which he had already incurred from the Croats. The pages of Serbia's history are blackened by many royal assassinations. Her kings have frequently fallen victim to the violence of their followers.

Nor do the Regent Paul's chances of reconciling this old blood feud seem more promising. The Jugoslav, or National Coalition, on which the late King depended to end the parliamentary and governmental chaos of the country, has collapsed. M. Stoyadinovitch, who was twice Premier in 1936, has proved unable to maintain unity among the various nationalist groups. The prospects of a real parliamentary government, and the restoration of constitutional guarantees, seem more remote than ever. Internal revolution is only averted by the policy of the iron heel. The prisons are crowded. The opposition is bribed or gagged. The rare

politicians, whether Serb, Croat or Slovene, of Liberal
views and independence of mind are cowed and coerced into
silence. The plain truth of the situation is that the Serb
generals are in the saddle, and are determined to remain
there. So long as Pan-Serb ambitions remain the strongest
political force in the country, there is no alternative before
Jugoslavia other than Dictatorship or Revolution.

[5]

Meanwhile the foreign policy of Jugoslavia continues to
excite speculation and anxiety in more than one European
country. The assassination of King Alexander was the most
serious blow yet struck at the foundations of the Franco-
Jugoslav alliance. The late King had commanded the armies
of Serbia in the field, and had personally experienced the
horrors of the Serbian retreat. He was at once anti-
Austrian, anti-German and anti-Italian : that is to say
wholeheartedly Francophile. His successor, the Regent
Paul, is less affected by the memories of the Great War.
His brother-in-law is a Bavarian nobleman.

Since the death of Alexander the relations between
Jugoslavia and Germany have been intimate. General
Goering has paid several visits to Belgrade and has been
received with enthusiasm. And in the summer of 1936
the German Finance Minister, Dr. Schacht, had important
conversations in the Jugoslav capital with a number of
Jugoslav Ministers and bankers. During the past two
years German imports into Jugoslavia have almost doubled,
increasing in value from an annual total of 470 million
dinars to 751 millions. An economic and commercial
agreement recently signed between the two countries
promises to raise the annual total to 600 millions. Germany
undertakes for her part to buy an equivalent amount of
agricultural produce from Jugoslavia, and, moreover, to
accept payment in kind for the outstanding commercial
obligations of that country. These obligations are increasing almost daily, for the Jugoslavian Government has
during 1936 placed large orders for armaments, machinery
and other articles manufactured in Germany. Orders for
160 million dinars' worth of war material have been placed
with Krupp's, 500 million dinars' worth of railway rolling

stock ordered from other manufacturers, and telephone accessories to the value of 200 million dinars have been purchased. At the same time there has been a significant growth of political interest in Nazi Germany, accompanied by reciprocal gestures of friendship on the part of army officers, politicians and newspaper editors.

Jugoslavia's interest in securing the friendship of Germany is primarily one of self-defence. She seeks in it a double protection for her own post-war frontiers—a protection against Italy ; a protection against the danger of a Habsburg restoration. Her alliance with France is believed by an increasing number of Belgrade politicians to have outlived its utility. Profitable so long as Germany and Austria were disarmed, profitable and even vital so long as France was the strongest military power in Europe, it no longer suffices to guarantee Jugoslavia against a powerful revisionist movement in South-eastern Europe, or against the menace of Italian ambitions in the Adriatic now that Italy is fully armed, Germany rapidly arming, and Austria driven to choose a modification of the long-discussed Anschluss with Germany as an alternative to civil war.

[6]

The ties of the traditional Serb friendship with France were already weakening before the tragic visit of Alexander to Marseilles. They were almost broken by the coincidence of the assassination of Alexander and the French *rapprochement* with Italy. The signature of the Laval-Mussolini accord in Rome in January, 1935, barely three months after the death of the Jugoslav monarch, struck a blow to the post-war alliance between France and Jugoslavia from which it has never recovered. The German reoccupation of the Rhineland, without French resistance or reprisals, confirmed the Jugoslavs in their conviction that henceforth France was too preoccupied with her own internal and external problems to be reckoned with as an active ally in the Balkans. The strong Germanophile movement already perceptible in Belgrade gained enormous impetus upon that day of March 7th, 1936, which saw the Reichswehr march into the bridgeheads of the Rhine.

There is another reason for the *rapprochement* between

Belgrade and Berlin. It not only insures the Pan-Serb nationalists against the threat of Fascist Italy. It also insures them against the incorporation of their Croat provinces in a future Habsburg Austria, or possibly a Habsburg Austria-Hungary. The Croats can be depended upon to defend Jugoslav frontiers against encroachment from Italy. They definitely cannot be depended upon to fight against Austria or Hungary. For years now the Croat leaders in Zagreb have bitterly compared their present condition under the domination of the Serbs with their relative freedom under the Austro-Hungarian Empire. Then they enjoyed some degree of provincial autonomy. A local parliament met in Zagreb. They were comparatively prosperous under Habsburg rule. Twenty-two years after the fatal shots were fired at Sarajevo which brought the greater part of Europe to war, and proved disastrous to the empire of the Habsburgs, the once-discontented Croats look back almost wistfully to those halcyon days. Such is the irony of history.

In the event of attempts by Austria or Hungary to secure by force the revision of the Peace Treaties, the Croats might prove the fatally weak link in the Jugoslav federation. To conjure this peril of a Croat-Habsburg coalition, the Serb nationalists have bethought themselves of the Anschluss. They prefer Nazi domination of Austria to the return of the Habsburgs. And since the union between Germany and Austria is the most certain insurance against the triumph of the monarchist party in Vienna and Budapest, and is also the most certain means of combating the Austrian policy of Mussolini, Belgrade hopes for the success of the Austrian Nazis, as the lesser of two evils. By encouraging the success of German Fascism on the Danube, she hopes to conjure the peril of Italian Fascism on the Adriatic. The recent reconciliation between Germany and Austria was hailed in Belgrade therefore with a double satisfaction : it rendered more remote the dangers of a Habsburg restoration, and it ejected Mussolini from his dominant rôle in Austria.

[7]

The army of Jugoslavia is raised by conscription. Military service is obligatory for all fit men between the ages of 21 and 45, and in the event of war youths between 18 and 21 and men between 45 and 50 can be called to the colours. The peace-time strength of the army is roughly 7000 officers and 190,000 other ranks. On mobilisation, however, an army of one million men is immediately available, and this could probably be augmented in an emergency to two millions. The army has been organised on French lines, under the supervision of. a French military mission. The infantry is armed with French quick-firing rifles and Hotchkiss machine-guns. The artillery is equipped with Schneider-Canet guns of modern pattern, in addition to many war cannon seized from or abandoned by the Austrians.

The Jugoslav Navy consists of a sea-going squadron comprising a flotilla-leader, 12 torpedo-boats, 6 minelayers, 4 submarines, an aircraft tender and several smaller vessels, with a transformed German cruiser as flagship; a river flotilla of 4 monitors and several motor-launches for service on the Danube; and an air service using mostly French machines. The Jugoslav naval base is at Cattaro.

CHAPTER X

THE BALKAN PACT AND THE LITTLE ENTENTE

[1]

SIX Balkan countries have vital interests in the Mediterranean or its dependent seas. They are Greece, Turkey, Roumania, Jugoslavia, Albania and Bulgaria. The first four states are now united in the Balkan Pact of February 9th, 1934. Two of them, Roumania and Jugoslavia, are more closely bound in the Little Entente, of which the third associate is Czechoslovakia. Of the two remaining countries, Albania, as we have seen, is a mere political and economic dependency of Italy, and its freedom of action in foreign affairs is limited. The sixth, Bulgaria, is still without direct access to the sea, and relies upon a revision of the Treaty of Neuilly, by diplomacy or by force, to regain the Ægean port of Dedeagatch which she lost at the end of the World War.

The Balkan Pact was the first concrete result of the long efforts, begun several years before the outbreak of the World War, to achieve a measure of Balkan unity. It was intended to demonstrate to the world that henceforth the Balkan peoples would resist the domination and interference of the Great Powers. It was also, as the reaffirmation and strengthening of the Little Entente had been, a retort to the four-power dictatorship of Great Britain, France, Italy and Germany proposed by Mussolini in 1933, and inherent in the vague terms of the abortive Pact of Rome signed in that year.

Four years of conversations and conferences between the Balkan states, including Albania and Bulgaria, preceded the signature of the Pact of Athens on February 9th, 1934. In the end, however, Bulgaria and Albania refused their signatures to the document : Bulgaria on the ground that her signature would have implied voluntary renunciation of the hopes based on Article 19 of the League Covenant respecting the revision of unworkable treaties, and Albania for no reason except that Italy had ordered her to abstain.

The Pact as signed contained three public articles and a secret protocol. The terms of the protocol have never been admitted, despite protests in the Greek Parliament. But they have been communicated to the British and probably to other Governments, and during a debate in the Greek Chamber the then Premier, M. Tsaldaras, declared that they merely confirmed general principles which were not mentioned in the Pact itself, and that they created " no danger that by the Pact Greece might be led into a war with a non-Balkan power." The public clauses of the Pact are :

1. Greece, Roumania, Turkey and Jugoslavia mutually guarantee the security of their frontiers.

2. They undertake to concert between themselves as to the measures to be taken in the presence of eventualities capable of affecting their interests as defined by the present agreement. They undertake to take no political action towards any other Balkan state not a signatory of the present agreement without previous mutual notice ; and to assume no political obligation towards any other Balkan state without the consent of the other contracting parties.

3. The present agreement will come into force from the date of its signature by all the contracting powers, and will be ratified as quickly as possible. It will be open to every Balkan state.

[2]

The most significant feature of the Balkan Pact is the fact that it was signed by both Greece and Turkey. For the first time in their history the Turks, under Kemal Ataturk, are in solemn alliance with their hereditary enemies, the Greeks, Roumanians and Southern Slavs, who for centuries groaned under the despotic heel of the caliphs in Constantinople. Only one other pact equally astonishing has been recorded in the history of modern Europe—the ten-year treaty of friendship signed between Germany and

Poland in January, 1934. The event shows that under pressure of political or economic necessity, and on the initiative of an all-powerful leader, the most deeply-rooted national or international enmities and the most bitter memories of rivalry or oppression may give way to feelings of reciprocal amity.

In the case of Greece and Turkey the reconciliation has been enormously aided by the fact that neither country now contains nationals of the other. The exchange of alien populations has been successfully accomplished. The last Greek has left Asia Minor. The last Turk has departed from Greece, except for Western Thrace, where he is still tolerated. Greece has now no unsatisfied ambitions in Asia ; Turkey none in Europe. The existence of large, discontented and oppressed racial or national minorities, which since the war has poisoned the relations between Hungary and her neighbours, and which for twenty years has prevented a reconciliation between Bulgaria and Jugoslavia, has been eliminated as a factor of discord between Athens and Constantinople.

The other great source of rivalry in the Balkans is the competition, economic, political and financial, hitherto waged in the peninsula by the Great Powers. Before the war the principal rivals were Russia and Austria, and the war directly resulted from their long struggle to dominate that field. Since 1919 the respective rôles of those once-great empires have been played by France and Italy. France, strengthened by her common interest to conserve the territorial and political conquests of Versailles, quickly established herself in the position of overlord in Roumania and Jugoslavia, buttressing her diplomatic influence by the steady acquisition of economic and financial power, by granting loans, by selling arms, by lending military and technical missions. Italy retorted, as we have seen, by invading Albania.

A keen rivalry then began for the favours of Greece and Turkey. Alternately Italy and France were paramount in the councils of the one, and rejected in those of the other. French support for Kemal in the war with Greece, and the too obvious ambitions of Italy to acquire Turkish territory in Asia Minor, for a time eliminated the Italians. They turned their attention to Athens, and in spite of the Corfu incident in 1923, succeeded in gaining the major influence in Greek affairs : an advantage which they have retained until the present day. Italian lecturers visit Athens and dilate upon the glories of Fascist literature, art and political economy. Italian banks, industrial enterprises and shipping companies have established themselves in Greece. The largest hotel in Athens has been rented by the Italian Government for five years at an annual rent of £2000, for use as an Italian cultural centre. And relations between the two countries are so close that for long the Greek Government hesitated to sign the Balkan Pact lest its action might give offence to Italy, and then only did so on the express understanding that Greece would not take up arms against Italy in any war which might break out between that country and another power, so long as Greek interests were not directly involved.

The most interesting recent development in Greece is the restoration of the dictatorship by the Premier, General Metaxas. By a coincidence which is, to say the least, suggestive, the event closely followed a visit paid to Athens early in the summer of 1936 by Dr. Schacht, Germany's financial dictator. It also succeeded an abrupt unilateral intimation by Greece that she intended to withdraw from the Mediterranean Pact of Mutual Assistance created during the Italo-Abyssinian War—a Pact which Great Britain kept alive for some time as a purely one-sided undertaking, and only renounced at the beginning of August.

The dictatorship in Greece has been accompanied by the usual restrictions on the activities of non-governmental parties and newspapers, by the arrests of Socialists and Communists and by the establishment of a severe censorship. Its attitude in foreign relations may be surmised from the instructions given by General Metaxas to journalists in Athens not to write or publish any criticism of Germany or National Socialism, and not to publish any news from Moscow, and from the expulsion of several Jugoslav newspaper correspondents.

The democratic régime in Greece promised at the time of the restoration of the monarchy has thus been short-lived. The reaction against it is all the more surprising since there seemed little internal danger to the new régime. The death of Venizelos had removed the most powerful enemy of the reigning dynasty and of its supporters. The newly restored King George enjoyed, or appeared to enjoy, popularity among all classes of Greeks. The absence of any internal pretext for the sudden abrogation of constitutional rights, and the revival of the dictatorial régime of the late General Condylis, strengthen the suspicion that both are largely the inspiration of Germany, which has lately resumed in a subtler form her pre-war policy of the *Drang nach Osten*, and is now endeavouring to achieve the doctrinal conquest of the Balkans.

[3]

Meanwhile Italy has for some years been engaged on a similar policy of penetration in Bulgaria and Roumania.

The former country, as the hereditary enemy of Italy's rival, Jugoslavia, had especial claims to Italian sympathy, and might well be expected, as in fact it did, to reply with alacrity to Italian offers of financial and economic aid. The dictatorship of Professor Tsankoff, which followed the assassination of the Bulgarian Liberal Premier, Stambulisky, in 1923, and which afforded a significant precedent for the dictatorships established by Dollfuss, Stahremberg and Schuschnigg in Austria ten years later, again with Italian support and at Italian instigation, gave Italy the predominant influence in Bulgaria's external affairs. The Bulgarian refusal to join the Balkan Entente, although adequately explained by the reason already given, may well have been strengthened by pressure from Italy.

In Roumania the success of Italy's activities has varied with the recurring political crises in that country. Her interests have been confided now to one now to another of Roumania's venal politicians, all ready, at a price, to play Italy's game in internal or in external affairs. Her puppets have risen or fallen in exact ratio to the state of tension between Roumania and Hungary, in which country Italy has also gambled heavily for power and privilege. If the claims of the Hungarian nationalists provoke a crisis on the frontiers of Hungary, Italy's supporters in Roumania are immediately elbowed out of power by the party friendly to

France, which can alone be depended upon to resist the revision of the peace treaties. If the danger seems more imminent in ex-Russian Bessarabia than in ex-Hungarian Transylvania, the anti-Russian party in Roumania returns to office, and with the approval of Italy a fresh reign of terror in Bessarabia stamps out any Moscow-inspired protest against Roumanian oppression.

Since the return of M. Titulescu to the direction of Roumania's foreign policy the Francophile and anti-Italian party had been almost continuously triumphant. The signature, in 1933, of a pact of non-aggression with the U.S.S.R., containing Soviet recognition of the existing régime in Bessarabia, has destroyed the chief weapon of the pro-Italian party. The entry of the Soviet Union into the League of Nations, the growth of imperialism in Italy, the revived fears of a restoration of the Habsburgs, and the belief that Mussolini is not unsympathetic to such a restoration, have all contributed to destroy the remaining vestiges of Italian influence in Bucharest. But recently a new and more dangerous rival to France seems to have assumed the upper hand in Roumania : Germany. Fears of a Habsburg restoration have resulted in a recrudescence of the pre-war Roumanian friendship with Germany, since the Nazi Third Reich is regarded in Bucharest, as in Belgrade, as the chief obstacle to a Habsburg restoration in Austria. Close relations are, moreover, believed to exist between the Roumanian Iron Guard, a Fascist organisation, and the National-Socialist party in Germany, and it is significant that Codreanu, the leader of the Iron Guard, and a friend of King Carol's mistress, Mme Lupescu, claims the friendship of Hitler.

The first result of this recent pro-German orientation of Roumania's foreign policy has been the elimination of M. Titulescu, who is rightly regarded in Germany as chiefly responsible for the *rapprochement* with Soviet Russia. And the defeat of the Titulescu party, if it proves to be of any permanence, may have incalculable consequences on Roumania's relations with France and the U.S.S.R.

[4]

The population of Roumania at the last census (1930) was just over eighteen millions. Military service is compulsory and universal between the ages of twenty-one and fifty. The peace establishment of the army is roughly 15,000 officers and 226,000 men, and in war-time is capable of expansion, on the French system of *cadres*, to a strength of about 1,500,000 all ranks. The air force comprises about 12,000 officers and men, and has an equipment of between 800 and 900 machines, mostly of French construction. The army is armed with Mannlicher rifles, field batteries of French 75's, and some heavy Krupp artillery.

The Roumanian Navy consists of a Black Sea force of 4 destroyers, 6 ex-Austrian torpedo-boats, 4 motor gunboats, a submarine and a depot ship ; and a Danube river flotilla of 7 monitors of 600 tons each, armed with 4.7 inch guns, 7 vedettes and other small craft. The Roumanian naval base is at Sulina, on the Black Sea, and a naval school is at Galatz. The building of another Black Sea base is under consideration.

In Greece, which has a population of roughly 6 millions, military service is also compulsory and universal for males between the ages of 21 and 50. The strength of the army in peace-time is about 5000 officers and 80,000 men, and in an emergency a force of between 300,000 and 400,000 could be mobilised. The infantry is armed with Mannlicher and Lebel rifles and with Hotchkiss, St. Etienne and Schwarzgloze machine-guns. The artillery possesses mountain guns of 65 mm., Schneider 75's and 105's, and Schneider, Krupp and other field guns.

The Greek Navy has been reorganised by a British naval mission. It comprises two pre-war light cruisers, recently re-fitted, 12 destroyers, 4 torpedo-boats, 4 minelayers, 6 submarines and other lighter craft. A new naval arsenal at Salamis has been under construction since 1931.

The defence forces of the two other states in the Balkan Entente, Jugoslavia and Turkey, are described elsewhere in this work.

[5]

Significant as is the renewed attempt to achieve a Balkan coalition, its power and its permanence should not be exaggerated. The unity of the four powers which subscribed the Balkan Pact is, to say the least, precarious. It is conditioned by common interests alone, and there happen to be few subjects of importance on which the four powers have the same interests to serve. Their respective attitudes to Italy, for example, vary from vigilant hostility, as in the case of Jugoslavia, to active friendship, as in the case of Greece. The Greek Government, at the outset, hesitated to sign the Balkan Pact lest its action should be construed by the Italians as a pledge to support Jugoslavia in any future Italo-Jugoslav dispute. Its eventual signature was subject, as we have seen, to the express reserve that Greece should not be called upon to make war upon Italy. And Greek statesmen at the time publicly announced that they had no interests in the Adriatic, and would not be dragged into any quarrel in that sea. The reservations stipulated by Greece were accepted by her Balkan allies without much difficulty, since in any event she was not to be asked to do more than assure the neutrality of Salonica, and thus guard Roumania and Jugoslavia from any surprise attack in that quarter.

But the Italo-Abyssinian War, and the danger it created early in 1936 of a naval conflict in the Eastern Mediterranean, caused another member of the Balkan alliance to warn its allies that it must not be expected to take up arms against Italy. This new warning was uttered by Turkey, and it fell unpleasantly upon the ears of the Jugoslav and Roumanian ministers assembled at the Balkan and Little Entente conferences held at Belgrade early in May, 1936. It forced the European allies of Turkey to realise that she was primarily an Asiatic power, and that her interests were paramount neither in the Balkans nor even in the Ægean, but in Asia Minor and in the security of the narrow waters which bridge the continents of Asia and Europe. It checked the growing friendship between Turkey and Jugoslavia, the advantages of which the Belgrade Government had lately seemed to prefer to her earlier and less particular entente with Roumania and Czechoslovakia, and thrust the Jugoslav statesmen sharply back to a grouping of purely European states on which they might count with more assurance in the event of an ultimate struggle with Italy on the one hand and with Hungary upon the other.

[6]

This intimation of Turkey's policy of neutrality in European disputes was accompanied, if not actually preceded, by a demand for the re-militarisation of the Dardanelles. The latter action seemed of such ominous portent to the vigilant Czechs and Roumanians, already sufficiently alarmed by the precedent of unilateral treaty-breaking created on March 7th by Hitler's military re-occupation of the Rhineland, that the leaders of the Little Entente issued from Belgrade on May 7th a dramatic statement of their attitude towards treaty revision, and reiterated their warning that a restoration of the Habsburgs would provoke war.

This declaration is so explicit, and of such importance in the light of the rapid development of the Austrian situation, that it merits examination. The common policy of the three states, Czechoslovakia, Jugoslavia and Roumania, is therein defined as follows :

1. During the past sixteen years the Little Entente states have exerted themselves to defend the cause of the League of Nations, of peace, and of the respect of international undertakings.

2. In the desire to preserve peace they have vigorously opposed any attempt to overthrow the existing state of things in Central Europe. For this reason they have consistently supported the efforts of the Western Powers to maintain the independence of Austria. They are opposed to any change in frontiers effected by a maleficent revisionism, *and also to the return of the Habsburg dynasty to the throne, an event which would inevitably provoke the gravest conflict in the Danube basin.*

3. They solemnly declare, at a moment particularly troublous in European history, that the states of the

Little Entente see no reason to modify in the slightest degree a policy which has been pursued hitherto continuously and with unshakable firmness. They are more than ever attached to it to-day, and will pursue it in future with the same energy and to the end, in the interests of European peace.

4. For this reason they declare with especial emphasis that the vital interests and the comprehension of the historic necessities of yesterday, to-day and to-morrow oblige them to remain forever indissolubly united each to the other. This truth is more evident than ever now that the international situation has produced great difficulties and even grave menaces for the peace of Europe.

5. For this reason they underline the fact of the profound and complete unity of their common international policy, whether it concerns their attitude to the League of Nations, to the independence of Austria and the return of the Habsburg dynasty, the respect of existing frontiers and the military clauses of treaties, or of international engagements of any kind, or whether it concerns their relations with France and Great Britain, Italy and Germany, Hungary, Bulgaria, Austria, Poland, the countries of the Balkan Entente, or the U.S.S.R. Their policy remains absolutely identical, based on the same principles, on the same feelings and the same common interests. The states of the Little Entente desire to proclaim this in order to avert in their own countries and in others any misunderstanding and any error. The attitude of the three countries of the Little Entente to any or all of the aforementioned states will be always the same, collectively and mutually loyal.

A month later, during secret conversations between King Carol of Roumania, the Regent Prince Paul of Jugoslavia and Dr. Edward Benes, the President of the Czechoslovak Republic, held at the Roumanian sovereign's shooting-lodge at Skroviste near Bucharest, the foregoing declaration of policy was re-affirmed. According to an official report published after the meeting, King Carol insisted that the Little Entente was a single international unit, and in close collaboration with the Balkan Entente it would pursue the defence of peace and of its own interests. " The first of these interests is respect for existing frontiers, *which are to remain forever unaltered,* and respect for the peace treaties. We must remain faithful to the League of Nations, and if experience proves that certain modifications ought to be made in the Covenant, we will accept no attack on the principle of the equality of states, nor any proposal that would tend to enfeeble the Covenant."

To this singularly intransigent declaration, Dr. Benes, the Czechoslovak President, added : " The Little Entente is the keystone in the structure of Central Europe, and of European peace, a column without which the European edifice will tumble in the midst of a conflict the consequences of which would be incalculable. We are ready to defend with all our strength the pledges given and the treaties signed, ready to act together and defend ourselves to the last breath in case of necessity."

It is clear that the chiefs of the Little Entente states had particularly in mind, when they made these brutally candid announcements of policy, the imminent contingency of a Habsburg restoration in Austria. It is less clear whether Turkey, in announcing to her partners in the Balkan Entente her resolve to preserve neutrality in all European disputes, considered as more immediately threatening a naval war between Great Britain, France and Italy in the Mediterranean or a land war involving Italy, Austria and Hungary on the one hand and the Little Entente states on the other. At all events the Turks were making their own preparations, as we shall now see, to meet all possible emergencies.

CHAPTER XI

TURKEY, THE U.S.S.R. AND THE STRAITS

[I]

SINCE the fall of Constantinople in 1453 and the destruction of the Byzantine Empire, the Ottoman power had excited the fear, the hatred, the envy or the anxiety of Christian Europe for wellnigh five centuries. It provided its neighbouring states in the Mediterranean with the ever-recurrent problem of their security. It provoked crusade after crusade from the West. It made periodical inroads into Central Europe, and after repeated sieges was only beaten back from the gates of Vienna by the redoubtable Polish warrior-king, John Sobieski. Until almost the end of the seventeenth century its corsairs sailed unchecked from the Golden Horn to the Pillars of Hercules, and although the naval prestige of the Turks, for long thought invincible, had been seriously shaken by the victory of the Christian fleets at Lepanto in 1571, they continued for another hundred years to burn and ravage the coasts of Southern Europe, and their hold on the Balkan peninsula, and on the entire northern coast of Africa, was practically unweakened.

At the beginning of the nineteenth century the decaying power of the Sultan, challenged although it was by Napoleon in Egypt and Syria and threatened from the north by the Tsars of Muscovy, nevertheless gave the conqueror of the world cause for anxiety. In 1808 he was still preoccupied by the enigma of the Caliph who bestrode Europe and Asia. In that year he wrote : " Who is to have Constantinople ? That is always the crux of the problem."

Yet twelve months earlier Turkish possession of that city had proved of signal service to his own fortunes. In 1807 a British fleet under Admiral Duckworth had been sent through the Dardanelles to subdue Constantinople, destroy the Turkish fleet, and aid Russia, England's ally against France, to gain egress from the Black Sea.

The expedition failed, like its successor 107 years later, and the retiring fleet was heavily bombarded from the Turkish forts in the Narrows.

With the defeat of Napoleon and the rise of the British Empire in the East the policy of British governments towards Constantinople underwent the first of many changes. Russia, and not France, was now seen as the enemy. The fear of Russia and the possibility of a flank attack on British sea routes to India caused successive British expeditions to the Crimea, Egypt and the Persian Gulf, and inspired the seizure of Aden and Cyprus.

During at least one period in the nineteenth century the Western powers were faced by the prospect of a virtual Russian-Turkish alliance. The treaty of Unkiar Skelessi, signed on July 8th, 1833, established the now-familiar principle of mutual assistance between Russia and Turkey in the event of any attack by a third power. The Sultan prudently restricted his eventual assistance, however, to the closing of the Straits to enemy warships if material support could not be furnished by the Sublime Porte. This is the first occasion in history on which Turkey entered into any public engagement concerning the Narrows, and voluntarily renounced her liberty of action concerning them. Eight years later, in the Straits Convention signed on July 13th, 1841, the Sultan announced his determination to maintain as a fixed policy of his empire the prohibition of the entry of ships of war into the Dardanelles and the Bosphorus so long as Turkey remained at peace. For their part the rulers of Russia, Austria, Great Britain, France and Prussia bound themselves to respect this principle.

In 1853, when a British fleet made its next appearance in the Straits, it was as an ally of Turkey and not as an ally of Russia. The Treaty of Paris, which ended the Crimean campaign, reaffirmed the prohibition already made at the close of the Napoleonic Wars against the entry of foreign war vessels into those contested waters. A generation later, in 1878, Great Britain again intervened to prevent Russia from seizing Constantinople. When the powers negotiated peace at Berlin she forced the Tsar almost at the sword-point to renounce the more excessive of his claims against Turkey, although Lord Salisbury long afterwards declared that in fighting the Crimean War and opposing Russia Great Britain had been backing the wrong horse.

[2]

When the policy which for half a century had made Turkey an instrument of British imperial designs was finally reversed, its reversal was less due to any diminishing fear of Russian expansion in Asia or Europe than to a growing fear of the imperialism of Germany. The German naval menace in the early years of this century drove a British government to come to terms with St. Petersburg regarding spheres of influence in the Near and Far East. The Anglo-Russian agreement of 1907, which ended for a time the rivalry between the two powers in Afghanistan and China, and gave Persia as a close preserve to the Russian imperialists, effectually alienated Turkey and drove her inevitably into the camp of the Central Powers.

Nevertheless the Porte, after the Young Turk Revolution in 1909 and the flight of the Sultan, Abdul Hamid, hesitated repeatedly before throwing in its lot definitely with a power whose Emperor had ridden on a white horse into Jerusalem, had initiated the Berlin-Baghdad railway, and entertained dangerous ambitions of acquiring an Islamic empire. It accepted, it is true, a German officer, General Liman van Sanders, as commander of the 1st Turkish Army Corps, and a German military mission with him, thereby driving the Tsar's foreign minister Sazonoff to such fury that he demanded naval, financial and economic reprisals against Turkey, a financial blockade of the Turks by the Triple Entente bankers, and the occupation of Trebizond, Beirout and Smyrna by the combined British, French and Russian fleets. But on the other hand the Sultan's government appointed a British admiral to a similar position in the Turkish Navy. And in June, 1913, it even offered to enter into a defensive alliance with Great Britain, or alternatively with the Triple Entente, an offer which if accepted might have changed the course of history.

It was, however, refused by Sir Edward Grey, who dreaded the prospect of appearing to challenge the Central

Powers almost as sincerely as he believed in the pacific intentions of the Russian Court and its ministers. Moreover, the patient diplomatic efforts of the Russian Government to induce its Western allies to accept Russian domination at Constantinople had already succeeded, for on the eve of the outbreak of war France and Great Britain were prepared to hand over the capital of the Ottoman Empire to the Tsar. Thus irrevocably Turkey was driven into the German and Austrian camp. And when on August 10th, 1914, the German cruisers *Goeben* and *Breslau* violated the Straits Convention by appearing in the Dardanelles, it was with the secret consent of the Sultan's government, which thenceforth associated its destinies with those of the Central Powers.

[3]

The rest of the story of Constantinople and the Straits belongs to the history of the Great War and of the peace which followed it. An Allied expedition to break the Turkish stranglehold on the Straits and deliver the Russian war fleet from its prison in the Black Sea, and with it the Russian grain ships from Odessa, came to disaster. It failed gloriously, but it failed. Two years later the Russian Revolution had broken out, and with the collapse of the empire of the Tsars ended for the time being the long preoccupation of British foreign policy with the imperialism of a power which alternately threatened British dominion in India by the land gate of Asia and menaced British sea communications in the Mediterranean by its domination of the Balkans and its prospective command of the Straits.

The Treaty of Sèvres, imposed upon the defeated Sultan, left him in possession of Constantinople indeed, but of a Constantinople surrounded by but a few square miles of Turkish territory. It deprived him of Eastern Thrace in Europe, and of western Asia Minor. It deprived him of sovereign rights over Turkish waters, and forbade him to fortify the Straits, which were henceforth to be open to the ships of war or ships of peace of all nations—in other words, placed the power occupying Constantinople, and the littoral states of the Black Sea, at the mercy of the strongest naval force in the Mediterranean, which then, and for the next eighteen years, happened to be British.

That Treaty was signed in 1919. Three years later it was nullified, so far at least as its territorial and economic dispensations went, by the military resurrection of Turkey under Mustapha Kemal Pasha, who afterwards became the Ghazi, and ultimately was known as Kemal Ataturk. The Turks swept the Greeks out of Asia Minor and out of Eastern Thrace, regaining European Turkey as far as the Maritza River, and the farther limits of Adrianople. The Sultan was deposed. Republican Turkey denounced the ancient régime of the Capitulations, captured all the war stocks purchased by the Greeks with British money, and appeared triumphantly at the Conference table in Lausanne at the end of 1922 to negotiate a new treaty with the Western Powers. But the Lausanne Treaty, while it confirmed the Turks in their new power and independence, relentlessly reimposed upon them the obligation not to fortify or garrison the shores of the Dardanelles, although it permitted the maintenance of a small garrison in Constantinople ; and in establishing freedom of navigation through the Straits for all ships of war, it reversed a principle which had been a cardinal feature of British as well as Turkish imperial policy for nearly a century.

[4]

The Lausanne Conference was the first experience gained by the Turkey of Mustapha Kemal in European diplomacy. Her delegation to that conference was led by Ismet Pasha, the small, dark, gentle-faced and gentle-voiced warrior who had been chiefly responsible for the recent victories over the Greeks. Great Britain was represented by the late Lord Curzon, then Foreign Secretary. The recently established Fascist Government in Italy was represented for the first time in a diplomatic assembly. Mussolini himself made a brief and dramatic visit to Lausanne to confer with M. Poincaré and Lord Curzon. At the later stages of the Conference, when the future status of the Straits was to be decided, all the other interested nations—Soviet Russia, Roumania, Greece, Bulgaria—were invited to join the discussions. The late M. Tchicherin, then Soviet Foreign Commissary, arrived as chief delegate of the Soviet Union, accompanied by Rakovsky, later to be exiled to

Siberia, and Vorovsky, doomed to die before the end of the Conference at the hand of an assassin. The representative of Bulgaria was her Premier, Stambulisky, also destined to fall before many months a victim of assassination. Of the other principal delegates at Lausanne the only statesmen who have escaped death, exile or obscurity are Mussolini and Ismet Pasha—both the spokesmen of new dictatorial régimes.

To gain their ends at Lausanne—which were primarily the revision of the Sèvres Treaty, the recognition of their own newly constituted republic, and the abolition of the vexatious system of Capitulations which were a legacy from the Osmanli dynasty, the Turks relied chiefly upon their own record of military successes and upon the mutual jealousies of the Western Powers. France and Great Britain in particular had rival interests in the Near East. They had already quarrelled over the Greco-Turkish War. They were, moreover, seriously in dispute over German reparations, a dispute which was shortly to be made dangerously bitter by M. Poincaré's invasion of the Ruhr. Ismet Pasha contrived very skilfully to exploit these differences between the two great Western Powers to his own country's advantage. Turkey emerged from the Lausanne Conference largely liberated from the heavy burden of financial and political obligations which had weighed like a millstone about the neck of the old Ottoman Empire. The obligation not to fortify the Dardanelles, and to permit ships of war to pass freely through the Narrows, seemed to Ismet a very moderate price to pay for the almost complete revision of the Sèvres Treaty—all the more since it was accepted with the mental reservation that treaties were not eternal, and that this particular limitation of sovereignty would not forever be acquiesced in by Turkey.

Not so, however, reasoned Ismet's ally, mentor and critic, the Bolshevik diplomatist Tchicherin. The late George Tchicherin had been reared in the Tsarist school of diplomacy. For all his Marxism—a Marxism more than tinctured by the mild Liberal philosophy of the pre-war Bloomsbury in which he had long been a not over-discontented exile—he thought on traditional lines. He was preoccupied by the same dangers that had haunted the vision of his Tsarist predecessors in the direction of Russian

foreign policy. Many years earlier, as a young man in
St. Petersburg, he had read a long-forgotten work by Lord
Curzon on the struggle for power in Asia, and had been
impressed by its reasoning.

And now, at Lausanne, he met that redoubtable
imperialist face to face. The one, magnificent in his
triumphant complacency of asserted power, defended a
capitalist empire with far-flung lines of communication,
and great dependencies which bordered Russia's Asiatic
dominions in the East. The other, nervous, flustered,
with his mind filled with memories of the century-long
struggle between two great empires for the command of
Constantinople and for domination in Asia, represented a
Socialist republic just issued from a life-and-death struggle
with counter-revolutionaries and interventionists, and still
suspicious of real or imaginary combinations of capitalist
powers intent on destroying her.

Tchicherin battled long and angrily therefore against
the proposed demilitarisation of the Straits. He saw, and
rightly, that so long as the Dardanelles could not be closed
to fleets of war, and defended by a power which was either
the active ally of Soviet Russia or a benevolent neutral, the
Black Sea lay open to any powerful aggressor and the few
war vessels owned by the Soviet Government in that sea
were in danger of being overwhelmed. But in this he
fought a losing game. His Turkish ally supported him
without conviction. The other Black Sea states at that
time, and for years afterwards, were hostile to the U.S.S.R.
The Soviet diplomat was outmanœuvred. The coalition
of his adversaries was too strong for him. The utmost
concession that he could obtain was the provision that the
strength of any foreign war fleet entering the Straits should
not exceed the strength of the strongest fleet in the Black
Sea—a concession of little importance in peace-time, and
of none at all in time of war, since Turkey was denied the
power to enforce observance of the limitation.

[5]

Between 1923, the year in which the Lausanne Treaty
and the Statute of the Dardanelles were signed, and 1936,
no incident occurred to challenge either the naval security

of the Black Sea Powers, or the neutrality of the Straits.
On several occasions in 1934 and 1935 the Government of
Kemal Ataturk unofficially announced its intention of re-
opening the question of the Straits, but on each occasion
was urged by the diplomatic representatives of Great
Britain and France not to press the matter. In 1936,
however, the League of Nations dispute with Italy and the
imminent danger of war in the Eastern Mediterranean
provided Turkey with an opportunity too favourable to be
ignored. Either as combatant or as neutral, in the conflict
which seemed threatening, she was at a serious disadvantage
so long as the Straits were undefended, and Constantinople,
her greatest city, and the former capital of Turkey, together
with her European and Asiatic coasts lay at the mercy of a
hostile fleet.

Early in April, 1936, the government of Angora accordingly addressed a Note to each of the nine powers—Great
Britain, France, Italy, Japan, Greece, Bulgaria, Roumania,
Jugoslavia and the U.S.S.R.—which negotiated the Straits
Convention of July 24th, 1923, requesting the early revision
of the clauses of that convention which provided for the
demilitarisation of the shores of the Dardanelles, the Sea
of Marmora and the Bosphorus. In this Note the Turkish
Government declared that the political crisis had clearly
demonstrated the inefficacy of existing collective guarantees, the machinery for enforcing which was much too
dilatory in action. No real guarantee existed under the
present convention that the security and neutrality of the
Straits would be secured, and Turkey could not be expected
to remain any longer indifferent to the grave contingencies
that might arise. The Note ended with the statement
that the Turkish Government was ready to enter into
negotiations with the object of reaching a speedy settlement of the question of the Straits, and of securing at once
the security and inviolability of Turkish territory and the
greatest freedom of navigation for commercial vessels
between the Mediterranean and the Black Sea.

The Turkish demand was received with all the more
sympathy in British and French official quarters since it
was clearly understood that, failing a revision of the Statute
of the Dardanelles by friendly negotiation, Turkey was

prepared to emulate Hitler's unilateral denunciation of the Rhineland demilitarisation clauses of the Versailles and Locarno Treaties.

[6]

Delegates of all the signatories of the Lausanne Treaty assembled at Montreux in June, with the solitary exception of Italy, which declined official representation on the ground that the hostile combination of Mediterranean powers created during the Abyssinian campaign was still in being, but sent an observer. Among the eight powers represented at the Conference, agreement was readily reached regarding Turkey's claim to re-militarise the shores of the Straits. The British demand for freedom of navigation of all ships in peace-time was also accepted in principle but subject to important reservations. In war as in peace-time the free passage of merchant vessels through the Straits by day or night was agreed, with the sole reservation that, in case of war in which Turkey is a belligerent, merchant shipping of non-hostile powers may not carry cargoes for enemy purposes and is limited to passage in the day-time.

Chief among the subjects of dispute at the Conference was the clause relating to the passage of warships through the Narrows. The Soviet Union, Roumania and Bulgaria wished for obvious reasons to close the Black Sea to the war fleets of all non-littoral states. Turkey proposed that in peace-time all warships should be admitted by day through the Straits, with the exception of submarines. M. Litvinoff, the Soviet delegate, demanded that this exception should only apply to non-Black Sea Powers, explaining that the Soviet Union might require one day to send its fleet from the Black Sea to other Soviet ports. Great Britain and Japan, each for her own and quite distinct reasons, opposed the closing of the Black Sea to non-littoral war fleets. Soon the discussion centred in the interpretation of the various mutual assistance pacts signed between France, the U.S.S.R., Turkey and Roumania. M. Titulescu, the Roumanian delegate, bitterly accused Great Britain of pursuing one policy at Geneva, where she supported the principle of mutual assistance, and a different and contradictory policy at Montreux, where her delegates opposed that principle.

In the end the British Government, under pressure from France, made some concessions to the Russian and Roumanian attitudes, and Japan, somewhat to the general surprise, abandoned her general policy of opposing the U.S.S.R. so far as to accept the draft Convention with reservations.

The new Convention concerning the régime in the Straits was signed at Montreux on July 20th by eight of the original nine powers responsible for the Lausanne Treaty, and came into force immediately, so far as the re-militarisation of the Straits was concerned. It is valid for twenty years, but may be revised every five years. It contains twenty-nine articles and three annexes, and begins by " recognising and re-affirming " the principle of the liberty of passage and navigation by sea in the Dardanelles, the Sea of Marmora and the Bosphorus. The duties of the International Straits Commission are transferred to the Turkish Government, and the Commission is abolished. Article 25 of the Convention contains, in deference to the arguments of Russia, France and their allies, the important declaration that " no provisions of the present Convention violate any of the rights and obligations devolving from the Covenant of the League of Nations either for Turkey or for any other high contracting party."

The main provisions of the Convention are the following :

As to merchant vessels, it is established that in time of peace such vessels will have complete liberty of passage and of navigation in the Straits by day and night whatever their flag subject to certain sanitary supervision and restrictions.

In time of war, Turkey not being a belligerent, merchant ships, whatever their flag, will also have liberty of passage and navigation. If Turkey is a belligerent, merchant vessels flying a flag other than that of a country at war with Turkey will similarly have freedom of passage provided they do not assist the enemy in any way. The passage must be made by day and along a prescribed route.

In cases where Turkey considers herself menaced by war the principle of freedom of passage will still be maintained, but certain restrictions such as the prohibition of passage by night and compulsory pilotage along a prescribed route are enforceable.

As to warships a distinction is made between those belonging to the littoral and non-littoral Powers. Article 14 lays down that the maximum total tonnage " of foreign naval forces " which may at any one time pass through the Straits must not exceed 15,000 tons nor be composed of more than nine vessels. Littoral Powers, however, may send through the Straits more ships of the line even if the tonnage be greater. The passage must be made singly and with a maximum escort of two destroyers.

In time of peace light surface craft, small cruisers and auxiliary vessels may, whatever their flag, have liberty of passage into the Straits. Prior notice must be given and entry made by day.

Submarines of Black Sea Powers which have been purchased abroad may pass through the Straits for purposes of repair at foreign shipyards or for rejoining their base. (This article was inserted on the insistence of Roumania, most of whose submarines have been built in England.)

Prior notice for the passage of warships through the Straits must be given to the Turkish Government through diplomatic channels.

The Turkish Government reserves the right, despite the provisions of the other articles of the treaty, to invite on a courtesy visit to any harbour in the Straits foreign naval forces of any tonnage or composition. The maximum tonnage that non-Black Sea Powers may at any one time accumulate in the Black Sea must not exceed 30,000 tons.

If, however, at any future time the tonnage of the strongest Black Sea fleet shall exceed by 10,000 tons the strength of the strongest fleet on the date of signature, then the 30,000 tons may be raised by 15,000.

Should non-Black Sea Powers desire to send naval forces for humanitarian reasons into the Black Sea authorisation must be obtained from the Turkish Government. A reply must be given within 48 hours, and after consultation with other Black Sea Powers. The forces despatched to the Black Sea must, however, in no case exceed 8000 tons, and may not remain for longer than 21 days.

If Turkey considers herself " menaced by an imminent danger of war " she may exercise her discretion about the passage of all warships. Thus a " menace of war " is placed on the same basis as a " status of war."

Civil aircraft have the right of passage from the Mediterranean to the Black Sea and across the Straits from Europe to Asia subject to certain restrictions.

[7]

The population of Turkey according to the last general census (1927), which was also the first in Turkish history, was just over 13½ millions. At the present day it is probably about 15 millions; 92 per cent of the total live in Asiatic Turkey, and the remainder in Europe. Men are called up for military service at the age of twenty-one and remain liable to serve during the next twenty-six years. The strength of the peace-time army is approximately 20,000 officers and 120,000 men. In a national emergency probably an army of half a million could be put in the field. The President of the Republic, Kemal Ataturk, is supreme commander of the army, and is a general of proved capacity with a brilliant record both in the World War and in the Greco-Turkish War which followed it, and which resulted in the resurrection of Turkey and its reorganisation on modern European lines under the leadership of Kemal. The infantry is equipped with Mauser rifles; the artillery with Krupp 75's, and 10·5 and 12 cm. Schneider howitzers. The air force has been trained by French officers. The navy comprises the 22,500-ton battle-cruiser *Yavuz Sultan Selim*, formerly the German *Goeben*, built in 1911 and in 1930 completely refitted by French shipbuilders, and armed with ten 11-inch guns and other smaller guns; an old 9000-ton battleship, the *Tourgout Reis*, armed with six 11-inch guns and used as a training ship; two light cruisers, the 3830-ton *Hamidieh* and the 3300-ton *Medjidieh*, both built in 1903; 4 small gunboats, 4 new destroyers, 2 new

submarines and 2 old ones. A new naval base has been
built at Izmit. Four new submarines have recently been
ordered by the Turkish Government, and a depot-ship of
6000 tons has been purchased from Germany.

Little information is available regarding the U.S.S.R.'s
forces in the Black Sea. The official Soviet commentator
Karl Radek made a significant reference to Soviet naval
policy in an article published in *Izvestia* in May, 1936, in
which he stated that the U.S.S.R. must build not one battle
fleet but three, since its three zones of naval activity, the
Baltic, the Pacific and the Black Sea, were mutually isolated.
No reliable statistics have been published regarding the
vessels under construction or projected in the Soviet Union.
Most of the additions made since the Revolution to the
Russian Navy are in the categories of light cruisers, light
destroyers and submarines. The latest official figures concerning the strength of the Soviet fleet attribute to it the
possession of 4 battleships (3 of which date from 1914),
5 cruisers, 2 cruiser minelayers, 19 flotilla leaders and
destroyers, 23 submarines, 4 sloops, 2 gunboats and 6 minesweepers.

[8]

During the first fifteen years of the Soviet Union's
existence the question of the demilitarisation of the Straits
had a purely defensive interest for Moscow. The Black
Sea, so far from being a Russian lake closed to outside intervention by the bottleneck of the Dardanelles, became—once
those narrows were open to any war fleet from the Mediterranean, and were undefended by their natural custodian—a
prison instead of a refuge. But since 1934, the year of the
entry of the U.S.S.R. into the League of Nations, the
Bolshevik leaders have contracted certain obligations in
Europe which oblige them to think of the Straits in terms
of offensive strategy. Soviet Russia is now bound, both by
the League Covenant and by her treaties of non-aggression
and mutual assistance with other Eastern Europe states, to
intervene in any European dispute in which League interests
or those of her allies are threatened. She could not remain
aloof from a Mediterranean war in which either the League
collectively, or France, Turkey and possibly Roumania
individually were concerned.

One of the consequences of her acceptance of the League of Nations Covenant and the system of collective security based thereon, is that, henceforth, the Soviet Union cannot be content with a Black Sea fleet barely adequate for defensive purposes. She is obliged, so long as a general limitation of armaments continues to recede into the unpredictable future, to build up to the level dictated by her moral and political commitments in the Mediterranean. In January, 1936, the Soviet Committee of National Defence reported : " Hitherto we have devoted all our efforts to building up a submarine fleet. But we must also possess a strong surface force. Our navy must be very powerful in every respect if we desire it to conform to our other armaments."

Since the war the Black Sea fleet of the U.S.S.R. has been of negligible importance. Even with the return to Russia (under the Franco-Soviet Treaty) of the remnants of the Wrangel fleet for many years sequestered by the French Government in the Tunisian harbour of Bizerta, the Soviet naval forces in that sea are still inconsiderable. The stubbornness of the struggle put up by M. Litvinoff at the Montreux Conference against the proposed limits to the tonnage of Black Sea fleets in transit through the Straits suggested that early steps are to be taken by the Moscow Government to increase its naval forces in those waters. And the readiness shown by the British Government to meet the wishes of the U.S.S.R. in regard to the disputed Article II of the Montreux Convention may well have been inspired by a desire to establish a certain equilibrium in the recently disturbed Eastern Mediterranean. The permission given to Turkey to re-fortify the Dardanelles, the fortification by Italy of the islands of Rhodes and Leros, the existence of French naval bases at Beirout and Tripoli in Syria, and the prospective construction of British bases at Alexandria and Cyprus, are all eloquent of the importance which the Eastern waters of the Mediterranean have recently acquired in British eyes.

Doubtless Downing Street has been impressed by Soviet Russia's zealous interpretation of the League of Nations Covenant in the anxious controversies of 1936, and also by her decision to sign a Naval Pact with Great Britain analogous to the Anglo-German Pact. And it may be that

British uncertainty of Japan's ultimate designs in the Pacific has been another important factor in influencing recent British policy with regard to the naval ambitions of the U.S.S.R.

However this may be, it is uncontested that the real success of the Montreux negotiations was the liberty of movement claimed for and obtained on behalf of the Soviet Union's Black Sea fleet by M. Litvinoff. The text of Article II of the new Statute of the Dardanelles, which may, one day, acquire historic significance, is as follows :

" The Littoral Powers of the Black Sea are authorised to despatch through the Straits their ships of the line of a tonnage in excess of that laid down in paragraph 1 of Article 14 (in which foreign warships are limited to 15,000 tons) on condition that these vessels pass singly through the Straits, escorted by not more than two destroyers."

The question of free egress from the Black Sea into the Mediterranean has another and equally vital interest for the Soviet Union. It contains her only ice-free port in Europe. Leningrad, Cronstadt and Archangel are virtually closed for several months of the year, despite the use of the most powerful ice-breakers in the world. The bulk of Russia's export of grain is carried from the Black Sea port of Odessa. The whole of her export of oil is piped into tankers in the Black Sea port of Batoum. The security of her oil supplies, moreover, may have an important bearing on the next war. Oil has become the first of the essential raw materials of naval warfare. The U.S.S.R. possesses, after the United States, the largest oilfields in the world, and its potential resources in oil are possibly even greater. Its output in crude oil is roughly one-tenth of the world output. If by any act of war the supply of oil from the United States were cut off, or were greatly diminished in volume, Russia would become the greatest producer of oil in the world outside the American continent. Its supplies would become of paramount importance to European governments, for the Mosul oilfield, whose yield reaches Europe by pipe-lines at Tripoli (in Syria) and Haifa (in Palestine) after hundreds of miles of journey across the dangerous Syrian desert, will not for many years become a great producing centre.

PART THREE

THE SHORE OF AFRICA

CHAPTER I

MOROCCO

[1]

THE British Empire was founded upon the acquisition of India. The French Empire, at a later stage of the colonial struggle, began with Morocco. Both dependencies were originally protectorates. Morocco, in theory, is still one. Its modern history, the story of its subjection to Europe, of its exploitation and development, of its part in the intrigues and bickerings which foreshadowed the World War, belongs to the twentieth century. The whole of the story is far from written, is not even conjectured. Its resources are not yet fully known, and hardly tapped. Its economic possibilities, its strategic utility, its weaknesses and dangers will only be fully realised when a new war shakes Europe to its foundations. Its future is bound up with the future of Africa, the last of the great unknown continents. Its destiny is at the mercy of hazard, or the outcome of the ultimate struggle for the mastery of the Mediterranean.

A great country, as large in land area as France and two and a half times larger than Great Britain, and known to its inhabitants as Moghreb-el-Aksa—the Farthest West. A country which in the European winter is a green paradise, in summer an arid tract of desert, sirocco-scorched, locust-ridden, with dried-up rivers and bleak mountains in whose clefts alone the sheep of the Berber find pasture. But a country for all that capable, in its brief seasons of fertility, of producing three crops a year, growing wheat, barley, oats, beans, maize, linseed, cotton, tobacco and early vegetables for the European markets. A country rich in lemons, oranges, almonds, figs and dates, in cork, cedar, oak, arar and argan trees ; in great herds of cattle and horses, sheep, pigs and goats. And finally a country with vast resources in oil, phosphates, lead ore, and smaller but not negligible quantities of manganese, gold, silver, tin, antimony, copper, coal and iron.

Its population is small (always an inducement to the conqueror)—roughly six millions, in all, of whom five millions are within the limits of the French zone. The inhabitants are, in the majority, Islamised Berbers and Arabs, with a small admixture (about one in twenty) of native Jews and foreigners.

[2]

The story of France's diplomatic conquest of Morocco has been told in the earlier chapter on Tangier. By successive conventions she purchased British approval (at the price of a similar disinterestedness in Egypt), narrowed the interests of Spain to a coastal zone in the north, bought off Germany by concessions elsewhere, and finally, under the Treaty of Versailles, eliminated that power from Africa altogether. Great Britain's primary interest in Morocco lay in its strategical command of the Straits of Gibraltar, and care has been taken in both the public and the secret articles of the Anglo-French Convention of 1904 respecting Egypt and Morocco to ensure the permanent neutrality of that part of the Moroccan coast which confronts Europe across the narrow sea.

It was expressly stipulated that "in order to secure the free passage of the Straits of Gibraltar" a stretch of Moroccan coast comprised between, but not including, the future Spanish town of Melilla on the Mediterranean and the right bank of the river Sabu on the Atlantic was to remain unfortified. In one of the secret clauses of the Convention it was prescribed that France should endeavour to reach an understanding with Spain defining and limiting that country's interests in Morocco, and another secret clause stipulated that the Spanish zone of influence should not exceed the hinterland of the African littoral opposite the coast of Spain, and that any territory thus attributed to Spain should never be alienated by her. Finally it was provided that the Anglo-French agreement should remain in force whether Spain accepted it or not.

A few months later, however, negotiations between France

and Spain were successfully concluded, and a separate
Franco-Spanish Convention confirmed the Anglo-French
agreement. By it France sub-leased to Spain a portion of the
territory which she hoped eventually to lease directly, but
over which she as yet had no juridical or other rights, from
the Sultan of Morocco. Those rights were only conceded,
in effect, in the French Treaty signed with the Sherifian
Government in 1912.

[s]

Thus the diplomatic conquest of Morocco anticipated its
political conquest by eight years. Military subjugation of
the country was not to be completed until 1925, when the
insurrection of the Riffi under Abdel Krim, undertaken first
against the Spaniards and ultimately extended to the French
zone, was finally crushed. But in the meantime the greater
portion of Morocco had been steadily brought under
French control by that remarkable soldier-administrator,
the late Marshal Lyautey. Lyautey directly reversed the
colonial policy pursued for upwards of eighty years past by
the French in Algeria. There the method employed had
been that of assimilation. Algeria was treated as a province
of metropolitan France. Native laws and customs were
replaced by the less flexible Code Napoléon. French colonists, soldiers and functionaries had paramount influence and
privileges in the country. The Arab was forced to acquire
the language, the customs and the law of the French overlord—a subjection to which, after the revolts of 1830–1847,
he resigned himself all the more philosophically since for
centuries Algeria had already known the even more arbitrary if less energetically pursued domination of the Sultans
of Turkey.

But the Moroccan Arabs and Berbers were of a different
mettle. They had never submitted to the yoke of the
Ottoman Empire. Although of the Islamic faith, they
recognised as Caliph their own Sultan in Fez and not the
Sultan in Constantinople. They were of a hardier and
wilder breed, with a long tradition of culture, freedom and
independence, and moreover with still vivid memories of
the Moorish domination of Spain, and the splendour of
their own ancient royal court in Granada. It was Lyautey's
especial genius that he sensed this difference, and rising

above the limitations of his own profession demanded and exercised the right to administer Morocco, of which he had been appointed Resident-General, in his own manner.

His policy was one of collaboration, not of domination. It was based on the sound maxim that " the adversaries of to-day are the colleagues of to-morrow." He pacified wild and rebellious regions by the simple Roman expedient of building good roads through them, believing and demonstrating the palpable truth that civilisation follows communications. He encouraged fairs, trading, schools, land settlement, agriculture. He proclaimed himself the minister and the right hand of the Sultan (in 1927 Mulay Youssef, who had reigned from 1912, died, and was succeeded by his third son, Sidi Mohammed, the present ruler), insisted upon respect for native customs and tribal laws, pacified dissident tribesmen south of the Atlas and in the black and dangerous Taza zone, not fully subdued until 1928, by the adroit nomination of their chieftains as local administrators, and brought prosperity to Morocco by stimulating the sale of native products in France and other European countries.

In the end he had acquired wide and sincere popularity in the country. He alone had been able to keep Morocco free from internal disturbance during the Great War, without asking for a single additional French soldier to augment his small force of occupation. He had turned a dangerous liability for France into a definite asset, and the result was that Morocco became a source of raw material, food and man-power during the perilous years in which her conquerors and protectors were fighting for their existence in Europe.

[4]

The most dramatic evidence of the success of the Lyautey method of colonisation was furnished by the Riff rebellion in the neighbouring zone.

Until the advent of the Republic in 1931, Spanish colonial methods had not greatly changed since the sixteenth century. The arrogance, the indolence, the corruption, the inefficiency, and the sombre military pride which had successively caused the ejection of the Spaniards from the Netherlands, in the sixteenth and seventeenth centuries, and from the Central and South American states in the beginning of the nineteenth century, were displayed at their crudest in Spanish Morocco between 1904 and 1921. The Riff mountaineers, like the border tribesmen in North-West India, revolted primarily because they were cut off from the opportunities of trade and barter in the plains. Hunger, and not the impulse to independence, drove Abdel Krim originally to attack the Spaniard. An early victory over the slothful and unprepared Spanish army caused all the malcontents in Northern Morocco to crowd in sudden enthusiasm to his banner.

The war dragged on for years, and in April, 1925, overran the loosely-defined boundary into the French zone. The French took a hand in the operations against the Riffan leader, and their intervention, more vigorously and efficiently undertaken than the war had hitherto been, led to the encirclement and surrender of Abdel Krim, who was deported with his wives and children and a not ungenerous civil list to an island in the Indian Ocean. The Riff war gave Lyautey's political enemies in France a new weapon. Worn out, disillusioned, and resentful of the critical and discouraging attitude shown to him by the Painlevé Government in Paris, the veteran administrator resigned.

Nevertheless his work had, in the main, been accomplished. His methods were not renounced by the series of civilians (ending in the present administrator, M. Peyrouton) who succeeded him as Resident-General. The immense legend he had acquired persists in Morocco after his death. He had succeeded in that rarest of all colonial enterprises—the difficult art of making the conqueror not only respected but held in friendly esteem, on a footing of equality, by the conquered. And the result is that in Morocco even to-day, in a time of intense economic and financial depression, when the native is, according to a statement made to the author by a French colonist during a recent visit, *criblé d'impôts* (literally, riddled with taxes), the relations between the two nations are intimate, friendly and peaceful. In the Spanish zone, despite the reforms introduced since the creation of the Republic in Madrid, the Spaniard has not succeeded in making himself liked by the native. At the most, as I have had occasion to note, he is tolerated, in spite of the infinitely lighter burden of taxation he has imposed, and his indifference to the religion, customs, and hygienic habits of the native. Whereas in the French zone, although the native is subject to a complicated and vexatious system of taxes, laws, traffic and civic regulations, and is on occasion forcibly ejected from his vermin-ridden tent or hut, and rigorously washed, de-loused and reclothed by a French sanitary patrol, Moor and European have achieved a relationship of moderate amity.

[5]

The reason may be sought partly in the political character of the French nation, partly in its racial character. The principles of the French Revolution, however insincerely invoked or bitterly derided on occasion in the Chamber of Deputies, have nevertheless had vital and lasting consequences for the relations between the French and their dependent peoples. The French colonial functionary, like all French functionaries, is usually the son of humble parents. Frequently he is born of peasant stock, in which the equalitarian principle of the Revolution of 1889 is most deeply ingrained. He has not a moral but an instinctive sense of the equality of peoples. He is not influenced by distinctions of colour or race.

The French colonist is even more fiercely individualist than the administrator. His strongest instinct is to found a family and to defend it against the encroachments of his neighbour or his Government. Next in order after that primitive instinct is his passion for land. So long as these twin interests are not threatened, he has little class or race prejudice. He recognises the equal rights of negroes, brown men, yellow men and white. His motive in colonisation is neither moral nor political nor humanitarian, but purely economic. He leaves his ancestral village, buys land in semi-barbarous countries, raises crops, intermarries with the native races, mixes socially with his native rivals in agriculture and trade as easily and successfully as in his native France the black lawyer-deputies from Senegal enter the Chamber, practise law in Paris, marry white women and are completely free from ostracism, social inhibitions and taboos. He carries with him the tolerant republican spirit, the graces of the French language, the amenities of French life, the culture and the traditions of France. In

whatever country he establishes himself the familiar and
friendly features of the French scene follow him : the
café with its terrace, the multi-coloured French apéritifs,
the wines and dishes of France, newspapers, the shabby but
distinctive uniforms, the diverse accents of the mother
tongue, the small comforts, the cynical, shoulder-shrugging
tolerance of official confusions or contradictions, the
passionate interest in politics everywhere.

Moreover, he readily accommodates himself to the
climate, the cooking, the atmosphere, the customs and the
mental processes of the country in which he has become a
voluntary exile. The result is that whereas in British India
official architecture, churches, barracks, clubs, restaurants,
schools, social life, sports and all other evidence of conquest
are upon rigidly and unforgettably British lines, in Morocco,
Indo-China and the other French dependencies there has
been a spontaneous and admiring interest in native art and
customs. Official buildings, mosques, cafés, villas, barracks,
museums and shops all conform to the natural and native
arts and habits of the people.

British India looks appallingly like Aldershot, when it is
not a painful attempt to imitate Balmoral, Cheltenham and
St. Pancras. In Rabat, Fez, Meknes, Marrakesh and other
cities in Morocco (with the solitary exception of Casablanca,
which is an entirely European commercial city, neither
better nor worse than a thousand others in Europe and
America, and built upon malarial marshes at the edge of
the sea) the buildings of modern French construction have
either grown up alongside the Moorish city, and independently of it, in conformity with local design and colouring
and with the most agreeable of results, or have been so
cunningly interposed (as in Marrakesh) among houses of
Moorish architecture that they do not offend the eye. In
Rabat the whole of the administrative city newly built
outside the old walls of the Moorish town is a model of
grace and dignity, and faithfully although not slavishly
follows the principles of native architecture. French
Rabat, although nothing like so ostentatious as British
New Delhi, and costing but a fraction of it, may well seem
to an unprejudiced posterity the more admirable example
of imperial architecture.

[6]

Morocco is capable of almost limitless development. It is, in many parts, more fertile than Algeria, and richer in mineral wealth. It is the most promising of all the regions of Northern Africa. It has in recent years been the subject of a land boom as sudden and as sensational as any ever recorded in European history. Between 1926 and 1929 real estate in Casablanca changed hands as often as twenty-five times in a single day. In one year capital values appreciated by 500 per cent. There was a boom in wheat, in phosphates, in oil-bearing properties, in sheep-farming, in hotels, cafés and restaurants. Thousands of young and active French settlers from France or from Algeria bought land in Morocco at high prices and prepared to enjoy the fruits of the long period of prosperity which seemed ahead.

Then came the world depression. The over-capitalised business enterprises collapsed. Hotel proprietors, manufacturers and farmers went bankrupt. The colonists who had sunk everything they owned into land held grimly on and waited for a rise in agricultural prices. Their patience and their hope have not yet been rewarded. The country is still suffering from an unparalleled economic crisis. Nevertheless the public finances of Morocco are healthy. In the years of prosperity a considerable reserve fund was accumulated from recurring Budget surpluses, and this has been drawn upon since 1930 to help meet the deficit in the Budget caused by the collapse in prices.

Thanks to such contributions from the reserve fund, and to an increase in taxation, the Budget of the Sherifian Government has been regularly balanced. The total receipts in the ordinary Budget for 1935 were estimated at 890,003,000 francs, as compared with 878,811,000 francs for 1934. The total imports for 1934 amounted to 879,961 tons valued at 1,319,704,000 francs, and the total exports to 1,990,716 tons valued at 667,395,000 francs. Compared with the previous year, imports had declined by 126,800 tons and 212·7 million francs, but exports had increased by 265,900 tons and 67·1 million francs.

The largest proportion of Morocco's trade (roughly one-half of the whole) is with France : but all countries trading

with her, including Great Britain, have in recent years lost
ground to Japan. In 1934 the competition in Japanese
textiles reduced the imported cotton-piece goods from
Lancashire to one-half of the 1933 figure, which itself was
but a small proportion of the earlier import total. It is
noteworthy that the adverse trade balance of French
Morocco has been halved during the past five years, and the
process of reduction continues. During the first six months
of 1935 the French zone increased its exports by 50 per
cent over those for the corresponding period in 1934, and
reduced its imports by about 15 per cent. In the period
January–June, 1935, the exports of phosphates reached
645,000 tons, vegetable fibre 36,700 tons, manganese 6700
tons, beans 8000 tons, early vegetables 24,300 tons. The
wheat exports during the same period were 64,000 tons
higher than those of the previous year.

The capital invested in urban buildings in Morocco
(including the value of the sites occupied) reaches the
considerable total of 6500 million francs. Building activity
has naturally fallen off since the economic crisis made its
effects felt in Morocco, and the falling-off in the total
value of building permits between the years 1933 and 1934
is officially estimated at 197 million francs. In the earlier
year the customs duty alone on imported building materials
had brought 74 million francs into the Sherifian Treasury.

[7]

French sea communications with Morocco fall under
three heads :

1. The route from France's Mediterranean ports to the
   ports of Algeria—via Marseilles–Algiers, or Marseilles–
   Oran, or Port Vendres–Oran—whence goods are
   carried by rail or road to Morocco.
2. The route from Marseilles to Tangier, via Barcelona.
3. The routes from France's Atlantic ports, Bordeaux,
   Nantes and Brest, to Casablanca, Port Lyautey, Saffi
   and Agadir, all new and developing ports on the
   Atlantic seaboard of Morocco.

The security of these routes depends upon a number of
diverse factors. The distance between Marseilles and

Algiers is 410 miles, and in mid-voyage the French steamers on this route are within 250 miles of the Italian air bases in Sardinia. The same route is also commanded by Spain, whose naval and seaplane bases in the Balearic Islands practically intercept the steamship communications between France and Northern Africa. If at any time the Mediterranean became a battle-field between the Great Powers, it is no longer certain that superior naval power alone would assure the safety of French sea routes to Africa. Air power has added a new imponderable to the existing dangers of mines and submarines. In the event of a Mediterranean war France would be obliged to depend almost entirely on her Atlantic communications with North Africa, and this explains the recent construction of harbour works in the Atlantic ports of Saffi and Agadir, in Southern Morocco.

It is for this reason, too, that successive French Governments during the past ten years have spent much time and money on the development of an air service between the metropolis and Morocco. At present a daily service of French machines carrying passengers, mail and merchandise, and flying winter and summer, connects Paris with Casablanca, via Marseilles, Barcelona, Alicante and Tangier. Twice a week a supplementary service connects Oran in Algeria with Alicante. For two years past a weekly service has been successfully run between France and South America, via Dakar, the rapidly developing air and naval station in Senegal, on the west coast of Africa.

[8]

The Spanish zone of Morocco is just over 13,000 square miles in area, which represents about one-fifteenth of the area of the French zone. It is administered by a Spanish High Commissioner in Tetuan, assisted by a Khalifa chosen by the Sultan from a list of two candidates nominated by Spain. Its soil is less fertile than that of French Morocco. It is predominantly a mountainous country, with stretches of good pastureland for sheep and cattle at the foot of the bleak range of the Riff. The zone was pacified much more recently than French Morocco, and in parts is still under military authority. It is largely undeveloped, and outside the towns of Tetuan, Larache, Ceuta and Melilla is thinly populated. Its contiguity to Europe, however, its mild Mediterranean climate, its picturesqueness, its rich mineral deposits of lead, antimony, iron, with smaller quantities of gold, silver and copper, the beauty of its coast, and the strategic value of its coastal cities in regard to the Straits of Gibraltar, make Spanish Morocco an enviable possession in the eyes of Powers seeking territorial expansion in Africa.

CHAPTER II

ALGERIA

[1]

ALGERIA is the arch-symbol of the conquest and
domination of Africa by extra-African races. Nine
centuries before the Christian era the Phœnicians
overran it and set up the great empire of Carthage. For
five centuries, from the fall of Carthage to the fall of Rome,
it was the Roman colony of Mauritania, and to this day
innumerable traces of the Roman occupation litter the
Algerian plains. Then in rapid succession followed invasion
after invasion ; the Vandals, the legionaries of the Byzantine
Empire, the Arabs, the Hillal tribesmen from Arabia, the
Turks. In the sixteenth century it became a pashalik of the
Ottoman Empire. The great corsair Barbarossa ruled it in
the name of Suleiman the Magnificent. The Emperor
Charles V tried vainly to seize Algiers. A hundred and
thirty years later Duquesne and the Marshal d'Estrées
assailed it at the head of French expeditions. Asia had held
it triumphantly since the fall of the Roman Empire.
Europe was not destined to conquer it again until the
nineteenth century, when on June 14th, 1830, a French
army landed at Sidi-Ferruch, and a month later captured
Algiers. In 1836, not without fierce fighting, it captured
the once-imperial city of Constantine, which stands out
from the plains of Eastern Algeria on a great natural fortress
of rock.

During the 100 years which have succeeded that conquest
the French occupation of Algeria has progressed steadily.
The conquest of the coastal territory was complete in 1847.
That year saw the end of major military operations in French
Africa. The conquest of the southern territory proceeded
piecemeal. In 1900, with the occupation of the Touat

region, the whole of the ancient Mauritania, and a part of the ancient Numidia, from the Mediterranean to the Sahara, was in French hands.

With Morocco, Tunisia and Senegal, Algeria constitutes a quarter of all Africa. Its land area covers over 800,000 square miles—four times the area of France. Its coast-line extends over a distance of 700 miles, and faces three European countries across the Mediterranean—Spain, France and Italy. It is the northernmost portion of a colonial empire which extends from below the Equator in Central Africa to Cape Bon in Tunisia, a point under 100 miles·from Sicily in Europe. It contains the great economic reserves of France, a harbour (Oran) which is the third French commercial port, and immense capacities for producing wheat, wool, cotton, iron, vegetables, tobacco and fibre. It is also the channel through which France has in one war already tapped, and in another war will certainly tap again, the great reserves of man-power in French Occidental and French Equatorial Africa.

[2]

Algeria, administratively and politically, is divided into two regions : the fertile northern territory to a depth of 250 miles from the coast, which has been prospected, exploited and cultivated, and which is under civil administration ; and the much larger southern territory, which includes the Sahara mountains and desert, is inhabited only thinly by nomad Mozabites and Touaregs, and remains under military government. The northern region, considered as Algeria proper, comprises the three departments of Oran, Algiers and Constantine, which form part of metropolitan France, and send Deputies to the Chamber and Senators to the Senate. Since 1900 Algeria has been allocated a separate Budget for which the Governor-General is responsible, and which requires the approval of the Minister of the Interior in Paris and the signature of the President of the Republic to acquire the force of law.

Except that its citizens of French nationality (and within this category come all Jews and all Mussulmans, above the age of twenty-five and monogamous, who have either served in the war, or are proprietors and farmers, or can read and write or hold a French decoration) enjoy the same civic and political rights as Frenchmen in the mother-country, and are directly represented in its Parliament, the relation of Algeria to France is in many respects analogous to that of British India to Great Britain before the passing of the Constitution of India Act. The Governor-General is appointed by the President of the Republic on the nomination of the Minister of the Interior in Paris. He is through his advisory council responsible for finance, con-cessions and loans, police and defence, and public health. His duties and functions combine those of a departmental Prefect in France with those of the Paris Prefect of Police. He is, in other words, the direct representative of the executive body of the French Republic.

The Algerian Budget is prepared by his staff in consulta-tion with the Ministry of the Interior. It is submitted for the approval of a mixed committee known as the Financial Delegations, and consisting of elected representatives of the population in the following proportions : 24 colonists, 24 non-colonists, 15 Arabs and 6 Kabyles. It is then examined by the Upper Council, the highest consultative body in the province, composed of 7 members appointed by the Governor and 31 elected members. Two Govern-ment departments alone are withheld from the Governor-General's jurisdiction and controlled directly from Paris— the Departments of Justice and Education. These are dependent upon the corresponding Ministries in France. The military force in Algeria and Tunis, which comprises one army corps, including the Foreign Legion, numbers roughly 3000 officers and 70,000 men. Its commanding officers, like those of the naval establishment in the colony, are subject to the Governor-General, through whom pass all communications with the Ministries of War and Marine in Paris.

Algeria exports an increasing quantity of wheat, wool, wine, tobacco, vegetable fibre, olive-oil and early vegetables. Its foreign trade has steadily increased since the war. In the five years before the world depression imports averaged annually between 5 and 6 milliards of francs, and exports between 4 and 5 milliards of francs.

The population of Algeria has increased steadily during

the last sixty years. The first census was taken in 1872
and showed a native population of 2,125,052, and a French
population of 164,175. Since then the figures have almost
trebled. In 1931 the total population was 6¼ millions, of
whom between 700,000 and 800,000 were French. The
great majority of the colonists are engaged in agriculture,
wine-growing, tobacco-raising, sheep and cattle farming
and mining. The mineral resources of the colony are
considerable, and include iron, copper, lead, zinc, phosphates
and some coal and petroleum.

[3]

France offers a notable exception in the history of
colonial empires in the fact that she has no surplus population for which to find an outlet. Alone among the colonial
powers she has a population which is actually diminishing.
Thus her chief problem in North Africa has been to
maintain a reasonable balance between a native population
rapidly increasing, thanks to her own improvement in
education, housing and hygiene, and a French colonial
population which although considerable in itself, and
slowly augmenting, remains relatively slight in proportion
to the indigenous peoples. In Morocco and in Algeria the
problem, although not yet grave, is still serious. In Tunisia,
as will be seen later, it is further complicated by a third
element : the existence of a numerically equal, and in
reality larger, European minority of Italian stock.

French colonisation in North Africa differs radically
from that practised by Great Britain in the southern
territories of that continent. It resolves itself, in the main,
into a direct economic struggle between white workers and
black or brown. Its pioneers are not the disinherited
younger sons of the middle or the landed classes, but the
offspring of struggling and land-hungry working farmers.
For the French colonist, as has been pointed out, is not in
the majority a soldier or a functionary, but a peasant. He
cultivates African soil, raises vines, wheat, barley, vegetables,
with the same patience, knowledge and experience with
which he raised wine or olives on the hillsides of Provence,
or wheat, potatoes and mutton in the green lands of
Brittany. He does not become a large-scale farmer. He

continues to work with his own hands, employing one or two native day labourers at most.

Like France, Algeria is a country of small agricultural estates. Before the war 149,000 small French agriculturists were settled, with their families, on an area of over two million acres. On this land they produced as great a yield as the natives engaged in farming an area three times as large. They supplied France with one-tenth of her wheat, and one-fourth of her mutton. They planted vines from Bordeaux and Burgundy on the hillsides of Algeria, and within thirty years were almost rivalling the French growers in the production of popular classes of table wine. They sent 45,000 tons of early vegetables, raised in the fertile coastal region near Algiers, to the French markets, therein competing successfully with the market gardeners of Nice.

At the end of the war, however, a good deal of this rich agricultural activity had passed into native hands. The balance of numbers between the French and indigenous populations had fallen dangerously low. Lower still had fallen the proportion of French to the other white races. In 1921, of the total white population of 831,000, only 400,000 were French, the others being of other European stocks, Spanish, Italian, and Anglo-Maltese, with the Spanish predominating. During the next five years the French Government made great efforts to increase the numbers of its own nationals in Algeria. The 1889 nationality laws were enforced in the colony, and large numbers of non-French colonists were encouraged to become naturalised Frenchmen, or, having been born in Algeria of non-French parents, were declared as having acquired citizenship on reaching their majority.

The result of this intensive process of naturalisation was that in the 1926 census the white population had risen to 872,431, of which the French proportion had increased to 690,124. Five years later, in 1931, the figures were even more significant. Of a total white population of 920,788, the French claimed 762,852. Thus in ten years, while the total European population had increased by only 11 per cent, the French population had increased, legally if not ethnically, by 90 per cent. And during the same period the proportion between the French and the natives had been

increased from roughly one in twenty to one in eight.
Unlike the Italians in Tunisia, the Spanish settlers in
Algeria (about one-sixth of the European total) have readily
accepted French citizenship. They form the largest non-
French ethnical group in the colony, and are concentrated
in the province of Oran, where they have proved sober,
diligent and prosperous colonists.

[4]

After a century of French colonisation Algeria has become
the most stable province in the French Empire. It reacted
almost not at all to the world-movements of Communism
and Nationalism which swept the East and the West after
the Great War. During the years 1914–1918 it sent large
numbers of native labourers and troops to France, and when
the war ended the French Chamber wisely anticipated any
native unrest in Algeria by voting a series of financial and
political reforms, re-distributing taxation more equally as
between colonists and natives, and giving the indigenous
Arab and Berber a share in local government. Large numbers of natives who had served in the war were at the same
time offered French citizenship without losing, as previously
they had been compelled to, their traditional and personal
rights as Moslems, and this fact goes far to explain the
extraordinary increase already noted in the French population as recorded by census.

The first serious signs of post-war unrest in Algeria were
not manifest until 1935, and then were confined to disturbances and race riots between Moslems and Jews in
Constantine—a significant sequel of the racial warfare in
Germany and an equally ominous precursor of the race
riots in Palestine of 1936. A fresh outbreak of native
agitation occurred in the months which followed the Left
electoral victories in France in May, 1936, and the formation
of the Popular Front Government of M. Léon Blum. It
was, however, like the incidents in France, largely of an
economic character.

Nevertheless, as in all countries where economic problems
are complicated by race rivalries, the race problem is
steadily emerging into the foreground of Algerian politics.
The recent assassination of the Imam of the Mosque of

Algiers and the attempted murder of the Grand Mufti of Constantine, in each case by Mahommedans who accused the leaders of the Moslem community of undue attachment to French interests, are significant signs of the growth of Arab nationalism in French North Africa. It is of interest to note that such sporadic outbreaks of disaffection in Algeria and Morocco have invariably followed the election successes of the democratic parties in France, with their consequent democratisation of relations between the central government and its subject populations.

The Moslem world from Morocco to Syria is a sensitive sounding-board which magnifies the least whisper of impending political disintegration or class conflict in Western Europe. The mass strikes, the wholesale occupation of industrial plants, and the disorganisation which preceded and followed the formation of the first Popular Front Government in France seemed to many Arab minds, more familiar with the ancient Oriental notion of despotic power than with the myriad uneasy manifestations of democracy in evolution, the precursor of the downfall of the West. The civil war in Spain has provided an even more dramatic symbol of the apparent disintegration of the Christian world. And the successful insurrection of General Franco in Spanish Morocco, the recruiting of Moors to crush a European government, and their transport in airplanes from Africa to the coast of their ancient empire in Spain, there to avenge the fifteenth and sixteenth-century persecutions of the Moors and the twentieth-century defeat and expulsion of Abdel Krim, are portents which have encouraged every Arab and Berber nationalist from the Atlantic to the Levant, and have filled with foreboding and dismay the hearts of the European colonists in Algeria, Tunisia and Morocco.

CHAPTER III

TUNISIA

[1]

TUNISIA is the third and most easterly section of
French North Africa : a great land spur thrown
out by the African continent to meet the European
spur of Sicily, and with it narrowing the Mediterranean to
a channel less than a hundred miles wide. It carries the
tricolour from Cape Rosa on the coast of Algeria round the
great promontories of Cape Blanco and Cape Bon to the
coast of Tripoli. It is bounded on the north and east by
the Mediterranean, on the west by Algeria, on the south by
the Libyan and Saharan deserts. It covers a land area of
about 48,300 square miles—between one-fourth and one-
fifth of the area of France. At the last census, taken in
1931, the population comprised 2,215,399 natives, mostly
Arabs and Bedouins, with a small sprinkling (about one in
forty) of Jews ; and a European population of 195,293.
Among the Europeans the French numbered 91,427 and the
Italians 91,178, and from this practical equality in numbers
arise most of the problems created by Tunisia in
Mediterranean politics.

The differing attitude of France towards her North
African dominions may be seen in the variety of ministries
which direct their respective internal economies. Algeria,
the first acquired, is regarded, in its most fertile regions at
least, as an integral part of France, and is administered by
the Ministry of the Interior. Morocco, although nominally
a protectorate, is directed from the French Ministry of the
Colonies, through the French Resident-General in Rabat.
Tunisia, also a protectorate, but less fertile than Morocco,
and less open to French economic exploitation owing to its
equal and at one time preponderant population of Italians,

is dependent upon the French Ministry of Foreign Affairs.

In Tunisia hitherto the French Resident-General has been nominally a mere lieutenant of the native ruler, or Bey, as in Morocco he is that of the Sultan. His nominal rôle in the native government is that of Minister of Foreign Affairs. Actually, of course, he is the real ruler of the country, as the representative of the paramount Power. The native sovereign has long since been relegated, in Morocco and in Tunisia, to a purely titular and decorative rôle. His authority is only acknowledged in native affairs. Of the eleven members of the Government of Tu..is, eight are French and only three Tunisian. The nineteen districts into which the country is divided are governed by French *contrôleurs*, who have authority over the local caids and sheikhs. Justice between Europeans, and also between Europeans and natives, is administered by French tribunals. Disputes of criminal charges concerning natives alone are under the jurisdiction of native courts.

[2]

The French protectorate over Tunisia dates from 1881, when a French force invaded the country, compelled the reigning Bey to acknowledge France as a protector power in the treaty of Kasr-es-Said, signed on May 12th, 1881, a treaty confirmed two years later by the convention of June 8th, 1883. Yet older as the French occupation of Tunisia is by twenty years, it is far less firmly established than the similar occupation of Morocco. The paramount Power has had to contend with two local agitations : the agitation of the Italian settlers, encouraged and supported by Italy ; and the agitation of the Tunisian natives, encouraged by all the Islamic world. Both arise, in a sense, from the peculiar history of Tunisia, a country which has been successively the seat of the Carthaginian Empire, a frequently rebellious fief of the Ottoman Sultans, and a military out-post of Spain and the Empire under Charles V, reconquered by the ambition of Don John of Austria, and lost again by the procrastination of Philip II.

The fierce struggle between Turkish janissaries and the captains of Philip ended in the triumph of the Moslem and the expulsion of the Christian king from Africa. In the stormy events of the sixteenth century both Tunisian Arab and Tunisian Italian find occasion for pride. If the one, aided by the Turk, succeeded in expelling the Christian warriors, the other had borne the lion's share of the burden and the heat of the day. An Italian soldier-engineer, the great Serbelloni, built the new fortress with which Don John proposed to dominate the capital of his dreamed-of African kingdom, and defended it to the last, seeking to remedy by Italian patience, energy and courage a situation already doomed by Spanish indolence and slothful pride.

During the nineteenth century a peaceful legion of Italian colonists crossed the narrow straits from Sicily to farm a soil on which the memories of Carthage, Rome and Renaissance Italy were still tangible and vivid. The French invasion of 1881 alarmed and infuriated Italy, but the peaceful occupation was not thereby interrupted. The Italian urge to migrate proved irresistible. Tunisia was the nearest African shore to Italy, and more fertile than her own future colony of Libya. Italians settled in the French protectorate in greater and greater numbers, clung desperately to their nationality, and refused to be assimilated. By 1921 the Italians still outnumbered the French, who comprised only one-third of the European population, and their families, more fruitful than the French, prospered and multiplied. In 1931, in spite of ten years of intensive French propaganda and assimilation, and desperate attempts to increase the number of French nationals in the colony, the Italians still achieved a practical equality with the French, and it is certain that ethnically and linguistically, the real Italian population to-day greatly exceeds the French.

[3]

When the French invaded Tunisia a treaty was already in existence between the Bey of Tunisia and the Italian Government by which Italy enjoyed special rights in the Bey's dominions. That treaty, signed in 1868, did not expire until 1896, and although by the Franco-Italian Agreement of 1884 Italy surrendered her consular juris-diction over her nationals in Tunisia, she expressly retained her other rights under capitulations and treaties. In 1896 three new Franco-Italian agreements were signed in Paris which recognised Italy's claim to special privileges. The second of these conventions provided that " persons who shall have retained Italian or Tunisian nationality according to the laws of their country shall be regarded as Italian subjects in Tunisia and as Tunisian subjects in Italy." The *status quo* was equally to be maintained for Italian schools in Tunisia.

Thus Italian settlers in Tunisia were expressly exempted from the provisions of French or Tunisian nationality regulations, and were recognised the right, long since accorded to foreign residents, their descendants, in other parts of the Ottoman Empire, to retain their nationality of origin from generation to generation. The three conventions of 1896 expired in 1905, but in that year and during the next fifteen years, France was too heavily engaged in Morocco and Europe to risk a dispute with Italy over their denunciation, and the privileges of Italians in Tunis were therefore not challenged. In 1918, at the close of the war, France denounced the first and second of the 1896 conventions, but proposed that pending the negotiation of a new treaty they should be tacitly renewed for periods of three months. It was clearly intimated, however, that the special status of Italians in Tunisia was in the near future to be terminated, and that henceforth Italian children, born of parents who were themselves born in the colony, would be considered as of French nationality.

Before the new treaty could be negotiated Mussolini had become master of Italy. Italian colonial policy was revived in its most aggressive form. Franco-Italian relations, never cordial, and recently embittered by Italy's disappointments during the Peace Conference, entered upon a long phase of tension. The Tunisian question remained a thorn in the side of both countries. No Franco-Italian co-operation or reconciliation was possible until the status of the Italians in the colony was regularised by mutual consent. The suspicion and covert hostility which subsisted between Paris and Rome during the years 1922–1935 were reflected in the relations between French and Italian colonists in Tunis. The grievances of the Italian settlers were aired in the Italian press. Fascist officials, generals, consuls and propagandists kept the resentment of the Italian population alive and embittered by speeches, demonstrations and newspaper articles. The situation resembled that created in more recent times by the Nazis in Austria, and the Germans in Danzig and Memel.

The agitation only subsided in January, 1935, when the pact of friendship and reconciliation was signed by Mussolini and Laval. The question of Tunis was among the subjects then relegated from the controversial sphere to that of mutual tolerance and conciliation. Since then the Franco-Italian problem in Tunis has given precedence to the native Tunisian problem, although during the Italo-Abyssinian War the reluctant French acquiescence in sanctions threatened to reopen the old sore, and with it all the other grounds of hostility and rivalry between France and Italy.

[4]

The native problem remains. The Italian ferment came to a head in the heated atmosphere of Fascism. The other source of anxiety to the paramount power—the nationalist agitation—reached its critical phase before the Fascist revolution in Italy, in the troubled years which followed the war. Tunisia had always responded to European political movements more quickly than the other Islamic countries.

It anticipated the rise of nationalism in the neighbouring state of Egypt, with which it is in close geographical, linguistic and cultural affinity. Its first attempt to overthrow the despotism of Bey and Sultan, and achieve constitutional government, was made before the French occupation. The effort failed, and was not repeated until half a century later, when Europe was in the throes of a new outbreak of rival nationalisms ; when Turkey was reorganising herself under Mustapha Kemal ; and India and Egypt were demanding independence. In 1920 a Nationalist Party was, for the first time, successfully organised in Tunisia. Finding ready adherents, as in Egypt and India, among the educated middle class, wealthy but politically irresponsible, it soon dominated the native Press, and obtained great influence over the illiterate and inarticulate peasantry. In March, 1920, the Nationalist Party presented its programme, a document under nine heads. It demanded a deliberative assembly comprising Tunisian and French representatives, elected by universal suffrage, possessing equal voting powers, and power to vote the financial Budget. It demanded that the Government should be an elected organ of, and responsible to, this popular assembly; that the executive, legislative and judicial powers should henceforth be separate; that Tunisian candidates should be admitted to official posts if they were capable of filling them; that the salaries of French and Tunisian officials should be equal for equal duties; that municipal councils should be elective; that freedom of Press, speech and assembly should be established; that education should be compulsory and free; and that State lands should no longer be colonised exclusively by French settlers, but shared with the natives.

The Nationalist petition was presented (as in the case of Egypt) by native delegations which visited the capital of the dominant Power. It was not rejected outright. The French Government promised to give heed to the agitation for reform, and as a measure of its sincerity created in 1921 a Tunisian Ministry of Justice which admitted native officials to a certain control over native jurisdiction. But this concession proved inadequate to stem the rising tide of nationalism. A year later, in April, 1922, the Bey had been persuaded to join in the popular revolt, and a crisis of some gravity had arisen.

[5]

It arose directly out of a curious incident. The Resident-General, M. Lucien Saint, somewhat indiscreetly put pressure on the Bey to announce his hostility to constitutional reform in a newspaper interview. The Bey gave the interview required of him, but significantly hedged on the all-important question of the Constitution. The version of the interview transmitted to the French press by the Resident-General represented the Bey as stating that in his view a Constitution was unnecessary. The Bey indignantly denied this version, and invited the Resident-General to withdraw the offending statement. The Frenchman refused, whereupon the Bey intimated, on April 4th, 1922, that he intended to abdicate.

This happened, embarrassingly enough for M. Lucien Saint, on the eve of a State visit to Tunisia by the President of the French Republic, then M. Alexandre Millerand. The city of Tunis was in a ferment. Crowds massed outside the palace of the Bey and demonstrated their approval of his action. The Bey himself, alarmed at the consequences of his gesture, and probably regretting it, issued a denial of the report of his abdication. Nevertheless, in deference to the Tunisian nationalists he showed enough spirit to present their demands to the Resident-General in person, accompanying them with a hint that he would abdicate unless they were conceded. After several days of excitement M. Lucien Saint ended all uncertainty as to the French Government's intentions by paying a State visit to the Bey. He was significantly escorted by a strong body of French troops, in sufficient numbers and in attitude aggressive enough to overawe the population.

The threat of force (which two years later, in November, 1924, was to be adopted in similar circumstances by Lord Allenby in Egypt, the British High Commissioner calling upon Zagloul Pasha with a formidable escort of lancers) was completely successful. The Bey yielded, and withdrew his demands. A number of his Ministers were dismissed—according to the French, for their nationalist leanings; according to the Tunisians, because they had failed in support to the Sultan in an emergency. The President of the Republic landed in Tunis and completed his visit without untoward incident.

[6]

Nevertheless the nationalist demonstrations had not been entirely without effect. They forced the French Government to introduce long-delayed measures of reform. Shortly after M. Millerand's departure from the now submissive protectorate, six administrative decrees were announced. They were issued under the *firman* of the Bey, and were approved and confirmed in an *Arrêté* of the Resident-General. The first three, dated July 13th, 1922, established mixed administrative councils in each region of that part of Tunisia under civil control, and created a Grand Council designed in some sense to function like the legislative assembly demanded by the nationalists. The second batch of three decrees, issued on the following day, provided for slight increases in native control in administrative matters. Nevertheless the concessions were largely illusory. The Grand Council was severely limited in its functions. It consisted of a *section française* and a *section indigène*, and never were the twain permitted to meet. They deliberated apart, they were forbidden to discuss constitutional or political matters, they could only discuss the all-important question of finance under rigid supervision of the French Government, as impersonated by the Resident-General. When, as often occurred, the rival sections of the Grand Council recorded contradictory votes on any matter, the deadlock was only broken, and then only superficially, by the creation of an arbitral committee wholly nominated by the Resident-General.

The result was that the nationalist agitation, temporarily quieted by the dual policy of force and concessions in 1922, flared up again. But now the leadership came not from the educated middle class, some of whose members had found occupation at least in the Grand Council, ineffectual although it was as a political or governing instrument, but from the lower sections of the native population. The wave of Communist and nationalist agitation, then sweeping over the Far and the Middle East, and over Eastern and South-eastern Europe, sent ripples of political disturbance which broke upon the shores of Northern Africa. The French Communist Party, which between 1920 and 1924 was at the height of its activity in France, established flourishing sections in Tunisia, both among the French population and among the natives. Thus France was faced in her African protectorate with a double problem : the threat of Fascist imperialism, and the equal threat of Communist internationalism.

[7]

The problem was curiously complicated for France by the fact that at Bizerta, the northernmost point of Tunisia, and the chief naval station in French North Africa, lay rusting at its anchors the remnant of Wrangel's White Russian fleet. After the collapse of the counter-revolution

in Soviet Russia the fleet had taken shelter in Bizerta
harbour, and its crews, a band of adventurers henceforth
without a country or a government, and liable to prove a
grave danger to the security of an already troubled African
colony, were prudently disarmed by the French authorities.
The destiny of this fleet, which represented the greater
part of the former Tsarist force in the Black Sea, remained
for long in doubt. The Soviet Government claimed it in
vain. France held it as security—although a valueless
security in itself—for the eventual repayment of the
Tsarist debts. The restoration of the long-idle warships
to Russia was delayed for fifteen years, and was only finally
promised in the Franco-Soviet Treaty of friendship and
non-aggression concluded in 1935 and ratified in the spring
of 1936.

The security of Bizerta and Tunis has since become as
anxious a problem to the French Government as that of
Malta has become to the British. All three places are within
easy bombing range of the Italian air stations in Sicily.
All three lie in that dangerously narrow and contested zone
which divides the Western Mediterranean from the Eastern.
The British decision to strengthen the naval and aerial
defences of Malta, as a direct consequence of the Anglo-
Italian crisis of 1935–1936, will undoubtedly find its
counterpart in a French decision to provide for the similar
defence of the principal ports of Tunisia against aggression
by sea or air.

During the years of France's preoccupation with Morocco,
Tunisia was the Cinderella of the French colonial empire.
The fact already noted that it came under the jurisdiction
of the French Foreign Ministry, which had the best of
reasons for wishing to avoid any risk of conflict with Italy,
deprived its administration of the same vigorous and long-
sighted energy which distinguished the rule of Lyautey in
Morocco. Yet there are, for imperial France, the soundest
of reasons for regarding Tunisia no longer as an isolated
African dependency but as an inseparable part of French
North Africa. If in the past Tunisia has been more accessible to European and Asiatic influences than the rest of
North Africa, in the present day it still retains its religious
and cultural contacts with Islam. It possesses, in the holy

city of Kairouan, the second sanctuary of Islam after Mecca. It is the real gateway of the East, the bridge between African and Asiatic Islam. The Tunisian experiment, properly utilised, might have afforded the French the knowledge of the Oriental, as distinct from the African Moslem, which alone could have averted the series of blunders and disasters which accompanied the exercise of the French mandate over Syria, and which are now being repeated in the British neighbouring and mandated territory of Palestine.

[8]

A candid warning to the French Government of the perils and disillusionments which may result from the present negligent administration of Tunisia was published in the *Revue des Deux Mondes* in March and April, 1936, by General Paul Azan, the commander-in-chief of the French forces in the protectorate. " Situated in the heart of the Mediterranean, at one of the world's cross-roads," wrote General Azan, " Tunisia is of the first importance, strategically, politically and commercially. As a result of its geographical situation it can play a rôle out of all relation to its small area and its modest resources. . . . It must not be considered as an isolated unit. It must never be separated from Algeria and Morocco, from the French North African trinity. It must be treated in its proper place in the chess-board of overseas France, and even be considered in its place among the nations of the world. Further it must be constantly examined in its contacts with the Islamic world, and its reactions thereto. If such precautions are neglected, the problems of Tunisia may be superficially regarded as settled when in fact the primary factors remain unchanged, and temporary successes may be followed by grievous disappointments. If Tunisia were to be directed by incompetent or inexpert hands, it would soon witness scenes of disorder and ruin which would rapidly spread all over French North Africa. If, on the other hand, it is guided by leaders with experience of Islam and of local customs, and capable of showing both suppleness and firmness, justice and generosity, Tunisia may enjoy a brilliant destiny. . . ."

This warning was uttered after the transfer of the

French Resident-General, M. Peyrouton, to Morocco, and was intended to express the anxieties felt by the military command in Tunisia at the appointment of a successor more radical in politics and less suspect than M. Peyrouton in the eyes of M. Sarraut and his fellow-Radicals. Since then the Radical M. Sarraut has been succeeded by the Socialist M. Blum. Members of the Front Populaire in France and in Morocco are clamouring for the removal of M. Peyrouton from the Residency-General in Rabat. And General Azan's fears of scenes of disorder spreading through French North Africa have already been echoed by the French soldiers and administrators in Morocco.

CHAPTER IV

LIBYA ITALIANA

[1]

SOUTH of Italy, and occupying 1200 miles of
Mediterranean coast-line on the northern shore of
Africa, lie the twin colonies of Tripolitana and
Cyrenaica, which the Italians call by their ancient name of
Libya. Libya is one of the strangest of the African enigmas.
Under its desert sand three civilisations lie buried. Many
centuries before the Christian era, at the junction of the
three great caravan routes to Lake Chad, Timbuctoo and
Darfur, the Phœnicians founded the three cities of Oea,
Sabrata and Leptis Magna on the site of the modern
Tripoli. In the seventh century B.C. the Greeks had
flourishing colonies in Cyrenaica. In the heyday of the
Roman Empire Libya was the granary of Rome, and wheat
ripened where now the desert wind blows hollows in the
barren dunes of sand. Of those three civilisations no trace
persists in Libya to-day. They have vanished as completely
as if they had never been. But of a fourth and infinitely
older civilisation, a Neolithic age resembling that which
flourished in the Iberian peninsula, in Brittany and Britain,
a multitude of witnesses survive in the several hundred
thousand monolithic and other monuments, stone barrows,
sacrificial stones and mounds, carved rock cells, dolmens
and stone circles strewn over the Libyan plains.

Before the Italians entered Libya it was the No Man's
Land of North Africa. The Sultan of Turkey held a
nominal suzerainty over the coastal region. Beyond that
narrow strip of barely fertile territory the nomad Arabs,
the Senoussi Berbers of the Fezzan and the migrant negroes
from the Sahara roamed unchallenged and unfettered save
by their own tribal feuds and rivalries.

Italy seized Libya less for economic reasons than for

reasons of national pride and prestige. The disappointment of the French occupation of Tunisia still rankled fiercely in her heart. France held, in addition to Tunisia, Algeria and Morocco. The British were in Egypt. Germany, as was seen in the Agadir affair, bent greedy eyes on Africa. In 1911, before the diplomatic world had recovered from its nervous shock over the *Panther* incident, Italy took the plunge and landed in Tripoli. Her preparations for that expedition were preceded by a campaign of nationalist and imperialist hysteria similar to that which preceded the war with Abyssinia.

As in 1935, no declaration of war accompanied the military occupation. The Italians occupied Tripoli ; the Sultan of Turkey retorted to this act of war by a declaration in form. The war dragged on into 1912 without notable successes on either side, and only ended in Italy's favour when Turkey found herself beset by other hostile nations in the Balkans. The Treaty of Ouchy, signed by Italy and Turkey on October 18th, 1912, confirmed the Italians in their annexation of Tripoli, and this annexation was subsequently recognised by the Great Powers. During the next two years the Italians consolidated their occupation of Tripolitana, but in Cyrenaica, the neighbouring colony, the Senoussi tribesmen, secretly aided by Turkey, stubbornly resisted their authority.

[2]

When the Great War broke out the Senoussi and Fezzan revolted. The native troops recruited by Italy in Libya deserted to the enemy. The Italians, who by this time had entered the war in Europe, prudently abandoned further attempts at colonisation and retired to several strategic points on the coast, notably Tripoli and Khoms. The rest of Libya was left under the authority of native chiefs armed and aided by Constantinople. The Senoussi leader Suleiman-el-Baruni, who had been driven by the Italians out of Africa in 1913, reappeared with a mandate from the Sultan appointing him Pasha of the vilayets of Tripoli, Tunis and Algiers. His brother ruled in Fezzan. Another Berber chief, Ramadan-el-Shtewi, set up an independent state of Tripoli with his capital at Misurata.

By 1917, however, the military fortunes of the Turks were on the wane, and the Senoussi chiefs, no longer bound by common allegiance to the Turk, were quarrelling among themselves. In 1918, when the Italians reappeared on the scene in force, a compromise was effected without much difficulty whereby the dominant power agreed to govern through the native chiefs, by the medium of political officers attached to them. Ramadan-el-Shtewi and Suleiman-el-Baruni acknowledged the King of Italy as overlord. An Italian decree of June, 1919, granted the natives a status described as " complete local citizenship " and a form of parliament.

But this promise of democracy was illusory. The Italians steadily strengthened their military occupation of the country. The process of subjugation and economic re-organisation carried on simultaneously by the Governor-General, Giuseppe (later Count) Volpi, were continued after the advent of Mussolini by an even more energetic and more ruthless policy of conquest. In 1928 the territory in effective occupation was vigorously pushed still farther southwards and eastwards. The unsubmissive province of Fezzan was conquered. The oases of Gialo, Augila, Marada, Zella and Socna were occupied, and as the result of concessions made by the Government of Egypt, in the Italo-Egyptian agreement of December 6th, 1925, ratified in Notes exchanged between Great Britain and Italy, the oasis of Jarabub was added to Libya, and an awkward salient straightened out. Meanwhile, by an arrangement concluded with France in 1919, the western frontier of Libya had been extended to include territory formerly in Tunisia. Two French salients were eliminated, and the Italian frontier now extends in a curve from the west of Ghadames to the south of Tummo, including the oasis of Ghat, and gives Italy uninterrupted control of the great caravan route from Lake Chad to the Mediterranean. Finally, under the Laval-Mussolini agreement of January, 1935, France ceded to Italy a further strip of territory on the southern frontier of Libya, of an area of 44,000 square miles.

[3]

In 1929, for administrative and military purposes, Libya
was divided into two territories named Tripolitana and
Cyrenaica, the former with its capital at Tripoli, the latter
at Bengazi. Tripolitana, the larger and more valuable
colony, has an area of roughly 351,000 square miles and a
population of under 600,000, of whom 22,700 are Europeans
(20,000 being Italians). The official languages are Italian
and Arabic. All the towns of any size are on the coast :
Tripoli with 60,000 inhabitants, Misurata with 14,000 and
Khoms with 5000. The other centres of activity are
chiefly caravan halts and oases. Climatically and agri-
culturally the territory is divided into three zones : the
coastal zone, about 17,000 square miles in area, rich in date-
palms, olive and orange trees, and suitable for wheat and
barley ; the sub-desert, of little agricultural value except
for the alfa plant which grows profusely ; and the desert,
over which fertile oases are found at rare intervals. A
caravan trade of very ancient origin thrives between
Tripoli and the Central Sudan, and Tripoli is one of the
chief ports of export for the African trade in ostrich
feathers, the London market receiving an annual consign-
ment valued between £40,000 and £50,000.

The occupied zone of Cyrenaica is about one-fifth of the
size of its neighbour, having an area of only 75,000 square
miles. If its great hinterland of Cufra is included, however,
its estimated area swells to 285,000 square miles. At the
1931 census the population was recorded as 225,000, of
whom 10,000 are Italians. Cyrenaica is more fertile than
Tripolitana. It has large pasture lands, and is capable of
raising large herds of cattle. In recent years an attempt
has been made at large-scale colonisation, and Italian
colonial centres or nuclei have been established at Guarscia,
Soluk, Tocra and other oases. A beginning has been made
with the cultivation of cotton, olives, grape vines and
bananas ; barley is already extensively grown by the natives.

[4]

Libya acquired political importance for the outside world
for the first time in 1935, when Great Britain became

gravely concerned for the security of Egypt and the Sudan. It is the obvious jumping-off place for any Italian military enterprise against those territories. During the Italo-Abyssinian War the military forces in the colony, which in normal years had not exceeded 1100 officers and 35,000 men (of whom 26,500 were natives and the rest Italians), were increased to three times those numbers, and a large force of aircraft was stationed in hastily created air bases within easy distance of the Egyptian and Sudan frontiers. At the same time the naval defences in Tripoli and Bengazi were strengthened, and large stocks of oil and aircraft material were concentrated in the aircraft depôt outside Tripoli and in other new air stations inland.

With the Italian annexation of Abyssinia the importance of Libya has been enormously augmented. It is no longer an isolated and unprofitable territory squeezed in between the great French and British possessions in Africa, but a strategic outpost and half-way halt on the road to Italy's new African Empire. Between Italian Libya and Italian Ethiopia are 900 miles of Libyan and Nubian desert, and once that barren and uninhabited region is crossed by Italian long-range aircraft, the Italian flag flies over Africa from the Mediterranean to the shores of the Indian Ocean and the Red Sea. In the new road of Imperial Rome to the Eastern seas, a road 4000 miles long, and hitherto Britain's undisputed passage to India, the only non-Italian territory that remains an obstacle in the path of the Fascist legions is the Anglo-Egyptian Sudan.

[5]

Since Libya is likely to be taken by Mussolini as the model for the future colonisation of Abyssinia, a brief description of Italian methods in the North African territories may be of interest. The form of government is frankly despotic. The Governor-General, or Viceroy, has the power of a Roman proconsul. His authority is not limited by any popular assembly or even, like that of Mussolini, moderated by the advice of a Fascist Grand Council. He has, since the departure of Count Volpi, invariably been a high military officer. He is appointed by the King of Italy on the recommendation of the dictator.

Both the civil and the military affairs of Libya are vested in the Governor-General, who is assisted by a Deputy-Governor, a commander-in-chief and a military staff. In five-sixths of Libya, comprising the province of Fezzan and the great southern territory of Koufra, which are but partially pacified, the military authority is supreme. In the north-western region of Tripolitana, and in the narrow coastal region of Cyrenaica as far south as Nalut, a civil administration has been created.

The Italian Government hopes that when the colony is fully developed it may be able to support 300,000 Italians and their families. At present the number of actual colonists, as distinct from functionaries and military, hardly exceeds 15,000 in Tripolitana and 7000 in Cyrenaica, and these figures include wives and children. Land suitable for cultivation is left in native hands when it is actually so employed : otherwise it is bought or confiscated by the Government and sold to Italians in plots varying from 125 to 2500 acres. Land in urban areas or near the railways is sometimes distributed in plots as small as twelve acres, but small holdings are discouraged by the authorities as unprofitable. During the first twenty years of their possession colonists are exempt from land taxes. In the pacified areas they are lodged in former military huts and barracks until State-built or State-aided houses are available for them.

The Italian attitude to the native population differs from that of other colonial powers. It is regarded not as the actual and natural possessor of the soil, and not even as a source of cheap man-power, the serf class of a white *élite*, but as a tenant on sufferance, to be gradually eliminated as the colony develops and adequate numbers of Italians settle in Libya. The Government watches the growth of the native population with anxiety. If it should show signs of outstripping the severely limited economic resources already allocated to it, drastic measures, among them that of expulsion, would unhesitatingly be taken by the authorities. Meanwhile the Arabs and Berbers are heavily taxed. Natives living in urban areas pay a house tax fixed by the municipality. Agricultural and nomadic tribes pay a collective tax assessed according to their numbers, the value of their crops, and the extent of their wealth in sheep, horses and goats.

In the small area under the civil administration justice is administered by native courts if the dispute concerns merely affairs of family and succession, but in all civil and commercial matters the Italian regional courts alone have jurisdiction, whether the litigants be natives, Italians or foreigners. Serious crimes are dealt with according to the law of Italy by an Assize Court. Appeals in both civil and criminal cases are heard by the Court of Appeal in Tripoli, with a final appeal to the Court of Cassation in Rome. In the vast southern territory there is little semblance of public law. The regional military commissioners have power of life and death. Natives are shot or hanged without the formalities of court, judge and jury. The only justice practised is military justice, swift, ruthless and without appeal.

[6]

For all the uncompromising nature of their rule in Libya, the Italians are not actively disliked. Count Volpi once admitted : " We naturally cannot expect the Arabs to love us. The best we can hope for is that they do not hate us : and I do not think they do." The reason for this lack of hatred, or this carefully dissembled affection, is to be found in the class and racial tolerance shown by the Italian conquerors. There is a degree of social intercourse between Europeans and natives unknown between the British and the Hindus or Mahommedans in India. The Italian has more sense of racial equality than the Anglo-Saxon. To him the Arab is not a man of a different colour, but a man of a different political or military order. Between the lowest caste of both races, the manual labourers in the fields, the domestic or military servants, and the sailors and dock-workers in Tripoli, there is almost complete social and economic equality. In the highest degrees of the social scale the intimacy between Italian officer and wealthy Arab chief is friendly and equal. It is, as in all countries of mixed races, the middle social orders of the rival peoples between which mutual suspicion and dislike are most displayed.

CHAPTER V

EGYPT AND THE SUDAN

[1]

EGYPT is the oldest of the Mediterranean states. Her history has also been the most chequered. When the waters of the Atlantic flooded the Mediterranean basin there was probably a civilisation already firmly established on the Nile. For wellnigh seventy centuries her sun waxed and waned and waxed again. She knew splendour and decay in long cycles during which Northern and Central Europe were plunged in barbaric night. She was overrun almost ceaselessly by Asiatic hordes whom she assimilated and absorbed. Invader after invader fell under the mysterious fascination of the Nile. Glittering dynasty succeeded dynasty. There seemed no end to the secret resistance of this people of shepherds and cultivators, whose youth was renewed eternally, like the Nile itself, by untamed forces drawn from the dark heart of Africa.

And then there came the last great migrations to the shores of the Levant : the Persians and the Medes from the East, the Nordic barbarians out of the forests and mountains of the North. As she had thrown off that of the Semitic shepherd kings, Egypt had thrown off the yoke of the Assyrians only to fall victim to the Persian Empire of Darius I. She fell in turn to the ambitions of Alexander, and under him and his general, Ptolemy I, she knew a new renaissance, not of military power but of learning, and for several centuries the Egyptian city of Alexandria became the cultural centre of the world. From a Greek colony Egypt became a Roman colony. The Roman occupation ended thirteen centuries ago, upon the rise of the Ottoman Empire, and for long centuries thereafter Egypt was a vassal of the Turk. Her subjection to foreign Powers has lasted, with but brief intervals of revolt and precarious independence, for nearly three thousand years to the present day.

[2]

The Mediterranean coast-line of Egypt extends from the Gulf of El Sollum, due south of Crete, to the town of Rafah, on the border of Palestine, a distance of nearly 600 miles. Egypt proper, which covers the quadrilateral composed by the Libyan desert, the Nile valley and the Sinai peninsula, has an area of roughly 383,000 square miles. Of this great region only the part comprised by the delta and valley of the Nile and the scattered oases, is cultivable, and this portion has an area of no more than 13,600 square miles. Within the narrow limits of this area, no larger than that of Belgium, Egypt supports a population of over 15 millions, more than twice the population of Belgium. Cultivated Egypt is probably the richest and most densely populated region of its size in the world. Cairo, the capital, has a population of about 1,100,000, and is, after Barcelona, the largest city in the Mediterranean basin. Alexandria, the largest port and commercial centre in Egypt, has a population of about 600,000. Over 60 per cent of the population are fellahin, or small agriculturists, a large proportion of them being landless labourers. Cotton is the principal crop of the country, although large quantities of wheat, barley, lentils, beans, maize, rice and sugar-cane are also grown. As a result of intensive irrigation works in the Nile valley and at the junction of the White and Blue Niles, and the construction of a dam at Assouan and barrages at Esna, Nag Hammadi Asyut and Zifta, over 2,000,000 acres have been added to the cultivable area in Lower Egypt during the present century. In addition, over half a million acres have been converted since 1920 from the old basin system to perennial irrigation.

Since 1922 Egypt has been recognised as a sovereign state, and since 1930 has nominally been endowed with a constitution and the privileges of representative government. In practice, however, owing to the existence of Capitulations, by which foreigners in Egypt enjoy extra-territorial rights, with their concomitant of jurisdiction by mixed tribunals

and immunity from taxation except by consent, and to the
facts that the defence of Egypt is expressly reserved by
Great Britain, and that the Western Powers, through their
control of the foreign debt (roughly £90,000,000 at the
present day), exercise a virtual power of mortgage over
the country, the independence of Egypt has hitherto been
a polite fiction.

Capitulatory rights have been claimed and exercised by
foreign powers in Egypt since the middle of the last century,
and the Constitution granted to Egypt in 1930 expressly
leaves these rights, and the treaties and conventions on
which they are based, untouched. In Alexandria and thirteen other towns in Egypt, local administration and taxation
are in the hands of Mixed Commissions composed of
Europeans and Egyptians in equal numbers. The foreign
debt of Egypt originated in 1862, with loans of just over
£3,200,000. Since then the total indebtedness of Egypt
to foreign creditors has been multiplied thirtyfold. As
long ago as 1879 England and France assumed joint control
of Egypt's finances. A year later the other powers took a
hand in the task. The modern Constitution gives the
Egyptian Parliament the power of voting money supplies,
but in fact the Budget remains closely scrutinised by the
governments and bankers of the great European Powers.

The question of defence remained reserved to Great Britain
under the terms of the British recognition of Egypt's independence. The native Egyptian army is raised by conscription, but only 4 per cent of the men annually called to
the colours are required to serve. The army does not
comprise more than about 13,000 all ranks, and certain of
the higher posts in the army are held by British officers.
In normal times the British force in Egypt is numerically
almost equivalent to the native force. It comprises 2
regiments of cavalry, 3 batteries of heavy and 2 of light
artillery, 2 companies of engineers, 5 battalions of infantry
and 2 armoured car companies. During the Mediterranean
crisis of 1935-1936 the strength of the British army in
Egypt was increased from roughly 10,000 all ranks to over
20,000. The port of Alexandria became the headquarters
of the Mediterranean Fleet, reinforced by a number of
powerful units from the Home Fleet. Egypt, which in

normal times is the headquarters of the Middle East Air Command, and contains four squadrons of aeroplanes and a number of air depots, also witnessed an impressive concentration of British air power.

[3]

The Constitution of 1930 leaves undefined and subject to subsequent negotiation Egypt's rights in the Sudan, and the full title of the King of Egypt in that respect has not yet been established. The Sudan extends for over 1600 miles southwards of Egypt as far as Uganda and the Belgian Congo, and eastwards from the Red Sea and the frontiers of Abyssinia into the heart of Central Africa. Its area is just over 1 million square miles. Its largely nomadic population is approximately assessed at between 5 and 6 millions, of whom only 55,000 are non-natives.

Egypt's authority over the Sudan, which had been gradually extended during the nineteenth century under the reign of Muhammed Ali and his successors, was brought to an abrupt halt by the revolt of the Mahdi in 1882. For thirteen years the Mahdi and his successor, the Khalifa, ruled despotically. In 1896 a joint Anglo-Egyptian force entered the Sudan, and two years later destroyed the government of the Khalifa. British influence in the Sudan dates from that rebellion and its suppression. The Anglo-Egyptian Convention of January 19th, 1899, which followed the recovery of the insurrectionary provinces, placed the whole territory under the joint rule of Great Britain and Egypt. In that Convention it was stated that Great Britain was " by right of conquest " entitled " to share in the settlement of a true working and development of the Sudan."

The country thus became a joint protectorate of Great Britain and Egypt. The authority of the Sultan of Turkey was simultaneously abolished in the Sudan, although it was not to be denounced in Egypt until the outbreak of the World War fifteen years later. The administration of the country was entrusted to a Governor-General appointed by Egypt with the consent of the British Government, and invested with full civil and military power. The flags of Great Britain and Egypt were to have equal rights of display. No customs barriers were to exist between Egypt and the Sudan ; slavery was abolished and the traffic in slaves heavily punished ; and the Brussels Arms Convention of 1890 was to be rigorously enforced. In 1924 Egyptian troops were withdrawn from the Sudan, and its defence was subsequently entrusted to a locally recruited Sudan Defence Force, acknowledging only the authority of the Governor-General.

The Sudan is administered on a system resembling that which prevails in the north-west frontier province of India, and the penal code enforced is adapted from the Indian penal code. In recent years the territory has become one of the world-producing centres of cotton. It is the chief source of the world's supply of gum arabic, and also exports considerable quantities of gold, ivory, papyrus, millet, hides, sesame, ebony and vegetable fibre.

[4]

The autumn of 1936 sees the beginning of a new phase in the relations between Great Britain and Egypt, and Egypt and the Sudan. A long period of Egyptian vassaldom is at its end. The new Anglo-Egyptian Treaty signed in London on August 26th, 1936, will establish upon a new and, it is hoped, a permanent footing of alliance an arbitrary relationship which has existed between the two countries since 1882, when Great Britain first occupied Egypt as a result of the war with Arabi Pasha. The British entered the country as an inevitable consequence of their acquisition of a financial interest, seven years earlier, in the Suez Canal. It is probable that that primordial imperial interest will continue to dominate British policy with regard to Egypt, for it is that country's fate to lie astride two great waters, the Suez Canal and the Nile, and to be at the mercy of any power capable of dominating the one or drying up the other.

During the fifty-four years since the expedition against Arabi Pasha British privileges in Egypt have risen from those of financial adviser, banker and mentor to those of a despotic military power in permanent occupation. A British protectorate over Egypt was first formally proclaimed soon after the outbreak of the World War in 1914, and a Khedive nominated by the Sultan of Turkey was replaced by a British nominee, the late Hussein Kamil, with the title of

Sultan. In 1922 the protectorate was abolished, and the nominal independence of Egypt recognised. Ahmed Fuad, who had succeeded his brother Hussein Kamil on his death in 1917, was created King of Egypt under the style of Fuad I, and a constitution was granted to the Egyptians.

Nevertheless the British occupation of Egypt continued. Parliamentary government became a triangular duel between Zagloul Pasha, the greatest of the post-war Nationalist leaders in Egypt, a would-be despotic King, and an occasionally despotic British High Commissioner. Egyptian policies became a farce in which the elements of buffoonery, intrigue and assassination were incongruously and often tragically mixed. The policy of Great Britain fluctuated between conciliation and coercion. Lord Allenby was the first of the modern British negotiators in Egypt to recognise that a whole nation stood behind the suspected or the derided figure of Zagloul, and that only the concession of complete independence would satisfy the Egyptian nationalists. But even Allenby, conciliatory as he was, rode down from the Residency to the Cabinet of Ministers, grim-faced and with a regiment of lancers for escort, to exact the last pound of flesh out of Egypt for the murder of Sir Lee Stack.

[5]

Three separate negotiations between Great Britain and Egypt failed to create a permanent and friendly basis for the anomalous relationship between the two countries. Mr. Ramsay MacDonald failed with Zagloul in 1924; Sir Austen Chamberlain failed with Sarwat Pasha in 1927, despite the offer of greater concessions even than those offered in 1924; and the late Arthur Henderson failed with Nahas Pasha in 1930. The negotiations initiated by the present High Commissioner in Cairo, Sir Miles Lampson, in the early part of 1936, when the Anglo-Italian tension over Abyssinia was at its height, and successfully concluded by the signature of the Treaty on August 26th, were the fourth to have been attempted since the protectorate was withdrawn in 1922.

In each case the previous negotiations for a treaty broke down over the four immutable reserves formulated by Great Britain as the safeguard of her imperial interests in Egypt and the Canal. These reserves had been explicitly outlined in the declaration of February 28th, 1922, by which Great Britain signified the termination of her protectorate over Egypt, and which ran as follows :

" Whereas His Majesty's Government in accordance with their declared intentions desire to recognise Egypt as an independent Sovereign State, and :

" Whereas the relations between His Majesty's Government and Egypt are of vital importance to the British Empire, the following principles are hereby declared :

" (1) The British Protectorate over Egypt is terminated and Egypt is declared to be an independent Sovereign State.

" (2) So soon as the Government of His Highness shall pass an Act of Indemnity with application to all inhabitants of Egypt martial law as proclaimed on November 2nd, 1914, shall be withdrawn.

" (3) The following matters are absolutely reserved to the discretion of His Majesty's Government until such time as it may be possible by free discussion and friendly accommodation on both sides to conclude agreements in regard thereto between His Majesty's Government and the Government of Egypt :

" (a) the security of the communications of the British Empire in Egypt ;

" (b) the defence of Egypt against all foreign aggression or interference direct or indirect ;

" (c) the protection of foreign residents in Egypt and the protection of minorities ;

" (d) the Sudan.

" Pending the conclusion of such agreements, the *status quo* in all these matters shall remain intact."

With reference to the last paragraph of this Declaration, it may be said without delay that in the absence of any agreement, the *status quo*, i.e. in its essentials a military occupation of Egypt, has subsisted from 1922 to the present day. Of the four reserves above formulated three alone were seriously discussed during the negotiations with Zagloul and Adly Pasha in 1920 and 1921. These reserves were : (a) which concerned the future of the **Suez Canal**, (b) which concerned the size, distribution and privileges of the British forces in Egypt, and (c) which concerned the régime of Capitulations. Reserve (d), concerning the future of the Sudan, was sedulously kept in the background.

In January, 1922, however, after the arrest and deportation of Zagloul to the Seychelles, the time for plain speaking had come. The four British reservations were laid down, and the Sudan was publicly included among them. The British Government sent a Note to the other Powers interested informing them bluntly that " the termination of the British Protectorate over Egypt involves no change in the *status quo* as regards the position of other Powers in Egypt. The welfare and integrity of Egypt are necessary to the peace and safety of the British Empire, which will, therefore, *always maintain as an esssential British interest* the special relations between itself and Egypt long recognised by other Governments, and in calling attention to these special relations as defined in the declaration recognising Egypt's independence, *we propose to declare that we will not admit them to be questioned by any other Power, that we will regard as an unfriendly* act any attempt at interference in the affairs of Egypt by another Power ; and that we will consider any aggression against the territory of Egypt as an act to be repelled by all means at our command."

[6]

Strong words these ! They were written in 1922, and represented the aggressive attitude of the Lloyd George Coalition Government, then the strongest in Europe. Their author was that redoubtable British imperialist, the late Marquess Curzon, then Secretary of State for Foreign Affairs, who possibly felt that the destinies of a near-Oriental country like Egypt came within his own especial province, as a man who had devoted his life to the study of imperial questions. Such words conveyed to Egypt as well as to the outside world the unmistakable warning that so long as the British Empire existed it would never withdraw its armed protection over Egypt, nor its armed forces (whatever fiction concerning their title or objective might be mutually consented to) from Egypt. The demand

put forward even by such moderate Egyptian Nationalists
as Adly Pasha that the British force in Egypt should be
confined to the vicinity of the Suez Canal and should be
limited in numbers was uncompromisingly rejected.

Even stronger words than those of Lord Curzon were used
by the then British Premier, Mr. Lloyd George, in which he
refused in a speech in the House of Commons the Egyptian
demand for a share in control of the Sudan.

" His Majesty's Government," he then said, " will never
allow the progress which has already been made (in irrigation
and dam-building) and the greater promise of future years
to be jeopardised. . . . Nor can His Majesty's Government
agree to any change in the status of that country which
would in the slightest degree diminish the security for the
many millions of British capital which are already invested
in its development. Egypt on the other hand has an
undeniable right to the most ample guarantees that the
development of the Sudan shall never threaten or interfere
with her existing water-supply or with that which she may
require in order to bring her own territory under full
cultivation. Such guarantees His Majesty's Government
will be ready to afford and there is no reason why they should
in any way hamper or retard the progress of the Sudan."
In other words, in the view of the British Government
then—and it has not changed in the interval—Egypt's
legitimate interest in the Sudan is in *Water*, whereas
Great Britain's legitimate interests are dual : (a) Security
for Capital Investment and (b) Security for Imperial
Communications.

[7]

The question of the Army and the question of the Sudan
had remained since 1922 the two great stumbling-blocks
in the path of peace in Egypt. Negotiation after negotiation
had been wrecked upon these fatal obstacles. Since 1930,
when the last attempt at treaty-making failed, there had
been an ominous lull in Egypt. The *status quo* had been
indefinitely prolonged. The fiction of the independence of
Egypt had begun to wear thin. The virtual domination of
the British in Egypt was quietly but unmistakably enforced.
Two major events in the early part of 1936 occurred to
change, superficially if not fundamentally, the relations

between Great Britain and Egypt and their respective attitudes towards the four reserves of 1922. These two events were the death of King Fuad, and the Italian annexation of Ethopia, with its implicit consequences for Egypt and the Sudan.

The first factor removed one of the most subtle elements of discord in the Egyptian scene : a would-be despotic monarch of Italian sympathies, surrounded by interested and intriguing court officials, with one foot in the British and the other in the Nationalist camp, who often held in their not incorruptible hands the destinies of the country. The second factor, by bringing home vividly to Egypt the weakness of her own defence system, and the risks she ran, with the Sudan, from the imperial ambitions of a powerful aggressor, changed the long attitude of hostility to the presence of a force of occupation to one of relief and security if not of enthusiasm.

The offer of the British Government to negotiate a new draft treaty with Egypt was made in February, two months before the death of Fuad, and was made, moreover, in circumstances of disorder in Cairo which seemed to some critics of the Government ill-chosen for a display of conciliation. After three months of laborious conversations between Sir Miles Lampson and Nahas Pasha, held in the sumptuous old palace of Zaafaran which the Khedive Ismail built for his harem, the limits of the British army to be permanently left in Egypt after the signature of a Treaty of Alliance again proved a serious obstacle to accord. The Egyptian Government demanded, as a concession to the prestige and dignity of a self-governing state, that no foreign troops should be quartered after the present crisis in its two principal cities at Cairo and Alexandria. There was, however, less insistence shown on the original demand for the limitation of the British defence force.

Recent events in the Eastern Mediterranean have brought many Egyptians to admit, however reluctantly, that there is security as well as indignity in submitting to the military domination of a foreign power. Lord Lloyd, one of the most energetic of post-war High Commissioners in Egypt, has pointed out very cogently that if the military clauses of the abortive draft Treaty of 1930 had been in operation during the Italo-Abyssinian War, Great Britain would have only been permitted to maintain 8500 troops on Egyptian territory, and these would have been forbidden to emerge from their confinement in the Suez Canal zone without special permission from the Egyptian Government. Moreover, under the 1930 Treaty Egypt would have become a member State of the League of Nations, and if she had given permission to Great Britain either to bring her troops out of the Canal zone or to increase their numbers, such permission might have been considered by Italy as an act of war. As events proved, a British force of more than twice that size was maintained in Egypt during the Eastern Mediterranean crisis, and was not hampered in its freedom of movement in any part of Egyptian territory. Further, the Egyptian Government so clearly recognised the dangers that had arisen on its own frontiers that it offered to the British authorities the free use of ports, aerodromes, military buildings, munition depots and roads for the duration of the crisis.

[8]

The political negotiations which were conducted both in Cairo and London during the summer of 1936 were enormously facilitated by this new attitude on the part of Egypt. The prospects of permanent peace are as a result better than at any time since 1922. For the first time in modern Egyptian history, some degree of unity of view has been achieved between the statesmen of Great Britain and Egypt. It has been reluctantly conceded in Cairo that a certain solidarity exists between the security of British imperial interests in the Near East and the security of Egypt, and upon that narrow basis the terms of a permanent military alliance between the two countries have been outlined.

At the end of July agreement was reached by the British and Egyptian delegations in Cairo on the terms of the new military clauses of the Treaty. The final text of the Anglo-Egyptian Treaty was signed in London on August 26th, 1936, by the Egyptian Prime Minister, Mustapha Kemal Pasha, and by the British Foreign Secretary, Mr. Anthony Eden. The Treaty gives Great Britain full facilities for the defence of fundamental British interests in Egypt, the Sudan and the Canal. The Egyptian Government, on the other hand, assumes responsibility for the maintenance of order at all times and in all parts of Egypt, and is relieved of the indignity of a permanent military occupation by a foreign power. The British troops now stationed in Cairo, Alexandria and Aboukir will be eventually withdrawn to Gineifa and other bases in the Suez Canal zone. A limit of 10,000 is placed upon the strength of the British force, and a time limit of twenty years upon the occupation; at the end of which time Great Britain agrees to evacuate the Canal zone if Egypt is in a position to undertake its defence. In the event of a dispute as to the date of evacuation, the League of Nations is to be invited to arbitrate. The British air bases at Heliopolis and Aboukir will be transferred to aerodromes near Suez and Moascar. A British Military Commission will be created to train and reorganise the Egyptian Army, which like the Egyptian Air Force will be increased and equipped with modern material. In the time of war British troops will have freedom of movement in any part of Egypt, and the British Navy will have full use of Alexandria and other Egyptian ports, although they will not officially become naval bases in peace-time.

The first article of the Treaty states explicitly that " the military occupation of Egypt by the forces of His Majesty the King and Emperor "—an occupation that has lasted fifty years—" is terminated." For the virtual protectorate of Egypt is substituted an Alliance between two free and sovereign states, an alliance subject indeed to certain mutual obligations and undertakings, and moreover *perpetual*. For the first time in modern history a treaty contains the unusual provision that although the treaty itself may be revised after twenty years, any revision must provide for the continuation of the alliance between Great Britain and Egypt.

The recognition of Egypt's new status is accompanied by certain material concessions on both sides. The British High Commissioner in Egypt is raised to the rank and style of Ambassador, and Egypt will be represented by a similar dignitary in London. Egypt undertakes to apply for membership of the League of Nations, and Great Britain, having recognised Egypt as a sovereign and independent state, will support her request for admission. " Each of the High Contracting Parties undertakes not to adopt in relation to foreign countries an attitude which is inconsistent with the alliance, nor to conclude political treaties inconsistent with the provisions of the present treaty." In other words, the alliance with Great Britain is implicitly recognised to be an exclusive alliance, so far as Egypt at least is concerned.

The most important feature of the Treaty is that which ensures protection for British imperial interests in Egypt and the Suez Canal. The relevant passages are the following :

ARTICLE 6

Should any dispute with a third State produce a situation which involves a risk of a rupture with that State, the High Contracting Parties will consult each other with a view to the settlement of the said dispute by peaceful means, in accordance with the provisions of the Covenant of the League of Nations and of any other international obligations which may be applicable to the case.

ARTICLE 7

Should, notwithstanding the provisions of Article 6 above, either of the High Contracting Parties become engaged in war, the other High Contracting Party will . . . immediately come to his aid in the capacity of an ally.

The aid of his Majesty the King of Egypt, in the event of war, imminent menace of war or apprehended international emergency, will consist in furnishing to his Majesty the King and Emperor on Egyptian territory, in accordance with the Egyptian system of administration and legislation, all the facilities and assistance in his power, including the use of his ports, aerodromes and means of communication.

It will accordingly be for the Egyptian Government to take all the administrative and legislative measures, including the establishment of martial law and an effective censorship, necessary to render these facilities and assistance effective.

ARTICLE 8

In view of the fact that the Suez Canal, whilst being an integral part of Egypt, is a universal means of communication as also an essential means of communication between the different parts of the British Empire, his Majesty the King of Egypt, until such time as the High Contracting Parties agree that the Egyptian Army is in a position to ensure by its own resources the liberty and entire security of navigation of the Canal, authorises his Majesty the King and Emperor to station forces in Egyptian territory in the vicinity of the Canal, in the zone specified in the Annex to this Article, with a view to ensuring in co-operation with the Egyptian Forces the defence of the Canal.

The detailed arrangements for the carrying into effect of this Article are contained in the Annex hereto. The presence of these forces shall not constitute in any manner an occupation and will in no way prejudice the sovereign rights of Egypt.

It is understood that at the end of the period of 20 years specified in Article 16 the question whether the presence of British Forces is no longer necessary owing to the fact that the Egyptian Army is in a position to ensure by its own resources the liberty and entire security of navigation of the Canal may, if the High Contracting Parties do not agree thereon, be submitted to the Council of the League of Nations for decision in accordance with the provisions of the Covenant in force at the time of signature of the present Treaty or to such other person or body of persons for decision in accordance with such other procedure as the High Contracting Parties may agree.

ANNEX TO ARTICLE 8

1. Without prejudice to the provisions of Article 7, the numbers of the forces of his Majesty the King and Emperor to be maintained in the vicinity of the Canal shall not exceed, of the land forces 10,000, and of the air forces 400 pilots, together with the necessary

ancillary personnel for administrative and technical duties.

These numbers do not include civilian personnel, e.g., clerks, artisans and labourers.

2. The British forces to be maintained in the vicinity of the Canal will be distributed (a) as regards the land forces, in Moascar and the Geneifa area on the south-west side of the Great Bitter Lake, and (b) as regards the air forces, within five miles of the Port Said–Suez railway from Kantara in the north, to the junction of the railway Suez–Cairo and Suez–Ismailia in the south, together with an extension along the Ismailia–Cairo railway to include the Royal Air Force Station at Abu Sueir and its satellite landing grounds; together with areas suitable for air firing and bombing ranges, which may have to be placed east of the Canal.

3. In the localities specified above there shall be provided for the British land and air forces of the numbers specified in paragraph 1 above, including 4,000 civilian personnel—but less 2,000 of the land forces, 700 of the air forces and 450 civilian personnel for whom accommodation already exists—the necessary lands and durable barrack and technical accommodation, including an emergency water supply.

In addition to barracks and water supply, the Egyptian Government undertakes to improve the railways in the Canal zone and between Ismailia, Alexandria and Mersa Matruh, and to construct roads from the Canal zone to Cairo and Suez; from Cairo to Alexandria via Ghiza and the desert; from Alexandria to Mersa Matruh in the western desert; from Cairo along the Nile to Kena and Kus; from Kus to Kossier and from Kena to Hurghada. Hitherto, as visitors to Egypt have sometimes found to their cost, the few existing roads in the country have been mere earth tracks, and prohibited to traffic at night owing to their danger from bandits and marauders.

The British troops in Egypt will not be withdrawn until these strategic roads and railways have been built. The necessary works in the Alexandria region are estimated to require eight years for their completion, and this period has been fixed as the maximum for the maintenance of troops in that garrison.

The Egyptian Government undertakes in addition to provide adequate landing grounds and seaplane anchorages for the Royal Air Force, and grants British military pilots freedom of navigation in any part of Egyptian territory. The British officers on the General Staff of the Egyptian Army are to be withdrawn, and the training of this army is to be entrusted to a British Military Mission.

Article 12 of the Treaty gives the Egyptian Government henceforth the duty of protecting foreigners in Egypt. The British forces are to enjoy special immunities and privileges outlined in a separate agreement which provides that " no member of the British forces shall be subject to the criminal or civil jurisdiction of the Egyptian Courts in any matter arising out of his official duties," and that " British camps in Egyptian territory shall be inviolable and subject to the exclusive control of the British authorities." With this solitary and important exception, however, the special privileges accorded to foreigners under the old Capitulation Treaties are to be withdrawn, after negotiations with the interested powers in which Great Britain promises Egypt full support, and after a reasonable period of transition. When this period expires, the existing mixed tribunals and consular Courts will disappear. Foreigners will be subject to the Egyptian penal code and to Egyptian fiscal legislation. The European Bureau of the Cairo police will be taken over by the Egyptian personnel, and after a period of five years the British members of the Egyptian police force will be entirely replaced by Egyptians.

Another important feature of the Treaty is the new régime to be established in the Sudan. Both Governments will resume their respective rights and duties under the Condominium of 1899, and will continue to administer the Sudan jointly. The Egyptian Army will again co-operate with the British forces and the Sudan Defence Force in the defence of the Sudan. No discrimination between British subjects and Egyptians will be made in regard to taxation or ownership of land. An Egyptian secretary and aide de camp will be added to the Governor-General's staff, and Egyptians will be equally eligible with British subjects for appointment to posts in the Sudan administrative services.

[9]

Thus the new attitude of Egypt towards the presence of a British military force on Egyptian territory has been accompanied by a change of opinion concerning the Sudan. That vast territory, which hitherto has been regarded with grudging and envious eyes by Egyptian Nationalists, as a source of wealth, fertility and man-power, unfairly diverted into British channels, is now seen for the first time as a source of potential danger to Egypt herself. The creation of a second Italian frontier east of the Sudan destroys the complacent Egyptian belief that the defence of the Sudan is a question for Egyptian forces alone. The Sudan is now hemmed in on three sides by the possessions of three great European powers— Italian Libya and French North-West Africa on the West, British Kenya and Uganda on the South, and Italian Abyssiania and Italian Somaliland on the East. The balance of power between these rival colonial empires can only be maintained by the closest community of interest and policy between Great Britain and Egypt.

That many Egyptians hitherto hostile to British influence on the Nile have been converted by the harsh logic of events to this new standpoint is evident. That the older political parties in Great Britain have been influenced by the recent incidents in North Africa, in Syria and in Palestine, and still more perhaps by the consequences for British naval strategy in the Mediterranean of the fortification of the Dardanelles and their possible denial of passage to ships of war in an international emergency, is equally evident. Out of this new reconciliation of mutual interests and common dangers it is likely that a new relationship between Great Britain and Egypt will be born. For good or evil, the country whose fate it has been to become the link between the Western and Eastern worlds, to hold the shores of the great artificial waterway between the Mediterranean and the Eastern seas, shares the destinies of the British Empire. It stands in a peculiar relationship to that empire, neither in it nor outside it. Its independence, however solemnly recognised by treaty and publicly sealed by its entry into the League of Nations, cannot but be precarious. Its history is inextricably linked with the history of the strongest naval power in the Mediterranean. Its economic security and its prosperity are conditioned by the goodwill of the power which holds the head-waters of the Nile. Its political development, its future, its military security are equally conditioned by the relations which bind it, as ally or as vassal, to the power which guards the neutrality of the Suez Canal.

CHAPTER VI

THE SUEZ CANAL

[1]

IT has long since ceased to be the engineering nine days' wonder of the world. The financial and mechanical difficulties which earth-bound the soaring ambitions of Ferdinand de Lesseps are forgotten. The proud achievement of French mechanical science was shortly to be engulfed in the collapse of the Third Empire and the disasters of the Franco-Prussian War. The last half of the nineteenth century was too crowded with industrial, political, and imperial adventure in Europe for men to dwell overlong in rapturous or fearful contemplation of the enterprise which had mingled the waters of the Mediterranean and the Red Sea, and cut a way from the ancient seat of European civilisation to the forgotten seats of other and older empires buried in antiquity.

Nevertheless the historian may be pardoned a brief evocation of that 17th day of November, 1869, which saw the apotheosis of the empire of the third Napoleon, which saw his smiling and beautiful empress Eugénie, on board the Imperial yacht *L'Aigle* (only one year before the French eagles were to fall on the field of Sédan), lead in triumph a procession of sixty-eight ships from Port Said to Suez. Not for another half-century, not until the day in 1919 when the German plenipotentiaries signed the humiliating terms of the Treaty of Peace in the Hall of Mirrors in Versailles, were the French to rejoice in another spectacle so flattering to national vanity. The Suez Canal was the culmination of an era in European affairs.

Suggestive as are its associations with French history, its part in the development of the British Empire has been infinitely more profitable. The events which gave

Great Britain a direct share in the ownership and administration of the enterprise of De Lesseps were of a dramatic simplicity more frequently encountered in fiction than in life. On a November evening six years after the opening of the Canal two men met at a dinner-table in Victorian London. One of them was a banker, Henry Oppenheim. The other was a journalist, Frederick Greenwood, the editor of the *Pall Mall Gazette*. The banker dropped the hint that the Khedive Ismail was endeavouring to sell his 176,602 shares in the Suez Canal Company to a French financial group. The editor went with this information to Lord Derby, the Foreign Secretary, who promised to convey it to Disraeli, the Prime Minister. Disraeli, who had the Oriental gift of seeing the world in the round, saw his historic opportunity. He telegraphed to the British Agent-General in Egypt to inform the Khedive that Her Majesty's Government could not stand idly by while he sold his interest in the Canal to an unknown third party. The Agent was requested to ask that the negotiations be suspended.

Nine days after the dinner-party in London the Khedive offered the shares to Disraeli for a sum of £4,000,000. On the following day Disraeli induced the house of Rothschild to guarantee the money. A day later, on November 25th, 1875, the sale was negotiated in Cairo. And on November 26th the share certificates were handed over to the British Consul. The shares gave Great Britain a 44 per cent interest in the Suez Canal. Their value has now increased to £25,000,000, or over six times the capital sum invested. They have proved in addition a profitable and ever-growing source of revenue to the British Treasury during the past sixty years.

[2]

On an average 6000 vessels pass through the Suez Canal every year, and roughly 60 per cent of their tonnage is British. The annual gross receipts of the Company from tonnage and passenger charges has steadily risen since the war. During the past six years they have averaged between eight and nine million pounds sterling. The Canal is owned and administered by an Egyptian Company registered in Paris (in which capital are its headquarters), and consequently subject both to French and to Egyptian law. Its President (at the present time the Marquis de Vogüé) is French. Of the thirty-one other directors twenty are French, ten are British, and one is a Dutchman. The seat on the board originally held by Germany was abolished during the war and has never been re-established, but with the revival of Germany's colonial ambitions it is not improbable that an effort may be made to regain it. Of the ten British directors three are appointed by the British Government.

Although the governing board of the Company is international, its financial direction is in Paris, and the technical administration of the Canal, the whole of the Egyptian staff of engineers, clerks, and traffic controllers are French, in part recruited from the French Navy. The whole length of the Canal—just over one hundred miles from Port Said to Suez—is patrolled night and day and is ceaselessly repaired, dredged and policed. The traffic through it is meticulously controlled, as regards speed and periodicity, by an intricate system of signalling and verification. The Company maintains control stations at every six miles along the Canal, owns all the roads, ferries, tugs, workshops and housing accommodation within the Canal zone, and possesses a private telegraph and telephone system linking every control station along the Canal.

It holds both banks of the Canal on a ninety-nine years lease from the Egyptian Government. The lease, which began on November 17th, 1869, expires on the same day in 1968. It has therefore but thirty-two years to run, and thereby hangs one of the gravest complications of the Anglo-Egyptian situation discussed in the preceding chapter. Under the original charter the Canal is to lapse, on the expiry of the lease, into the possession of the Egyptian Government, after proper compensation to the owners of the lease. When the time comes the Egyptian Government will, in theory at least, be free (a) to renew the concession to the present Company, (b) to grant a fresh concession to another financial group, or (c) to administer the Canal directly.

The problem of the ultimate destiny of the Canal has already begun to figure in interested discussions in both political and financial quarters in Paris, London and Cairo. The British, French and Egyptian Governments are vitally concerned in the political aspects of the problem. The present directors of the Suez Canal are equally concerned in its financial aspects. The day is fast approaching, as Sir Ian Malcolm, one of the British directors of the Company, has pointed out, when every programme of new works for the improvement of the Canal, involving a considerable expenditure of money, will have to be determined by the probable duration of the present company's effective administration of the enterprise and its consequent capacity of recovering its outlay.

[3]

An even more pressing political problem in connection with the Suez Canal was raised during the Italo-Abyssinian War—the problem of its neutrality during a prospective Mediterranean conflict, or during the execution of League Sanctions. The question of closing it to Italian troopships was first raised in the House of Commons in June, 1935, during the debate on Italy and Abyssinia. Italy had not at that time been declared an aggressor by the League of Nations, and the question of closing the Canal to her was therefore purely theoretical. Subsequently, however, the matter was frequently discussed in Parliament and outside it, but Ministerial opinion in Great Britain tended towards the conclusion expressed by the Marquis de Vogüé at the 1936 annual meeting of the Suez Canal Company. " If by act of force," said M. de Vogüé, " which nothing entitles one to anticipate, any Power thought of forbidding entry into the Canal to another Power, that gesture would be equivalent to an act of war, ·with all its consequences."

The Marquis based this declaration upon the terms of the International Convention respecting the Free Navigation of the Suez Maritime Canal signed at Constantinople on October 29th, 1888, by representatives of the following countries : Great Britain, Austria-Hungary, France, Germany, Italy, the Netherlands, Russia, Spain and Turkey. The First Article of this Convention stated in unequivocal terms that

" The Suez Maritime Canal shall always be free and open, in time of war as in time of peace, to all merchant or war vessels without flag discrimination.

" Consequently, the High Contracting Parties agree in no way to prevent the free use of the Canal in time of war as in time of peace.

" *The Canal shall never be used for the exercise of the right of blockade.*"

Of the sixteen other Articles of the Convention the following are also relevant to the question at issue :

ARTICLE IV.—The Maritime Canal remaining open in time of war as a free passage, even to the ships of war belligerents, according to the terms of Article I of the present Treaty, the High Contracting Parties agree that no right of war, no act of hostility, nor any act having for its object to obstruct the free navigation of the Canal, shall be committed in the Canal and its ports of access, as well as within a radius of three marine miles from those ports, even though the Ottoman Empire should be one of the belligerent Powers.

Vessels of war of belligerents shall not revictual or take in stores in the Canal and its ports of access, except in so far as may be strictly necessary. The transit of the aforesaid vessels through the Canal shall be effected with the least possible delay, in accordance with the Regulations in force, and without any other intermission than that resulting from the necessities of the service.

Their stay at Port Said and in the roadstead of Suez shall not exceed twenty-four hours, except in the case of distress. In such case they shall be bound to leave as soon as possible. An interval of twenty-four hours shall always elapse between the sailing of a belligerent ship from one of the ports of access and the departure of a ship belonging to the hostile Power.

ARTICLE V.—In time of war belligerent Powers shall not disembark nor embark within the Canal and its ports of access either troops, munitions or materials of war. But in case of an accidental hindrance in the

Canal, men may be embarked or disembarked at the ports of access by detachments not exceeding 1000 men, with a corresponding amount of war material.

ARTICLE IX.—The Egyptian Government shall, within the limits of its powers resulting from the Firmans, and under the conditions provided for in the present Treaty, take the necessary measures for insuring the execution of the said Treaty.

In case the Egyptian Government should not have sufficient means at its disposal, it shall call upon the Imperial Ottoman Government, which shall take the necessary measures to respond to such appeal; shall give notice thereof to the Signatory Powers . . . and shall, if necessary, concert with them on the subject.

The provisions of Articles IV, V, VII and VIII shall not interfere with the measures which shall be taken in virtue of the present Article.

ARTICLE X.—Similarly, the provisions of Articles IV, V, VII and VIII shall not interfere with the measures which His Majesty the Sultan and His Highness the Khedive, in the name of His Imperial Majesty, and within the limits of the Firmans granted, might find it necessary to take for securing by their own forces the defence of Egypt and the maintenance of public order.

In case His Imperial Majesty the Sultan, or His Highness the Khedive, should find it necessary to avail themselves of the exceptions for which this Article provides, the Signatory Powers . . . shall be notified thereof by the Imperial Ottoman Government. . . .

ARTICLE XI.—The measures which shall be taken in the cases provided for by Articles IX and X of the present Treaty shall not interfere with the free use of the Canal. In the same cases, the erection of permanent fortifications contrary to the provisions of Article VIII is prohibited.

After the World War the powers conferred upon the Sultan of Turkey by the foregoing Convention were transferred to Great Britain. In Article 252 of the Treaty of Versailles and in Article 107 of the Treaty of St. Germain

Germany and Austria respectively consented to this transfer. In the unratified Treaty of Sèvres, and subsequently under Article 17 of the Treaty of Lausanne of 1923 Turkey similarly agreed, formally renouncing all her rights and titles over Egypt and the Sudan as from November 5th, 1914, the date of her entry into the war.

[4]

During the Russo-Japanese War of 1904-5 the Russian Fleet passed through the Canal without incident, but on two other occasions the Canal has been closed, and on a third the full privileges of the Canal zone were denied to ships of war.

The first instance of closure occurred in 1882, before the International Convention was negotiated, and during the revolt of Arabi Pasha against the Khedive of Egypt. In the unwillingness of Turkey and France to support the Egyptian Government in subduing the insurrection the onus of quelling it fell upon Great Britain, who sent an expeditionary force to the Sudan, under Sir Garnet Wolseley. British troops were landed at Suez and Port Said, and a British naval force stationed at the latter port held the entrance to the Canal closed to all comers for three days. A decree of the Khedive, recognising " the military occupation charged to re-establish order in Egypt," sanctioned this precautionary measure on the part of the British authorities, and authorised them to occupy all the ports necessary. The action was therefore undertaken for the benefit of the state through whose territory the Canal passed, and at her invitation. And six years later the International Convention gave its sanction to such exceptional measures of security in the interests of Egypt.

The second occasion when the neutrality of the Canal or freedom of navigation through it was called in question was during the Spanish-American War of 1898. Then a Spanish fleet which desired to coal at Suez on its way through the Canal was denied such facilities by the Canal authorities, under Article IV of the Convention.

Finally the Canal was closed for a short period during the World War, when the safety alike of the Canal and of Egyptian territory was endangered by the advance of the Turkish army. When this danger was no longer imminent the Canal was reopened for navigation, and neutral vessels freely made use of it. An effective ban on the passage of enemy vessels, however, was exercised by the British Navy, whose command of the seas at each entrance to the Canal prevented the shipping of hostile powers from approaching it. At the outbreak of war several enemy ships were either actually in the Canal or hastily took refuge in it. They were offered free passage through the waterway by the Canal authorities, and on their attempting to ignore or to evade the invitation were conducted outside the three-mile limit of the Canal zone.

[5]

Since the World War no question of the neutrality or of the freedom of the Canal had arisen until the outbreak of the Italo-Abyssinian War, and in several European countries, notably in Great Britain, legal pretexts were sought for closing the Canal against Italian troopships and munitions of war. The relevant articles of the International Convention were eagerly examined for this purpose by jurists and sanctionists alike. They afford, however, but little legal basis for such action. Article I, as has been seen, declares unequivocally that the Canal shall at all times remain free and open to all vessels and all flags, and the Contracting Parties solemnly engaged themselves not to interfere with this freedom.

There is but one reservation to this principle. The rights of Egypt, as the state with sovereign rights over the territory through which the Canal runs, are left intact. To the Egyptian Government is allocated the task, under Articles IX and X, of assuring the execution of the Convention, and its right to defend its territory by its own forces is acknowledged. Article XI, it is true, provides that the measures which may be taken by Egypt under Articles IX and X shall not interfere with the free use of the Canal, but in a military emergency such as arose in 1882 and again in 1914–18 it is admitted that the sovereign rights of Egypt, when they are identical with the interests of the Canal, are a primary obligation.

It is clear, nevertheless, that subject to this reservation, and to certain limitations upon the rights of belligerents, the freedom of the Canal could not have been juridically denied to Italy as the aggressor in the Abyssinian dispute. It was accordingly suggested, by advocates of effective sanctions against Italy, that the Council of the League of Nations should be recommended to decide upon the closing of the Canal as a sanction under Article 16 of the Covenant, Italy having been condemned as an aggressor in disregard of its undertakings under Articles 12, 13 and 15, and thereby *ipso facto* being considered in a state of war with all other members of the League. It was objected, however, that the League had not the legal right to overrule an international convention which had been specifically recognised by the Treaties of Versailles, St. Germain, Trianon and Lausanne.

And to a further suggestion that the League Council be recommended to decide that the Convention was incompatible with the League Covenant, in that it restricted the liberty of action of the League, and should accordingly be abrogated under Article 20 (by which States members agree " that this Covenant is accepted as abrogating all obligations or understandings *inter se* which are inconsistent with the terms thereof . . ."), cogent arguments were returned in France and Italy that a Convention which is mentioned in two Articles of the Treaty of Versailles (which also forms the charter of the League of Nations) cannot be abrogated, on the grounds of inconsistency, under an earlier article in the same Treaty.

A third view was that the terms of the Suez Canal Convention might be reconsidered by the Assembly under Article 19 of the Covenant, which deals with the revision of inapplicable or inoperable treaties. But this solution was not one which could be effective in an emergency like the Italo-Abyssinian War, and the sanctionists were forced, in the absence of any legal basis for action in closing the Canal, to fall back upon more realistic considerations. If naval or military sanctions were taken against Italy, the closing of the Canal to Italian vessels would inevitably be effected in the same manner that German, Austrian and Turkish vessels were denied ingress to it during the war—by the British command of the seas at each of the channels of approach. Other grounds for closure might be found, if a similar contingency had arisen, in an Italian threat to Egyptian or Sudanese security, or to the security of the Canal itself.

Whatever the outcome of the dispute between Italy and the League, it is clear that considerations of the security and freedom of the Suez Canal have played a considerable part in the negotiations between Great Britain and Egypt for a treaty of alliance, and will figure prominently in any future discussions between the Mediterranean states with the object of concluding pacts of naval limitation or of mutual assistance. In an international conflict, of course, the freedom of the Canal is as illusory as the freedom of the seas. Its permanent neutrality, like the independence of Egypt, is a polite fiction. The naval power which holds the approaches of the Canal can effectively deny passage through it to hostile vessels. The naval power which holds Suez and Gibraltar can make of the Mediterranean a closed sea.

PART FOUR

THE SHORE OF ASIA

CHAPTER I

SYRIA

[1]

THERE is a curious historic resemblance between the destinies of the old Ottoman and Austro-Hungarian empires. Both collapsed at the end of the World War, partly as the result of military defeat, partly as the result of internal dissensions and the growing spirit of nationalism. In both cases an ancient system, half despotic, half tolerant, more and more loosely linked to the central authority, a patchwork of races, nationalities and religions with merely tradition and a certain economic cohesion to bind it together, was transformed by the war into a complex of rival and mutually suspicious states, armed against each other, economically isolated, internally intolerant of racial or national minorities, and with no common aim except that of the conservation of frontier territories arbitrarily attributed, or violently annexed. Such has been the post-war history of Austria, Hungary, Czechoslovakia, Roumania and Jugoslavia. Such has been equally the recent history of the Asiatic provinces of the old Turkish Empire—Syria, Palestine, Transjordan, and the Arab states of the Hedjaz, Nejd, Irak, and Yemen.

Formerly all the Asiatic shore of the Mediterranean acknowledged the rule of the Sultans of Turkey. Now the dominions of the Turkish Republic cease south of the Taurus mountains. The coast of Alexandretta to the Sinai peninsula is divided into mandated territories of France and Great Britain, with a vast and thinly peopled hinterland of greater or smaller Arab states. Italy, which under the secret London Treaty of 1915, the Sykes-Picot agreement of 1916, and the agreement of St. Jean de Maurienne of 1917, should have received the whole southern portion of Asia

Minor, including the zones of Smyrna, Adalia and Adana, was eliminated from any share in the spoils of the Ottoman Empire in favour of Greece, and although the Greeks failed to retain their foothold in Asia, the subsequent power and solidity of the new Turkey of Mustapha Kemal prevented Italy from reasserting her claim.

The shares of Great Britain and France in the dismemberment of Asiatic Turkey were considerable if of unequal value. Before the war had ended disputes arose between the two Western Allies regarding the mutual attribution of the spoils of war in the East. Damascus, the capital of Syria, had been captured by General Allenby and by the Arabs of Feisal and Lawrence, and in 1919-20 was the seat of the brief-lived Syrian kingdom of the Emir Feisal. In 1920, under pressure from Great Britain, Feisal abdicated and his kingdom was almost immediately afterwards handed over to the French, in virtue of their claim to Syria and Lebanon under the London Treaty and the subsequent secret agreements between the Allies. The French protectorate over these territories was recognised by the Allied Supreme Council at San Remo in 1920, and was subsequently confirmed by the issue of a League of Nations mandate in 1922.

[2]

The French mandated territory known collectively as the States of the Levant comprises four semi-autonomous republics or provinces—the republic of Syria, granted a Constitution on May 14th, 1930, and provided with a President, a Legislature, and an executive elected by the assembly ; the republic of Lebanon, which was proclaimed a state on September 1st, 1920, with its capital at Beirout ; the Government of Latakia, established in 1930 with their capital in the town of that name ; and the Government of Djebel Druze, with its seat at El Suweideh. The total area of these territories is about 60,000 square miles and its population nearly 3 millions, divided as follows : Syria, 1,700,000 ; Lebanon, 900,000 ; Latakia, 300,000 ; Djebel Druze, 60,000. The majority of the inhabitants are Arabs, but elements of all the other Levantine races are also present in the cities of Damascus, Aleppo, Beirout, Homs, Tripoli, Antioch, Latakia and Alexandretta. At Beirout there is, in addition to the French university, an American college with a faculty of medicine.

The history of the French occupation of the Levantine States has not been particularly happy. In the early post-war years they attempted to apply to territories inhabited largely by Arab and Alawite nomads the policy they had pursued with conspicuous success in Morocco. The country was governed by a military officer with the title of High Commissioner, and several battalions of the Foreign Legion were employed to police the country.

The results were disastrous. The Arabs found they had exchanged the easy, corrupt, antiquated and inefficient rule of a distant Sultan in Constantinople—a Sultan, moreover, to whom they readily paid religious tribute as Caliph—for the modern, militarised, efficient and less easily evaded authority of a Western state. All around them they saw their kinsmen ruled by Arabs. The sons of the Sheik Hussein of Mecca were enthroned as rulers in Irak and Transjordan. Ibn Saud, the warrior king of Nejd, was rapidly uniting the Arabs of Central and Southern Arabia. They alone, the Syrian and Lebanese Arabs, had been denied the fruits of the Arab revolt sponsored and organised by an Englishman of genius, the late Colonel Lawrence.

In 1925 they revolted against French authority. Damascus and the Djebel Druze were centres of a dangerous struggle for independence. For two years the rebellion smouldered, its embers being stamped out in one region only to flame up in another, In 1926 the French Government introduced a policy of conciliation. The military High Commissioners were succeeded by civilians. The first of these, the late Henry de Jouvenel, was sent out with full power to negotiate peace preliminaries with the Syrian nationalists and to sign a treaty recognising Syria's independence. He succeeded in his efforts to gain the goodwill of the agitators, and his conversations with the leaders of the revolt resulted in agreement on a draft treaty which assured a quasi-independence to Syria and the Lebanon. When M. de Jouvenel returned to Paris, however, a change of government and of policy had taken place in France, and his signature was repudiated. He resigned in indignation, and during the next four years the history of the French occupation of Syria resembled that of the British occupation of Egypt.

In 1930 a new policy of conciliation was adopted and certain concessions were granted to Syria. The territory was given a Constitution and an autonomous government. M. Henry Ponsot had succeeded M. de Jouvenel as High Commissioner, and had in turn been replaced by M. de Martel. The forms of self-government were conceded. But the substance was still denied. And all real authority continued to be exercised by the High Commissioner, fortified by further battalions of the Foreign Legion. The military occupation was extended and reinforced. Since 1931 the army of occupation has numbered roughly 300 officers and 14,000 other ranks.

Only in the summer of 1936, with the advent of the Front Populaire to power in France, and the formation of M. Léon Blum's first government, was a serious attempt made by France to convert its military occupation of Syria into a protectorate. One of the first acts of the new French Government, after conversations between M. Blum and the leaders of a Syrian Wafd or delegation, was to proclaim its intention of creating a federation of independent republics under the title of the States of the Levant, and to apply for their admission into the League of Nations. The precedent taken for this act was of course the British creation of the independent kingdom of Irak, which had done much to dissatisfy the Arabs in Syria with their existing state of subservience to an administration and a parliamentary assembly seated in Paris.

On September 9th, 1936, barely a fortnight after the signature of the Anglo-Egyptian Treaty, France made a somewhat similar pact with Syria, the first of a series of treaties by which the French mandate over the States of the Levant is to be withdrawn. The Franco-Syrian agreement then initialled is modelled on the Anglo-Irak Treaty, but in the words of M. Vienot, Under-Secretary of State for Foreign Affairs, the French Government has "been able to avoid the mistake committed by Great Britain in not ensuring at the same time the protection of Christian and other minorities," the latter being notably the Djebel Druze and Alawite communities.

The newly created Republic of Syria will come into existence by stages. During the next two years the machinery of the new State will be created. A third year will be devoted to a test of the machinery. In 1939, if the test is satisfactory, the Republic will function normally, and a 25-year treaty of alliance between France and Syria will enter into operation. In that year the French mandate will be withdrawn, the French High Commissioner will become French Ambassador, and Syria will be recommended by France for admission to the League of Nations.

The Franco-Syrian agreement initialled in Paris is subject to ratification by the French Parliament, and by the Parliament which will assemble in Syria after the impending elections. Formal signature of the treaty will take place after the formation of a Syrian Cabinet. It is hoped to negotiate a similar treaty with the Government of the Lebanon.

[3]

French interest in Syria is more strategic than political or economic. Its chief preoccupation has been to eliminate any other European power from a position of influence in the Moslem world second only to that of Great Britain. Hence the Peace Conference efforts to supplant Italy in Asia Minor by Greece, and France's post-war support of Mustapha Kemal in his struggle to eject both Italians and Greeks from Asia Minor.

There is yet another French strategic interest in Syria, and this of paramount importance to the French Navy, in war-time as in peace-time. The French share of the product of the Mosul oil-fields—fixed at 23.75 per cent by the San Remo agreement—is carried by pipe-line across the Syrian desert to the port of Tripoli, and thence shipped to Europe. The security of France's oil supplies from Mosul depends, therefore, upon the intimacy and cordiality of Franco-Syrian relations and upon internal order in Syria. The success of the British experiment in Irak, besides exciting to danger-point the spirit of in-dependence among the Syrian Arabs, has encouraged

France to hope that greater security for her interests in the Near East lies in a policy of co-operation than in one of coercion.

Despite the comparative contiguity of the Mosul oil deposits, and frequent indications of surface petroleum in Syria, attempts to work it have hitherto yielded little result. The country is not rich in minerals, although the ancient iron mines in Lebanon are still worked. The native industries are inconsiderable. The chief occupations of the population are agricultural, and their principal crops are wheat, barley, sesame, tobacco and cotton.

CHAPTER II

PALESTINE AND TRANS-JORDAN

[1]

BRITISH interests in the Levantine coast of the
Mediterranean differ from those of the French in
Syria in both character and in degree. Palestine
and its great Arabian hinterland are essential links in the
long chain of British imperial communications. France
has no vital interests in the Middle East. No great French
colonial possession borders that region. Her presence in
Syria is inspired partly by historic reasons—the memories
of the Crusades, the traditional protection extended by
the French kings over the holy cities and the Syrian
Christians—partly, as has been said in the preceding
chapter, by reason of precaution. As a power with great
Moslem dependencies in North Africa she is anxious not
to allow the Moslem Arabs of the Levant to pass under the
domination of a rival Mediterranean state.

Great Britain, however, has the double duty of protecting
the frontiers of Egypt and India, and of conserving intact
the great air routes to India and Australia and the fuelling
stations of the British Navy in the Persian Gulf. The whole
arid desert between the Mediterranean and the Gulf
bulks largely in considerations of Imperial defence. The oil
of Irak, the nationalist ferment in Egypt and Palestine,
the growing unity between the long-divided Arab nations,
have all enormously complicated the Middle Eastern
situation during the past few years. The tension in the
Eastern Mediterranean during 1935 and 1936, culminating
in the Arab-Jew riots in Palestine, the French Government's
intention to relinquish its mandate over Syria, and the
fresh Egyptian demand for full independence, has revived
world interest in this region of the Near and Middle East.

The great Arabian peninsula is washed by the waters of four seas—the Persian Gulf on the East, the Indian Ocean on the South, and the Red Sea and the Mediterranean on the West. Two-thirds of its Mediterranean coast-line, the narrowest portion of its immense seaboard and its frontage on the European world, is Syrian. The other third is included in Palestine.

Palestine is only one-sixth of Syria in size, having an area of but 10,000 square miles and a population of just over a million, of whom at the last census (1931) 73 per cent were Moslems, 17 per cent Jews and 8 per cent Christians. Since 1931, however, the Jewish population has grown considerably, partly as a result of its more prolific character, partly as a result of the increased immigration of Jewish colonists since the Nazi triumph in Germany. The influx of a great number of active, industrious and intelligent Jewish settlers, many of them equipped with capital, tools and machinery, has had the effect of precipitating a crisis long maturing between the Arabs and the Jews on the one hand and the Arabs and the British Government on the other : a crisis in part inspired by natural jealousy of the newcomer, in part by the growing spirit of nationalism among the Arabs.

[2]

In Europe and America there is a tendency among both Christians and Jews to lose sight of the political history of Palestine in the more grandiose spectacle of its religious history. The wealth of sentiment, religious, racial and historic, created by the Balfour Declaration and the mystic words " Jewish National Home," has obscured the real character of the country, its people and its problems. The real problem of Palestine is less a Jewish problem than an Arab problem. For over seven centuries until almost the end of the World War—a period as long as that since the Norman Conquest, and a much longer period of assimilation than is required to constitute ethnic, political and national unity in Europe—Palestine was in Moslem hands. Its chief town, venerated by the people of three faiths, had been captured by the infidel in 1244, two centuries before the discovery of America, and until the entry of Allenby and a British army in 1917 it had remained uninterruptedly since that date in Moslem hands.   In 1917 its Jewish population was probably less than 5 per cent of the whole.   In 1931, after thirteen years of British occupation and seven years of active Zionist colonisation, its Hebrew inhabitants did not muster more than 175,000, or 17 per cent of the total.

The Jewish character of Palestine at the time of its re-conquest by Great Britain was almost entirely Biblical. Since then intensive immigration has raised the strength of the Jewish minority, and in one generation, if the present rate of immigration continues, and the birth-rate in the thriving new Jewish settlements remains constant, the fears of the Arabs may be realised and their majority may well have shrunk to a minority.

Since the British conquest the administration of Palestine has been obstructed by the Arab refusal to take part in public affairs, and on three separate occasions, in 1921, in 1929 and now in 1936, the Arab protest against the British mandate took the form of violent attacks on Jewish citizens.   The British military occupation came to an end in 1920, and was succeeded by a civil government, under a High Commissioner who was also given the command of the military forces in the country.   The British mandate over Palestine was accorded by the League of Nations in 1922 and came into force in the following year.   Under the mandate Great Britain undertook to give effect to the pledges contained in the celebrated Balfour Declaration of November 2nd, 1917, in which it was stated that " His Majesty's Government view with favour the establishment in Palestine of a National Home for the Jewish people and will use their best endeavours to facilitate the achievement of that object, it being clearly understood that nothing shall be done which may prejudice the civil and religious rights of existing non-Jewish communities in Palestine, or the rights and political status enjoyed by Jews in any other country."

[3]

In September, 1922, soon after the issue of the League mandate, a new constitution was promulgated for Palestine. It provided for the replacement of the existing Advisory Council of the High Commissioner by a Legislative Council, an elective body to which were to be entrusted all public matters except defence and foreign affairs—both questions reserved to the British Government. During the following year, however, the Arab boycott of the British authorities had reached such lengths that the High Commissioner, with Parliamentary authority, suspended this provision of the Constitution, on the ground that Arabs had abstained in large numbers from the elections to the proposed Legislative body. The old Advisory Council, which consisted of the heads of the various government departments and the district commissioners of Northern and Southern Palestine, was restored, and this body has continued to assist the High Commissioner in the duties of government. Ordinances approved by this Council and signed by the High Commissioner have the force of law.

Since 1927 the Jewish population in Palestine has received official recognition as a religious community and has enjoyed, equally with the Moslem and Christian communities, full autonomy for its religious, cultural and communal affairs and with it the power of levying rates on its members. The community is governed by the Chief Rabbi and an elected assembly. The interests of the new and purely Jewish colonies in Palestine are in the hands of the Palestine Jewish Agency, to which has been delegated the right to treat with the British Government on behalf of its co-religionaries. A Moslem Supreme Council, presided over by the Mufti of Jerusalem, controls the internal affairs of the Arab community. English, Hebrew and and Arabic are all three admitted as official languages. Justice is administered in two kinds of courts, civil and religious. The higher civil courts are presided over by British judges assisted each by two Palestinian judges. The courts of each religious community, Moslem, Jewish and Christian, have jurisdiction in matters of religion and personal status. A special tribunal of British judges decides all disputes between the religious and civil courts. The native police force is also supplemented by a British Police Force of approximately 700 all ranks stationed in the towns of Jerusalem, Jaffa, Haifa and Nablus.

[4]

Arab opposition to the British mandate has been based on the charge that it is inspired primarily by regard for the interests of the Jews, and that it is aimed at the extermination, or at least the ultimate dispossession, of the Arab population. To the insinuation that Arabs are being driven out of Palestine Jewish authorities retort that so far from having decreased since the British occupation, the Arab population has actually increased, and is increasing at the steady rate of 20,000 a year. Stationary before the war, if not actually declining as a result of a high death-rate and migration overseas, their numbers have risen during the past sixteen years from roughly 500,000 to 800,000. The increase is ascribed less to any decrease in the mortality rate than to a large influx of Arabs from the neighbouring countries, attracted to Palestine by its more favourable economic situation.

As to Arab accusations that they have been driven off the land, the Jews reply that they can only acquire land in Palestine at exorbitant prices, and that many Arabs have been enriched and their status improved as the result of Jewish immigration. Moreover, the law protects Arab cultivators to the extent of insisting that they may not be displaced from their present holdings unless they are provided with acceptable farms elsewhere. A recent Government inquiry disclosed the fact that only a few hundred Arab farmers actually claimed to have lost their holdings as the result of Jewish purchases, and the majority of these refused the offer of land in compensation on the ground that they had found other and more attractive employment.

Palestine has few natural harbours and only four ports— Jaffa, Haifa, Acre and Gaza, of which only the two former are of any size. Gaza, however, is an important station on the England–India air route, and the Imperial Airways mail services leave once a week in each direction for Karachi via Baghdad, Basra and Bushire, and for London via Egypt, Athens and Salonika. There are also weekly services of flying boats between Alexandria, Haifa and Cyprus, and between Athens and Tiberias. The defence of Palestine is undertaken by the Middle East Command of the Royal Air

Force, and before the present disturbances in the country two squadrons of aircraft and four sections of armoured cars were permanently stationed in the country and in its neigh-bouring state of Transjordan, equally under British man-date. Normally two battalions of infantry suffice for extra police duties in Palestine. The Palestine–Transjordan border is guarded by the Transjordan Frontier Force, a body com-prising roughly 1000 men of all ranks, the maintenance of which is partly met by the British Government and partly by the Government of Palestine.

Early in September, 1936, the situation in Palestine had grown so serious that the British Government decided to place the country under martial law. Supreme authority over both the civil and military arms was entrusted to the new Commander-in-Chief, Lieut.-General J. G. Dill, who replaced the commander of the Palestine Air Force as military chief in the country. At the same time the British forces in Palestine—eleven infantry battalions—were con-siderably reinforced.

[5]

Transjordan, which was originally included in the Palestine mandate, has since 1928 been administered as an independent Arab state, under the Emir Abdullah Ibn Hussein, second son of the late Sheikh Hussein, ex-King of the Hedjaz, and elder brother of the late King Feisal of Irak. The British High Commissioner for Palestine, Lieutenant-General Sir Arthur Wauchope, has since 1928 acted also as High Commissioner for Transjordan, and is represented by a British Resident in Amman. The popula-tion of the territory is about 260,000, almost entirely Arabs, with a small sprinkling of Circassians. The quasi-indepen-dence of Transjordan was recognised in a Declaration made by the British Government in April, 1923, but not ratified until 1929, to the effect that His Majesty's Government proposed, subject to the approval of the League of Nations, to recognise the existence of an Independent Government in Transjordan, under the authority of the Emir Abdullah, provided such Government was constitutional and enabled the British Government to carry out its international obligations in respect of the territory. The Legislative Council provided for in this Declaration assembled in 1929 and ratified the agreement signed between the Governments of Great Britain and the Emir Abdullah regarding the important question of defence and the security of British air communications, which transverse the country from east to west.

During the later and more acute phase of the troubles in Palestine repeated attacks have been made on the Irak pipe-line, both in Palestine and in Transjordan. The Government of the Emir has inflicted heavy fines on villages in the vicinity of the damaged line. The Emir Abdullah himself has offered his services as mediator between the Palestine Arabs and the British Government, but made it known that his sympathies, like those of the Arabs of other neighbouring states, were with the Moslem leaders, and that the only condition on which a compromise could be reached was that Jewish immigration should cease pending the inquiry of the proposed Royal Commission.

In the Emir Abdullah's territory the provisions of the British mandate respecting the creation of the Jewish National Home have been abrogated. Jewish immigration and land purchase are completely prohibited. Notwithstanding the absence of Jewish competition in industry and agriculture, the general condition of the Arab population is stated to be inferior to that of the Arabs in Palestine, and the population has declined since 1920, chiefly as a result of Arab migration across the border into more prosperous Palestine.

CHAPTER III

THE ARAB RENAISSANCE

[1]

THE political renaissance of the Arabs, after their centuries of submission to the despotic power of the Ottoman Sultans, began in 1913 with the Wahhabi insurrection against the Turks. During the World War it was guided by the imagination of the late Colonel Lawrence into channels which ran for a brief period parallel with, if not identical to, the channels of Allied policy in the Middle East. After the war the divisions between the Western powers were reflected in the tribal and dynastic feuds of the Arabs themselves. Confusion reigned in the Arabian provinces of the old Turkish Empire. The dynasty of Sheikh Hussein of Mecca, upon which such unfulfilled hopes had been based by Lawrence, seemed near to collapse. Feisal had been deposed by the French in Syria. Hussein himself had been driven out of the Hedjaz by the brilliant warrior-statesman, Ibn Saud. Hussein's other son, it is true, ruled Transjordan under British protection, and Feisal had been found another kingdom in Irak, equally under British mandate. But while Hussein and Feisal lived no peace was possible with the usurper Ibn Saud. The two rival dynasties divided Central and Northern Arabia between them. In the south Ibn Saud and the Imam of Yemen were equally at war.

The death of Feisal removed one of the obstacles to reconciliation between the Arab states, and the Italian menace to the Arab shores of the Red Sea in 1935 and 1936 offered a solution to other difficulties. In the spring of 1936 a treaty of friendship was signed between the rulers of Irak and Saudi Arabia, and the Imam Yehia of Yemen is now reported to be favourably considering his adhesion to the pact.

The Irak-Saudi Arabian treaty is the third of a series of significant alliances which have recently linked Irak to Iran (Persia) and Iran to Afghanistan. If Yemen joins the other Arab states, and Egypt, which has a double interest, both as a Moslem and as a Christian country, in the Holy Places of Palestine and Arabia, responds to the friendly advances recently made to her by Ibn Saud and King Ghazi of Irak, a great Middle Eastern confederation will be created which will stretch from Africa to the frontiers of India and Asiatic Russia, from the Mediterranean and the Red Sea to the shores of the Caspian and the Indian Ocean.

The Arab renaissance has already borne fruit—both in Asia and in Africa. Syrian Arabs have forayed across the frontiers of Palestine to make common cause with their insurrectionary kinsmen in the Holy Land. In Algeria, in Tunisia, and in Morocco the advent of a Popular Front government in France has been greeted by simultaneous demonstrations of Arab unity, directed equally against the European colonists and the native Jews. British influences have undoubtedly played their part in the movement towards an Arab confederation, but it is too early to determine the political consequences of so ambitious an achievement, and the ultimate objective of the leaders of so unsettled and restless a people. At first glance the latest of the moves towards Arab unity seemed to be aimed against a possible Italian bid for domination of the Arabian peninsula, and thereby to favour British policy in the Middle East. But the Arabs who unite to repel the Italians from the eastern shores of the Red Sea equally unite against the French in Syria and against the British in Palestine. Their solidarity would seem to be directed against a race and not against any one nation, and the consequences of the present tendency towards unification may well prove equally disastrous for all the European powers with interests in the Middle East.

[2]

Irak, formerly known as Mesopotamia, the ancient seat of the Babylonian and Chaldean civilisations, is the richest and most prosperous of the Arab states. It lies between Syria and Palestine on the West and Persia (Iran) on the East, and on the South is bounded by Arabia and the

Persian Gulf. It has an area of 177,000 square miles and a population of nearly three millions, partly of Arab and partly of Kurdish stock. It comprises the former Turkish vilayets of Baghdad, Basra and Mosul, and was freed from Turkish rule during the Great War. From 1919 to 1927 it was ruled by Great Britain as a mandated state. The Emir Feisal, who had been forced to abdicate the throne of Damascus in 1920, was elected to the throne of Irak in the following year after a plebiscite in which 96 per cent of the population voted in his favour. In 1927 the British Government renounced its mandate; the kingdom of Irak was recognised as an independent state; and in 1932 was admitted, on the recommendation of Great Britain, as a member of the League of Nations.

Irak is an hereditary and constitutional monarchy. The present king, Ghazi I, the eldest son of the late King Feisal, governs with the aid of a senate of twenty nominated elders and an elective assembly of 88 deputies. The country has a rich soil and with adequate irrigation is capable of raising large crops of cotton, wheat, barley. Wool and dates are also important exports. The real potentialities of Irak, however, are in the development of its oil deposits.

The Mosul oilfield had been prospected before the war, and the Turkish Petroleum Company had been formed with British, German and other capital to exploit its rich possibilities. During the war Mosul and its oil-bearing region were the subject of long and secret discussions between representatives of the Allied Powers, and their future partition was provided for in the Sykes-Picot agreement of 1916. The arrangement then reached by Great Britain and France (to the exclusion of Italy) was modified after the war in the San Remo agreement and at the Lausanne Conference, and Italy was admitted to a small share of the future product of the Mesopotamian oilfield.

In 1925 the original concession of the Turkish Petroleum Company was replaced by a new concession granted by the Irak Government. Four years later, in 1929, the title of the Company was changed and it became the Irak Petroleum Company Ltd. The Company has a capital of £6,500,000, and its chairman is Sir John Cadman. Prospecting has been pursued with success in Mosul and in other regions, particularly in Kifri and Kirkuk, and over a dozen wells are now yielding oil. The Company's pipe-line is capable of transporting 40,000,000 tons of oil a year. The French share of the product (23·75 per cent) is carried from Kirkuk on the eastern bank of the river Tigris across the Syrian desert to Tripoli, on the coast of the Mediterranean, and a part of the British share to Haifa, in Palestine. By far the larger portion of the oil output of Irak, however, is piped to Basra and Abadan, Irak's two ports at the head of the Persian Gulf, and is there loaded into British tank steamers. A second oilfield, near the Persian frontier, is worked under concession by the Khanaquin Oil Company, a subsidiary of the Anglo-Iranian Company (formerly the Anglo-Persian), in which the British Government owns £7,500,000 Ordinary shares. The Anglo-Iranian Company (and thus indirectly the British Government) has also a large interest in the Irak Petroleum Company.

Recently the Irak Petroleum Company has considerably extended its activities in the Middle East by acquiring the Italian interests in Mosul Oil Fields Ltd., a company with an issued capital of £2,300,000, which was formed in 1932 to purchase the capital of the British Oil Fields Development Company. The last-named company enjoyed a concession of mineral rights in over 40,000 square miles of territory in Irak (originally negotiated by Mr. Francis W. Rickett, the British financier who first achieved world celebrity through his oil negotiations with the Emperor of Abyssinia). The deal gives Great Britain a large interest in the two principal oil prospecting companies in the Near and Middle East. It enables the Irak Petroleum Company to avoid the dangers of competitive production, and at the same time saves the Mosul Oil Fields Company the very great expense of constructing a separate pipe-line to the Mediterranean.

The defence of Irak is assured partly by the Middle East Command of the British Royal Air Force, which maintains several squadrons in the territory ; partly by the Iraki Army, created in 1929, and consisting of 3 cavalry regiments, 7 infantry battalions and an air squadron, and partly by a Levy Force, at the charge of the Imperial Budget. The police force comprises nearly 8000 officers and men, half of them mounted, and is assisted by two camel corps, ten armed car sections with Lewis and Vickers guns, and several wireless stations, fixed and mobile. There are large military and civil air stations at Basra and Baghdad, both important points on the England–India air route.

[3]

The Wahhabi rising against the Turks which gave the first signal for the re-emergence of Arab nationalism was directed by a warrior of genius and personality, Abdul Aziz ibn Saud. Ibn Saud captured the Hasa province from Turkey, and struck the first blow at an imperial edifice which was to be brought during the five succeeding years to complete collapse. At the end of the war the Turk had been vanquished in the further provinces of the Hedjaz, the Asir and the Yemen, and all Arabia was now free for the Arabs. The great peninsula thus liberated extends over an area of roughly 1 million square miles, an area of bleak mountains, barren coast, sandy desert and rock-strewn tablelands sloping gently down from the Red Sea to the shores of the Persian Gulf. A handful of ancient and historic cities—Mecca, Medina, Jedda, Riyadh, Hufuf, Wajh, Taif, Muwaila, Anaiza, Shaqra, Mubarraz and Sana—shelter the town-dwellers among the Arabs, and are more or less venerated places of pilgrimage to hosts of pious Moslems in Africa and Asia. The remainder of the seven millions of Wahhabis or Bedouins approximately estimated as the population of Arabia eke out a nomadic existence with their herds of sheep, goats and camels in the rocky clefts of the uplands and around the infrequent oases of the desert.

The warrior who reanimated the disillusioned heart of Arab nationalism after the blight had settled upon Arab hopes in Syria styled himself Sultan of Nejd, and established the capital of his first kingdom at Riyadh. Nejd is the largest of the Arab states. It comprises the central and part of the southern portion of Arabia. It has a population of roughly three millions, exports camels to Syria and horses to India, and boasts half a dozen towns with between ten and thirty thousand inhabitants. In 1925 Ibn Saud drove King Hussein out of Mecca, annexed his kingdom, had himself crowned in the holy city of Mecca, and later assumed the title of King of the dual kingdoms of Nejd and the Hedjaz. On May 20th, 1927, Great Britain recognised his title to the united territories in the Treaty of Jedda.

Nevertheless, the two kingdoms, although united under the rule of Ibn Saud, have not lost their separate status. The Nejd retains its old character of a despotically-ruled patriarchy, governed directly by its King without the aid of ministers, although the eldest son of the ruler resides in the capital of Riyadh and has the title of viceroy. The Hedjaz, although its capital city of Mecca, with 85,000 inhabitants, is the largest in Arabia, is smaller in area and population than its neighbour. Its inhabitants do not number more than a million. Its area does not exceed 150,000 square miles, about one-seventh of the total area of Arabia. It does a small trade in wool, hides, butter and dates, but the real source of its prosperity—interrupted in recent years owing to the disputes between Egypt and the Arabian states, but now reviving—is the annual pilgrimage to Mecca. The Hedjaz, which enjoyed a form of representative government under the reign of King Hussein, was granted a Constitution in the first year after Ibn Saud's conquest, and is endowed with a legislative assembly, municipal and tribal councils. The assembly, nevertheless, has no power over the ministers, who are appointed by the King. Its functions are purely consultative. The members of the municipal and tribal councils are also named or approved by the King.

[4]

Ibn Saud's victory over King Hussein of the Hedjaz left as his sole rival in Arabia proper the Imam of the Yemen. This ruler, Zaidi Yehia ben Mohammed ben Hamid el Din, reigns over a mountainous territory some 75,000 square miles in area and extending along the south-eastern coast of the Red Sea between the Hedjaz and the British protectorate of Aden. His subjects number between two and three millions, many of whom belong to the Ismaili sect of Mohammedanism. His capital is Sana, an ancient walled city with between 20,000 and 25,000 inhabitants. The long dispute between the Imam of Yemen and the victorious ruler of the Nejd-Hedjaz kingdoms over the tribal limits of their authority only ended in 1931, when a general treaty was concluded between them which attributed the fiercely contended territory of Asir to Ibn Saud. During 1936, as I have observed, the Imam is reported to have signified his adhesion to the pact of friendship concluded between the King of Nejd and the Hedjaz and the King of Irak.

The only other regions of Arabia with an independent existence as states are the Hadramaut, which adjoins the Aden protectorate on the east, and the sultanate of Oman (capital Muscat), and the little territories of the Sheikh of Kuwait and the Emir of Bahrein.

PART FIVE

PROBLEMS AND PERILS

CHAPTER I

THE CONQUEST OF ABYSSINIA

[1]

ALTHOUGH Abyssinia is not a littoral state of the Mediterranean, its past, present and future are intimately associated with the history of that sea. It was the immediate cause of the most serious crisis the Mediterranean has known, apart from the years of the Great War, during the present century. Its successful occupation, administration and occupation by Italy depend upon the security of her communications in the Mediterranean, the Suez Canal and the Red Sea. Its rapid conquest has cynically reopened a chapter in the history of colonial aggression which seemed closed for ever. It has provided Germany with a pretext for reviving her own colonial claims. Its ominous example has calmed the ardour of the most fanatical nationalists in Egypt and driven them to agree to a compromise with Great Britain on issues which a few months earlier seemed impassable barriers between the two nations. Finally, and without regard to the immense difficulties which still confront Italy in an only partially subdued country, it threatens to divide the scarcely conciliated Mediterranean powers on a number of controversial and vexatious questions, notably those of Lake Tana and the Djibouti–Addis Ababa railway.

[2]

Lake Tana and its water supply, as is clear from the British diplomatic correspondence concerning Italian claims in Abyssinia which preceded the war of conquest, are Great Britain's chief material consideration in the country. From that lake flow the head-waters of the Blue Nile, the source of the prosperity and the very existence of Egypt and the Sudan. As far back as 1902 the British Government made representations to the Emperor of Abyssinia regarding the future of that cherished water supply.

By the Anglo-Abyssinian Boundary Treaty signed in May of that year the Abyssinian Government engaged itself :

1. Not to permit any construction which would divert the Blue Nile, Sobat or Lake Tana waters from their normal course to the Nile ;

2. To lease a site for a trading station (afterwards established at Gambela) ; and

3. To reserve to Great Britain the right to build a railway through Abyssinian territory connecting the Sudan with Uganda.

A general understanding was also reached between Great Britain and Abyssinia that subject to " reasonable use of the waters in question by the inhabitants of the region," a dam should be constructed at the Lake in order to regulate the flow of its waters for the benefit of Egypt and the Sudan.

Not until nearly thirty years later, nevertheless, was any attempt made to carry this project into effect. In 1930 the J. G. White Engineering Corporation, an American firm, surveyed the Lake on the instructions of the Abyssinian and Sudan Governments. Operations were interrupted, however, owing to the considerable cost of the undertaking. In the following year, with the financial co-operation of the Egyptian Government, a second survey party was sent to the Lake. In May, 1935, the Emperor of Abyssinia invited the British, Egyptian and Sudan Governments to a conference at Addis Ababa with the object of reaching agreement on this question. But at that time the controversy with Italy was already acute. Great Britain, wishing to avoid any pretext which might be seized by Italy as a justification for breaking off negotiations, decided to postpone any discussion of Lake Tana. In Egypt, nevertheless, official interest in the barrage scheme was unabated, and the Cairo Government's five-year plan of expenditure on public works, approved by the Cabinet on May 22nd, 1935, allocated £E.21,000,000 for irrigation projects which included the building of a great dam at Lake Tana.

To all British expressions of concern, both official and

unofficial, at the possibility of any future alienation of the waters of the Lake from their present outlet, Mussolini has invariably replied with assurances that British and Egyptian interests will be scrupulously respected. Nevertheless, the fact remains that since the defeat of the Emperor Italy is for the first time directly interested in a question which hitherto has primarily concerned Great Britain and her Protectorates in North Africa. It may well be that in the inevitable negotiations between Great Britain and Italy over the Lake and its projected barrage, Mussolini will claim for Italian engineers and Italian labour the formidable and costly enterprise of building the dam.

Other British interests in Abyssinia are of a minor order. Chief of them is vested in the trading station, established in accordance with the Agreement of 1902 at Gambela, an Abyssinian town about 70 miles from the Sudan frontier. A considerable trade in Sudan ivory and ostrich feathers has been done through Gambela since the Anglo-Abyssinian Treaty of 1902, and its volume is steadily increasing. Until the Italian entry into Addis Ababa, moreover, a considerable proportion of internal trade in Abyssinia was conducted by British-Indian and British-Somali merchants. Another important, if purely local, interest is in the preservation of the rights of trans-frontier grazing between the British Somaliland and Abyssinian tribes in the Ogaden area. Finally, there is the important political consideration that nearly two-thirds of Abyssinia's frontiers march with British territory—Kenya, Somaliland and the Sudan.

Hitherto the frontier between Italian Libya and the Sudan was the only region in the world in which British and Italian territories were contiguous. The possibilities of conflict between the two powers arising out of minor frontier incidents or rival economic interests were until the present day almost non-existent. With the creation of the new Roman Empire in Libya and Abyssinia, however, along many thousand miles of frontier—represented by arbitrary lines drawn on the map, and largely undefined by physical or topographical landmarks—the British and the Italian Empires confront each other. In Lake Tana, Italy holds the key to the fertility of a great protectorate in which hundreds of millions of British capital have been invested. In the south of Abyssinia her new imperial frontier runs with that of Kenya, a colony in which British settlers have seen with alarm and indignation the overwhelming and subjection of a peaceful neighbour. The future of power politics in North and West Africa is therefore bristling with problems and perils.

[3]

The only other great European power with interests in Abyssinia is France. France has hitherto operated and owned the only large-scale commercial enterprise in the country—the Djibouti–Addis Ababa railway. A ninety-nine-year concession to build this railway was obtained by a French syndicate in 1894, and the Compagnie Impériale des Chemins de Fers Éthiopiens was created. Between 1896 and 1902 the company laid down 190 miles of a metre-gauge track, from Djibouti to Harrar, of which 56 miles lay in French Somaliland. The capital of the company then being exhausted, British investors were induced to join the undertaking. This was before the days of the Entente Cordiale, and the British and the French were still rivals in the Sudan and elsewhere in Africa and Asia. The growing French colonial party raised an alarm, and forced the French Government to accept a certain measure of responsibility for the railway. In February, 1902, the Government granted the company a subsidy of 500,000 francs annually for fifty years.

It was now the Emperor Menelik's turn to be alarmed. He had successfully resisted the influence of one foreign Government in his domains—that of Italy. He refused to allow France to acquire political control of a purely commercial concession. Two years later, however, he had so far yielded to French diplomatic and financial pressure as to authorise the company to continue the track as far as Addis Ababa, and the line was completed between the years 1909 and 1917. Its full length from Djibouti, in French Somaliland, to the Abyssinian capital is approximately 480 miles.

In the meantime France, Great Britain and Italy had reached agreement as to their future zones of influence in the Abyssinian hinterland of their respective Red Sea possessions. The Tripartite Agreement signed between the three powers in 1906 also regulated the position of the railway. The French Company was confirmed in its right to operate the existing railway as far as Addis Ababa, and it was laid down that lines should eventually be constructed from the capital to the Sudan under British auspices (as projected in the Anglo-Abyssinian agreement of 1902), and to Eritrea or Italian Somaliland under Italian auspices. In January, 1925, under the Mussolini-Laval agreement, France ceded to Italy 2,500 out of her 34,000 shares in the railway.

Difficulties in the operation of the line from Djibouti to Addis Ababa arose early in the Italo-Abyssinian War. With the defeat and flight of the Emperor all effective control of the railway passed into the hands of the Italian military authorities, and the French Government made urgent representations to Mussolini on the subject. As the result of the negotiations subsequently begun in Rome, however, agreement has been reached between France and Italy on a *modus operandi* pending the discussions which must sooner or later take place between the three signatories of the Tripartite Agreement of 1906 regarding their respective interests in the new Italian colony of Ethiopia.

[4]

Enough has been indicated of the problems created by the various interests of the Great Powers in Abyssinia to suggest the diplomatic difficulties which beset their ultimate recognition of the Italian conquest. It remains to be seen whether Italy, now that she has transformed her rights over a limited zone of influence in the Lake Tana region into political sovereignty over the entire country, will re-affirm the offer to recognise the special interests of Great Britain made on earlier and less privileged occasions. Thus in November, 1919, in the course of colonial discussions based on the pledges of the secret Treaty of London of 1915, the Italian Government proposed to Mr. Lloyd George's government that :

1. Italy should support Great Britain's claim for a concession to carry out works on a barrage on Lake Tana, within the Italian sphere of influence, pending the delimitation of the extent of the territorial zone

to be recognised as pertaining to Great Britain in respect of the latter's *predominant hydraulic interests.* 2. Italy should also support a British claim to construct a motor road from Lake Tana to the Sudan.

This offer, however, was " not entertained at the time," in the words of a British Note addressed to Italy in December, 1925, " chiefly owing to the strong objection felt to the idea of allowing a foreign power to establish any sort of control over the head-waters of rivers so vital to the prosperity and even to the existence of Egypt and the Sudan."

To-day Italy has established control over the head-waters of the Blue Nile and the Nile by force of arms, and the objections which the British Government felt so strongly in 1919 must now be swallowed with as good a grace as the circumstances permit.

They had, in fact, been so far mitigated in 1924 and 1925 as to encourage the first Labour Government to propose, and its Conservative successors in office to negotiate, an agreement with Italy based on the Italian offer of November, 1919. In December, 1925, in addition to territorial concessions to Italy on the Egyptian-Cyrenaic frontier, Great Britain undertook, in return for Italian support in obtaining from Abyssinia a concession to build a barrage on Lake Tana and a motor road from the Lake to the Sudan, to support an Italian request for the long-desired extension of the Addis Ababa railway to Eritrea and Somaliland.

On condition that Great Britain obtained the Lake Tana barrage concession, and subject to an Italian undertaking not to tamper with the water-flow into the Nile, the British Government in 1925 promised " to recognise an exclusive Italian economic influence in the west of Abyssinia and in the whole of the territory to be crossed by the above-mentioned railway. They would further promise to support with the Abyssinian Government all Italian requests for economic concessions in the above zone."

Ten years later, when Italy was beginning her plans for the invasion and conquest of Abyssinia, this British promise of 1925 was widely exploited by the Fascist press as evidence of the perfidy of Great Britain.

CHAPTER II

THE STRATEGIC ISLANDS

[1]

FIVE European powers and one Asiatic power possess strategic islands or island groups in the Mediterranean, either as integral parts of their national territory and its defence system, or as important bases for their imperial communications. The powers and their respective possessions are :

GREAT BRITAIN

Malta and Cyprus

FRANCE

Corsica

SPAIN

The Balearics : Majorca, Minorca and Ybiza

ITALY

Sardinia

Rhodes and the Dodecanese

Pantellaria (half-way between Sicily and Tunis)

GREECE

Corfu (in the Adriatic)

Lemnos, Mitylene, Chios, and Samos (in the Ægean)

TURKEY

Imbros and Tenedos (at the mouth of the Dardanelles)

During the Italo-Abyssinian War the strategic value of these islands was considerably enhanced by the military, naval and aerial concentrations of certain powers in the Mediterranean. Thus the Balearic Islands, off the Mediterranean coast of Spain, which during the World War were suspected of affording concealment for enemy submarines, were discussed as a possible base for the British fleet, if the harbour of Malta should become untenable by reason of its vicinity (within eighty miles) to the nearest Italian air stations in Sicily. Sardinia, which is within bombing range of the French ports of Marseilles and Toulon, became the centre of a great concentration of Italian long-range bombers. The Italian island of Rhodes, in the Ægean, only 350 miles from Alexandria and Port Said, also witnessed significant naval and aerial preparations by Italy. Leros and its neighbouring isles of the Dodecanese, which Italy seized from Turkey in 1912, were also hastily fortified and used as bases for submarines and aircraft. And the Italian island of Pantellaria, half-way between Sicily and Tunis, and in a position to dominate that comparatively narrow channel, suddenly acquired considerable importance in Italian eyes.

The Mediterranean crisis has thrown into greatest relief the strategical utility and security of the two British islands in that sea : Malta and Cyprus. Of the other islands in the Ægean, Imbros and Tenedos, which guard the entrance to the Dardanelles, have been disarmed since the Treaty of Sèvres, but Turkey, to whom they belong, has demanded and obtained the right to re-fortify them with the shores of the Straits. Similarly Greece, for the same reasons of security, proposes to fortify her islands of Lemnos, Mitylene, Chios and Samos.

[2]

The island of Malta lies exactly half-way between Gibraltar and Suez, and almost midway across the narrow channel between the southern-most promontory of Sicily and the coast of Africa. For three thousand years it has shared the vicissitudes of the Mediterranean's tumultuous history. It was conquered successively by the Phœnicians, the Greeks, the Carthaginians, and the Romans. The Arabs captured it in 870 in the course of their great northward advance into Europe. From 1090 until 1530, during all the period of the great crusades against the Turk, it was held against the corsairs of Africa and the Levant by the Norman kings of Sicily. In the latter year it was handed over by the Emperor, Charles V, as a refuge for the Knights of the Order of St. John, who had been driven out of Rhodes as they had previously been expelled from Cyprus and St. Jean d'Acre. The Knights built a city which they called La Valette (Valetta) after their gallant Grand Master, improved the harbour and strongly fortified it. In 1565 they had to withstand the last and greatest of their sieges by the Turk, and this time were successful in repelling him. For nearly two and a half centuries thereafter they remained in uninterrupted possession of the island.

An accident of the Napoleonic wars brought Malta into the keeping of the British Crown. In 1798, during his expedition to Egypt, Napoleon landed on the island and drove out the Knights. Three months later the Maltese rose in insurrection against the French, captured the town of Notabile and besieged the French garrison in Valetta. The islanders were supplied with arms and munitions by Saumurez, one of the captains of Nelson, and while the Maltese struggled to expel the French, British sailors landed on the neighbouring and smaller island of Gozo and took possession of it in the name of the King of England. The siege of Valetta continued throughout the year 1799 and the greater part of 1800, and the garrison only capitulated in September. Fourteen years later, under the Treaty of Paris, and at the petition of its inhabitants, the island was formally annexed to the British Crown. It has been in British possession for 122 years.

Malta is roughly the size of the Isle of Wight, with an area of 95 square miles. Its neighbour, Gozo, has an area of only 26 square miles. The population of both islands is about a quarter of a million. Both are bald, barren, sun-scorched rocks. In the middle of the larger island the old capital of Notabile (Citta Vecchia) raises its yellow mass of flat-roofed houses in terraces,. Two old forts, St. Elmo and St. Angelo, command the modern capital of Valetta and the Grand Harbour. Every inch of the coasts

of Malta, Gozo and the small intervening island of Comino
is defended by modern batteries, and since the Mediterranean crisis the defences of Malta have been thoroughly
overhauled and strengthened.

A Constitution was granted to Malta in 1921, but as a
result of the political troubles created by the language
problem the Constitution was on two occasions suspended,
in 1930 and in 1933, and ultimately, at the height of
the Anglo-Italian dispute over Abyssinia, was repealed
altogether. In consequence full authority in all Maltese
matters, civil and military, rests with the Governor, who
is appointed by the King on the recommendation of the
Minister for the Colonies.

[3]

With the recent and solitary exception of Abyssinia,
Malta is the only territory in the world in which British
and Italian interests are in direct conflict, and the language
dispute in the island, itself of no great importance, has
served since the advent of Fascism in Italy as a pretext for
an agitation entirely political in its aims and motives. Three
tongues are spoken in Malta : Maltese, English and Italian.
Maltese, an ancient language of Arabic and Phœnician
origin, is the mother tongue of all the islanders, and is
the language of native intercourse. It is taught as a compulsory subject in all elementary schools, and is spoken in
every home on the island, from the highest to the humblest.
English is the official language of Malta, the language of
the administration, of the garrison and fleet, of commerce
and domestic service. It was taught from 1902 up to 1923
as a second language in secondary schools, but parents
were given the choice between English and Italian, which is
the language of the law courts and of culture, Maltese
having little literature in spite of its ancient origins.

In 1923 (the first year of Italian Fascism) the pro-
Italian nationalists in the Maltese Legislative Assembly
succeeded by a majority of one vote in passing a bill making
both English and Italian compulsory subjects not only in
secondary but also in elementary schools, a measure which
resulted in neither language being adequately acquired.
The conflict which arose between the Governor and the
successive native governments as the consequence of

attempts to enforce this law resulted in the first suspension of the Constitution in 1930 and the creation of a Royal Commission of Inquiry.

When the Constitution was restored in 1932 the nationalists, defeated on the question of Italian as an obligatory school subject, attempted to evade the spirit of the Governor's instructions by ordering Italian to be taught on a voluntary basis *outside school hours*. The Governor, Sir David Campbell, upon orders from the Secretary of State for the Colonies, promptly forbade this proceeding, whereupon the Maltese Minister of Education, Dr. Mizzi, adopted such other expedients as the creation of intermediate schools, the subsidising of private schools in which Italian might be taught, and the sending of school teachers to study Italian in Italy at the public expense. The deadlock which subsisted between the nationalist majority and the British authorities in Malta during the three years which followed the second suspension of the Constitution, in 1933, reached a dangerous stage in 1936, when British relations with Italy were embittered by other and infinitely graver controversies. The situation which then arose was arbitrarily ended by the decision of the British Government to repeal the Constitution of Malta. Henceforth, it seems probable that British naval, military and aerial interests in the island will alone decide the form of Malta's administration and the languages to be taught her citizens.

Malta is one of the most important ports of call in the world. It is the headquarters of the British Fleet in the Mediterranean, and its base for repairs, fuelling and refitment. In normal times a comparatively large garrison is maintained in the island, comprising three infantry regiments, two brigades of Royal Artillery, a company of Royal Engineers, one company of the Royal Army Service Corps and another of the Royal Army Medical Corps. During the past year both the naval and the military forces at Malta have been very considerably reinforced, and it is probable that in future a part at least of this larger establishment will become permanent.

The British Government has also decided to strengthen the anti-aircraft defences of the island, and to increase very considerably the present accommodation for air squadrons.

[4]

Similar measures are being considered with regard to Cyprus, which seems destined to play a much greater rôle in Mediterranean strategy than hitherto. Cyprus lies in the Eastern Mediterranean, forty miles from the coast of Asia Minor and sixty from the coast of Syria. It is a beautiful island of ragged peaks and green valleys, about 140 miles long and 55 wide, and has a total area of 3,584 square miles. The island's history began in the dawn of Mediterranean civilisation. The Greeks, the Persians and the Phœnicians settled on it in comparatively recent times, and it was a Roman colony at the beginning of our own era. In 1191 Richard Cœur de Lion landed at Limassol and soon after his arrival married Berengaria, the daughter of the ruler. During the Crusades it formed part of the Latin kingdom of Jerusalem and the kings of that brief dynasty, driven out of the Holy Land, took refuge in Cyprus. When the sixteenth century opened it was a flourishing colony under the Venetians, and near enough to the great dominions of the Ottoman Emperors to be coveted by them. The conquest of the island was finally determined by the drunken Sultan, Selim II, a son of the great Sultan Suleiman. The siege of Cyprus in 1570 and 1571, its spirited defence by the Venetians, Bragadino and Baglione, the fall of Famagusta, the torture and death of Bragadino, and his avenging at the hands of a Christian fleet under Don John of Austria at the battle of Lepanto (1571), provided some of the most enthralling chapters of sixteenth-century history.

After its capture in that year Cyprus remained under the nominal suzerainty of the Sultan for three and a half centuries. In 1878 its administration was entrusted to Great Britain, but it was not formally annexed to the British Crown until the outbreak of the World War. In 1925 Cyprus was declared a Crown Colony, and its High Commissioner received the status of Governor. He is assisted by a Legislative Council with Greek, Turkish and British members. The island has a population of about 350,000, of whom roughly one-sixth are Moslem Turks, and five-sixths are Greeks, Armenians and others professing various branches of the Christian religion.

The importance of Cyprus to the security of British communications in the Eastern Mediterranean has been enormously increased by recent developments in that region. Before the crisis of 1935-6 the island received only one or two visits from British warships in a year. The Italian naval and aerial concentrations in the islands of Rhodes and the Dodecanese, and the imminent re-militarisation by Greece and Turkey of the larger of their respective possessions in the Ægean, may drive Great Britain to take similar measures of defence in regard to the great island of Cyprus. The construction and fortification of a naval base either at Limassol or at Famagusta, the ancient capital, is now being discussed by the British Admiralty. It seems likely that measures will also be taken to increase the aircraft defences of the island, which is already an important centre of aerial communications between Greece, Palestine, Syria and Egypt.

Early in August, when the tension in the Eastern Mediterranean had ended and the greater part of the Mediterranean Fleet had already been withdrawn from Alexandria, Air Chief Marshal Sir Robert Brooke-Popham, Inspector-General of the Royal Air Force, arrived in Cyprus and made a thorough examination of its facilities for accommodating and repelling aircraft. His report is now being examined by the Committee of Imperial Defence. Sir Robert's visit to Cyprus was followed by the arrival of a flight of British bombers, which will remain indefinitely on the island.

[5]

Reference has already been made to the possibility of utilising one of the Balearic Islands as an alternative naval base to Malta, in the event of a Mediterranean naval war in which Spain and Great Britain were allies. The future of these islands has become a question of urgent concern to France as well as Great Britain as the result of the civil war in Spain, with its threat of armed intervention by other powers, and the obvious sympathy between the Fascist insurgents and the authoritarian states in Europe.

CHAPTER III

THE SPANISH CIVIL WAR

[1]

THE outbreak of civil war in Spain has dramatically shifted the interest in European politics from the Eastern to the Western Mediterranean. It had provided the occasion for the first great naval demonstration by the European Powers—if the war years are excepted—since the Moroccan crises of the early years of the present century. It has given Germany her first opportunity of displaying the speed of her new pocket battleships, the nucleus of her reconstructed battle fleet. It has been followed by the spectacle, rare enough in history, of the main body of the British Fleet in the Mediterranean steaming westwards from Malta to make a demonstration in the western waters of a sea whose eastern zone had for many months within the same year been the scene of a similar demonstration.

Since the end of the seventeenth century the internal disputes of Spain have weighed heavily upon the politics of Europe. The legacy of the Spanish throne to a grandson of Louis the Fourteenth provoked the War of the Spanish Succession, which for long years devastated Flanders and Savoy. A century later the hereditary feud between England and France, revived and exacerbated by the ambitions of Napoleon, was fought out in the Iberian peninsula in the long and bloody campaign which revealed the military genius of Wellington. The fall of Napoleon did little to bring peace to Spain or friendship to France and England. During the nineteenth century the peninsula was the subject of many bitter and sometimes fatal controversies. In 1823 the expedition of the Duke of Angoulême to Cadiz provoked a fresh Anglo-French quarrel, and the disputes between Canning and the French chargé d'affaires, Marcellus, are familiar to every student of British foreign policy.

Twenty years later a new dispute broke out between the British and the French Governments over the Spanish Marriages. And the disastrous Franco-Prussian War of 1870-1871 was the indirect if not the direct consequence of the offer of the Spanish throne made by Marshal Prim to the German Prince von Hohenzollern-Sigmaringen, in defiance of French wishes and of the dynastic ambitions of Napoleon III.

During the present century Spain has lived happily remote from the rivalries of the great European war. Until the present she had seemed to belong rather to Africa than to Europe. Her modestly restricted interests in Morocco were not contested even by the powers who felt themselves cheated of their lawful opportunities of commercial and political expansion in North Africa. She remained severely neutral in the successive crises between France and Germany over Morocco and throughout the length of the war which broke out in 1914 as the inevitable result of that rivalry. It was not until the present year, and the beginning of what may prove a long and deadly struggle between dictatorship and democracy in Spain, that the Iberian peninsula resumed its old unhappy rôle in European affairs and threatened to become a new battle-ground between the Great Powers.

[2]

Europe is vitally interested in the Spanish civil war for various reasons, of which two are of paramount interest :

1. The consequences for the existing régime in North Africa of the disintegration of one of the principal parties to the Algeciras Convention and the Franco-Spanish agreement of 1912.

2. The probable emergence, at the end of the present struggle, of a Spain subject either to a Fascist or Bolshevik dictatorship.

Of the foregoing reasons the first is perhaps of more urgent concern. The Spanish zone in Morocco has always proved the weakest link in the system of European protectorates over the ancient dominions of the Sultan. Juridically it is held by Spain, as has been pointed out in an earlier chapter, not by direct concession from the Sherifian Government, but by lease from France. Under the agreement signed with France in 1912, Spain is required not to arm the natives and not to sub-lease any part of her territory in Morocco to another power. The agreement was intended to exclude Germany from any future interest in North Africa. The renunciation of Italy had already been purchased by France under a separate agreement which acknowledged Italy's exclusive rights in Libya.

But the insurrection directed from Ceuta and Melilla, with the support of most of the officers and men of the Spanish forces in Morocco, has directly contravened both the letter and the spirit of the 1912 Convention. General Franco, the leader of the southern rebel army, and the active spirit of the rebellion, has openly armed and recruited natives. He has instigated the despatch of Italian military airplanes to Morocco, and German machines and pilots to Seville. And he has received munitions landed from German vessels at Larache, and moral and political support, if not more material aid, from German warships at Ceuta. Both Italy and Germany have been given opportunities for demonstrating their interest in Morocco—opportunities which in the later years of the nineteenth and the opening years of the twentieth century were considered valid reasons for wars of expansion and conquest.

It was this more than any other consideration which drove the Front Populaire government in France to abandon its early attitude of sympathetic support to the democratic government in Madrid in favour of a hastily prepared pact of neutrality. The danger of intervention by other powers in the Spanish struggle was suddenly realised to be more menacing to French interests in Morocco than the possible triumph of Fascism in Spain. The goal of the interventionists was feared to be less the victory of an absolutist doctrine in Spain than the rich prize of Spanish Morocco. And to France the perpetuation of the existing régime in the Spanish zone, which lies between metropolitan France and her own share of the Sultan's territories, is a vital principle of her foreign and imperial policy.

There is another and even more incalculable danger arising out of the Spanish struggle. It lies in the rebel leaders' appeal to the Moors to support them against the Government in Madrid. The authority of Spain has never been very firmly exerted over the Moors. The insurrection of the Riffan mountaineers under Abdel Krim was only crushed after many humiliating losses, and then only with the active aid of France. Some regions of Spanish Morocco have been subdued in recent years, and now only acknowledge the rule of the conqueror under the constant menace of the machine-guns of the Spanish Foreign Legion. The spectacle of a suzerain Christian state divided and devasted by a long and bloody war, in which tribesmen recruited from the defeated legions of Abdel Krim are permitted to take terrible vengeance upon the populations of European Spain, is one to rejoice the hearts of the unregenerate Riffan hillsmen. It is, moreover, a suggestive example for the Moors in the contiguous French zone, which also has its unsubdued or but recently subdued and still restive areas.

Finally, the insurrection has led to a number of direct violations of the statute of Tangier. Spanish Government warships have fired at the rebel fortresses in Ceuta from the harbour or the territorial waters of the neutral international zone. Rebel vessels have taken refuge in Tangier harbour from pursuit by loyal warships. Rebel bands have pursued and attacked loyalists across the frontiers of the international zone. Both parties in the struggle claimed or ignored the neutrality of Tangier. The situation was rendered all the more complicated by the fact that although the Tangier Convention prohibits the use of the port and its hinterland for military purposes, the powers have previously recognised the Spanish Government's right of transit across the international zone in emergencies (such as the Riff War) in which the security of its own zone is endangered.

After some weeks of confusion and uncertainty, during which the insurgent General Franco repeatedly and menacingly demanded the expulsion of loyal Spanish warships from the harbour, the international committee of control decided to maintain absolute neutrality by requesting Spanish Government vessels to leave the territorial waters of the port, in the interests of the international colony ; and this request was complied with.

[3]

The question of the outcome of the struggle in Spain is one which interests more or less directly all Europe in general and France in particular. Although the Government in Madrid until recently contained neither Socialists nor Communists, it cannot be denied that the effective government of those regions of the country still loyal to Madrid has, since the outbreak of the civil war, been effectively exercised by proletarian committees. Socialists, Syndicalists and Anarchists have temporarily buried their ancient feuds—feuds peculiar to working-class history in Spain—in order to rally to the defence of the Republic as reaffirmed and reinvigorated by the electoral victory of the Popular Front in February, 1936. If they succeed in crushing the insurrection of the military and clerical elements in the country, they are likely to emphasise the Socialistic character of the Republic. In Catalonia the Government created by President Luis Companys in February, 1936, has already been replaced by one in which the trade unions—whether Communistic and pro-Moscow, or Anarchistic and anti-Moscow—are predominant. In Madrid a successful issue to the present struggle will almost certainly be followed by the consolidation of the present Government in which the left-wing Socialists of Señor Largo Caballero and the Syndicalists of the U.G.T. or General Workers' Federation are largely represented. Large-scale measures of socialisation ratifying and extending the emergency confiscation of landed estates, mines, factories, industrial plant, residential buildings, clubs and offices are the probable aftermath of victory.

In any case it seems likely that normal industrial life and parliamentary government in Spain will be suspended almost indefinitely. The Government of the extreme Left, if it is victorious, will be forced to exercise a virtual dictatorship for a long period to come. The danger of sporadic outbreaks in Navarre and other disaffected provinces will not end with the defeat of the present insurrection. Morocco will continue to be a source of rebellion. The peasants, although many of them have rallied to the Popular Front, for the same reasons that led the Russian peasants to hail the Bolshevik victory, in October, 1917, with its promises of " Bread and Peace," may be tempted, once their hunger for land has been satisfied by the confiscation and redistribution of the great landed properties, to turn against the Socialist or Communist workers in the towns. Faced with the same problems of counter-revolution and the threats of ivil war and foreign intervention that confronted the Bolshevik leaders in Russia in 1917 and 1918, the neo-Bolsheviks of Spain may well consider a period of proletarian dictatorship, with its concomitant restriction of democratic liberties, vital to their revolution. Similar problems face them, moreover, in the field of internal economy. They have to reorganise an army, a bureaucracy, an agricultural system, industry and finance and the creation of a strong central government based on the power—both economic and military—of the now armed and disciplined trade unions.

Whether that Government and its programme follow the precedent of Soviet Russia or not, the results of a working-class victory in Spain will be regarded with very different feelings by the Governments of Great Britain, France, Italy, Germany and Russia. Both the army and navy of a triumphant Spanish democracy will henceforth be officered and manned by Spaniards in more or less open sympathy with Soviet Russia, and with feelings of marked hostility to Italy and Germany, and in some degree to Great Britain. The prospect of a Red fleet at the gates of the Mediterranean, already noted in the preceding chapter, is not one to be viewed with equanimity by Great Britain, or even by France, warm although the sympathies of its own Popular Front may be towards their political co-religionaries in Spain.

[4]

But what of the prospect, no more remote, of a Fascist dictatorship established in the Iberian peninsula, and of Fascist naval bases at Ceuta and the Balearics ?

The aims of the insurgent generals were unequivocally set forth at the beginning of August by General Queipo de

Llano, the commander of the rebel forces in Seville. He stated that it was the intention of the leaders of the nationalist rising, if they were successful, to institute a corporative régime in Spain on the model of the régimes already existing in Italy, Germany and Portugal. The Fascist inspiration of the rebellion has been evident from the outset. The incidents of the Italian military airplanes landing in Morocco, of the German munitions unloaded at Larache, of the ostensibly courtesy visit of the officers of the pocket battleship *Deutschland* to General Franco in Ceuta, the attitudes of the German and Italian press, the comments of pro-Hitler and pro-Mussolini newspapers in Great Britain, leave no doubt as to the relations existing before and during the rising between its leaders and the Governments of Italy and Germany. Is a Fascist dictatorship in Madrid, modelled upon and in close harmony with the dictatorships in Berlin and Rome, any more attractive a prospect to the Western democracies than that of a Spanish Soviet? Does it offer any less danger to the already disturbed equilibrium of forces in the Mediterranean?

An earlier dictator in Spain, the late General Primo de Rivera, has already furnished Great Britain with a hint of the danger to British naval power in the Mediterranean inherent in an Italo-Spanish alliance. In 1926, the then master of Spain—who during the war had publicly demanded the return to Spain of Gibraltar—promised Mussolini a naval base in the Balearic Islands. At that time Great Britain and Italy were on cordial terms. Mussolini had just negotiated the cession by England and Egypt of Jubaland to Italy. English and Italian interests were not in conflict in any part of the world. There seemed no reason to apprehend, in the near or the remote future, any such dispute as that which dangerously disturbed the peace of the Mediterranean in 1935 and 1936. Mussolini did not reject the tempting offer of his Spanish disciple. But he discreetly did not attempt to exploit it. On the advent of the Spanish Republic in 1930 details of the secret correspondence between the two dictators were discovered in the archives of the Foreign Ministry in Madrid. The offer was withdrawn.

Nevertheless the precedent remains. And the prospect of its renewal by a second Fascist dictator in Spain is sufficiently disturbing to both the Governments of Great Britain and France. Great Britain has an historic interest in the Balearics. During the Mediterranean naval wars of the eighteenth century Minorca was a British naval base for eighty years. The subsequent capture of Gibraltar more than compensated Great Britain for its loss, and early in the nineteenth century the acquisition of Malta gave British sea power an adequate fuelling and repair station in the Mediterranean. But with the rapid growth of air power, and the discovery of the vulnerability of Malta, the once-British island of Minorca recovers its importance to the security of our imperial communication. If the power which occupies it is no longer closely bound to Great Britain, by political and commercial ties, Minorca, like the Spanish town and fortress of Ceuta across the Straits of Gibraltar, becomes a source of potential menace to British interests.

[5]

The danger to France of a Spanish dictatorship in open or secret sympathy with Italy or Germany is considerably greater. Spain is France's immediate neighbour, both in Europe and in Africa. Since the creation of the Third Republic in 1871 it has been a cardinal principle of French foreign policy to maintain terms of close friendship with Spain, irrespective of the form of its government, republican or monarchical. Hitherto Spain has replied to this policy of constant amity by entering into no alliance with any other Power, and by remaining a benevolent neutral in the war of 1914–1918, notwithstanding the dynastic and religious bonds between the Spanish and the Austrian Habsburgs, and the strong German sympathies of the higher officers of the Army.

The possibility of a Fascist Spain, united by political sympathy and tactical considerations to the Third Reich of Hitler and the Imperial Italy of Mussolini, bound doubly to Rome politically and spiritually, threatens France on the solitary land frontier on which hitherto she has been freed from military dangers, and has been enabled to dispense with garrisons. Spain is, moreover, in the direct line of communications between France and Morocco. The shortest route between Paris and Rabat, the capital of French Morocco, is *via* Madrid, Algeciras, Tangier and Larache. The direct road to French Morocco crosses both Spain and the Spanish zone. The French air services to Casablanca fly along the Mediterranean coast of Spain, with halts at Barcelona and Alicante. The security of French communications with North Africa, the source of French manpower in the next European war, depends to a great extent upon the neutrality or the complaisance of Spain.

There is a further threat to French security in the possibility, already referred to, of a third Power other than Great Britain being granted naval facilities in one of the Balearic Islands. These islands lie directly in the path of steamers between the ports of Southern France and Africa. Minorca, in particular, is exactly at mid-point of the steamer route between Marseilles and Algiers. Until the civil war broke out in Spain, and extended to the Balearics, one of the smaller harbours of Minorca was utilised as a halt for the daily seaplane service conducted by the Air France company between Marseilles and Algiers. A hostile power with submarines, destroyers and bombing planes based on the Balearics could effectively interrupt France's communications with both Algeria and Morocco, and could, granted possession of a naval force equal to that possessed by France in the Mediterranean, partially if not completely blockade the southern French coast.

In recent years the sea and air defences of Majorca, the largest of the Balearic Islands, have been considerably improved. The insurgent forces on the island put up a stubborn resistance to the attacks of Government ships and airplanes in August. The bombardment of Majorca and its defence are of interest in view of the British Government's negotiations with Spain during the Italo-Abyssinian war. At that time Spain was among the most active of the partisans of the League Covenant, and in fulfilment of her obligations under the Covenant might have been exposed, like Great Britain and France, to naval or aerial reprisals by Italy. In the winter of 1935–1936, according to reports current in Gibraltar and various cities along the Spanish coast, British naval officers made a careful examination of the harbours, landing grounds and strategic possibilities of the Mediterranean seaboard of Spain and the Balearic Islands, and it was confidently stated in Madrid that the Spanish Government had granted to Great Britain, for use in a general emergency, the naval base in the Balearics that had been offered to Mussolini under the Monarchy and withdrawn under the Republic.

CHAPTER IV

BRITISH SEA POWER AND SECURITY

[1]

THE British Commonwealth of Nations is at once the most powerful and the most vulnerable of the empires known to history. A quarter of the land surface of the globe acknowledges its sovereignty. Five hundred millions of people give allegiance to its hereditary crown, enjoy the blessings or submit to the rough justice of its law, and pursue their peaceful occupations in the security afforded by the Pax Britannica. But in the very immensity of this empire lies its inherent weakness. Unlike the Roman Empire, it is not, in majority, composed of members of the white race. Less than one-eighth of its vast population is of Anglo-Saxon stock. Its unity is no longer economic, and is in lessening degrees political. It is based not upon geographic or historic or racial ties, but upon collective loyalty to an abstraction : the idea of liberty, law and democratic government symbolised in the British Crown, and incarnate in the person of the British King.

The future of this vast confederation of peoples depends upon many factors : the security of 22,500 miles of land frontiers (5000 miles in India, 3500 miles in Africa, 3000 miles in Canada) ; the freedom of 80,000 miles of ocean routes ; the strengthening of the visible as well as of the invisible links between the mother-country and the dominions ; the permanence of the paradox of the democratic Crown, which reigns but does not govern ; and finally the realisation of self-government by India, and of a measure of autonomy by other and less politically advanced units within the empire. But the real factor which conditions the security and the continuity of the British imperial system is the security of Britain herself. For of all the links in the world-long chain of free dominions, self-governing colonies, dependencies and native States, Great Britain is the weakest. The Roman Empire did not long survive the fall of Rome.

Herself a world state, Great Britain finds herself daily more and more involved in the quarrels of her European neighbours. The dispute between two exclusively European nations which provoked the World War was but the prototype of half a dozen controversies which have sprung into dangerous activity since the peace, and which at any moment may bring the ponderous machine of the British Empire, however reluctantly, to fresh intervention in a primarily and preponderantly European quarrel. Politically, as well as socially and culturally, Britain has remained obstinately an integral part of the Old World. She is more interested in the political and economic régime of her continental neighbours than in that of any other country in the world. Bolshevism in Russia, which is largely Asiatic, concerns her more directly than would Bolshevism, say, in the United States of America. She is more prone to accept innovations in science, hygiene, industry, warfare, politics, philosophy, medicine, art or literature from France and Germany than from the United States, or even from her own dominions. Culturally, industrially and politically, she has hitherto acquired nothing from the overseas territories of her empire. The early triumphs of Labour in Australia and of Woman Suffrage in New Zealand left her indifferent. The Social Credit experiment of Mr. Aberhart in the province of Alberta seems likely to share the same fate.

But if she remains European in political theory, in outlook, in nationalist prejudices, in her social and cultural preoccupations, there is one notable advantage of her continental neighbours which Britain does not possess. France, Germany, Russia, Italy, Spain, and the Balkan and Scandinavian countries are largely agricultural states. In spite of their great industrial progress in modern times, they are still able to rely upon their own soil for the greater part of their food supplies. During the Great War Germany suffered indeed from a shortage of fats. Butter and margarine were heavily rationed, and the civilian population suffered heavily, but not much more heavily than in England, notwithstanding the fact that the British Navy held the seas. In France and Italy there was little shortage of foodstuffs. In France butter and meat were plentiful. The bread alone was of poor quality, owing partly to the invasion of the northern departments, but principally to the shortage of farm labour in the wheat-growing provinces. But not one of the European countries was faced with the imminent danger which menaced Great Britain in 1917. In that year, when the German submarine campaign reached its peak, the British people and their rulers were threatened with actual starvation. Food supplies sufficient for six weeks of the most rigorous rationing stood between them and a military collapse through hunger. The intervention of America at that moment would not have staved off the peril. The danger was conjured by the resourcefulness and the courage of the British Navy and of the British Navy alone. It remains to us as possibly the greatest lesson to be learned from the World War.

[2]

Great Britain is obliged by the deficiencies of her native agriculture to import 60 per cent of the food necessary to maintain life in her population of 45 millions. She imports 56 per cent of her consumption of meat, 85 per cent of her consumption of flour, 80 per cent of her sugar, 85 per cent of her milk, butter and cheese. Her total food imports reach the impressive figure of 20 million tons a year.

The requirements of British industry in raw materials are hardly less exorbitant. One-half of the pig iron used in the blast-furnaces and foundries of the industrial North is imported. All the non-ferrous metals—copper, zinc, lead, cobalt—come from other countries. Britain takes annually 200,000 tons of manganese from India, 25,000 tons of chromium from Rhodesia, 2000 tons of nickel from Canada and Norway, 300,000 tons of iron alloys from Scandinavia, 35,000 tons of tin from the Dutch East Indies, not to mention the cotton from India and Egypt, the rubber from Malaya and the petroleum imported from Mexico, from the United States, from the Dutch East Indies, from Venezuela, from Irak and Persia, and from the U.S.S.R. The British consumption of petroleum and petroleum spirit has increased ten-fold since 1913. It now exceeds 10,000,000 tons a year, and of this total not more than 400,000 tons at present can be provided by the distillation of coal products. In war-time the annual requirements of the Navy, of the Army, the Government and of industry are expected to reach 20 million tons.

The security of British food supplies, in peace and war, depends upon two factors : (1) the supremacy of the British Navy, and (2) the adequacy of the British merchant marine. At the beginning of the present century Great Britain owned just over 50 per cent of the world's merchant tonnage. In 1914 the proportion had decreased to 41·6 per cent. During the past ten years, according to Lloyd's Register Book for 1936-7, British shipping has shrunk by 2,122,000 tons. To-day, partly as the result of war-time losses, partly as a result of the considerable proportion of the world's carrying trade lost to other countries, our percentage of world tonnage is only 26·8. Although Britain is more than ever dependent on imported foodstuffs and raw materials, she has roughly 1,750,000 tons less shipping available for the purpose than in 1914.

The present low figure, moreover, includes the tonnage of a number of large passenger liners which at the outbreak of war would be armed as light cruisers and thus diverted from the transport of food supplies. At present the real resources of Britain in food-carrying tonnage probably amount to not more than one-fourth of her pre-war mercantile fleet. In addition to which it must be recalled that before the war British ships were coal-driven, and could be bunkered with British coal at home ports, whereas to-day the majority of them are oil-burning and to this extent themselves contribute to the growing burden of British dependency on foreign imports.

Even the considerable pre-war mercantile fleet proved insufficient for the war needs of Great Britain. She was forced to depend on the goodwill, the courage or the commercial acumen of neutral nations, and Spanish, Greek, Scandinavian and American vessels risked the increasing perils of the Atlantic or the North Sea for a by no means incommensurate reward.

The next European war, however, might place insurmountable obstacles in the path of assistance from friendly neutrals. If the submarine menace proved not to be a sufficient deterrent to neutral shipowners, shipmasters and crews, the enormous advances in military aviation and in naval science are more than likely to bridge the margin of sporting risk. The fear of air reprisals from belligerent states may well drive neutral governments to impose a war-time ban on the trading of their nationals. And even if such legal restrictions were inoperative, the modern development of light and fast motor-torpedo boats, capable of speeds approaching sixty miles an hour, has created a new and formidable danger to merchant fleets and their naval escorts.

[3]

The vulnerability of Great Britain has thus very considerably increased since the end of the World War. Her dependency on foreign supplies of food, raw materials and fuel has been doubled. Her effective merchant fleet (if fast passenger liners and fishing trawlers are excluded) has been reduced by nearly three-quarters. The war-time assistance to be expected from neutrals must be heavily discounted. The passage through Congress of the American Neutrality Act has created a new complication in the interpretation of the freedom of the seas. And the strength of the British Navy, the keystone of the imperial arch, has been reduced to such meagre proportions that the first challenge to be encountered by British prestige since 1914 finds little real opposition in England to the Government's resolution to restore the formidable breaches in the naval armament of the empire.

Before the war the British fleet comprised 69 battleships, 105 cruisers, 322 destroyers, and 76 submarines, besides a host of small craft. It was intended to equal in strength and fighting efficiency the combined forces of any two other fleets in the world. At the beginning of 1936 the greatly reduced strength of the fleet was officially given as follows :

 12 battleships
 3 battle-cruisers
 54 cruisers (of which 3 were to be sold)
 1 cruiser minelayer
 8 aircraft-carriers
 169 destroyers (of which 7 were to be sold)
 51 submarines

in addition to smaller craft, minesweepers, sloops, monitors, etc., making a total for the fleet of 388 vessels.

Following are particulars of the 15 ships of the line :

Name.	Date laid down.	Date of completion.	Displacement in tons.	H.P.	Speed in knots.	Armament.	Torpedo tubes.
Nelson type:			BATTLESHIPS				
Nelson .	1922	1927	33,500	45,000	23·0	9 16-in., 12 6-in., 6 4·7-in. AA (Nelson 28 smaller guns)	2
Rodney .	,,	,,	33,900	,,	,,		
Royal Sovereign type:							
Royal Sovereign	1914	1916	29,150	40,000	23·0	8 15-in., 12 6-in., 4 4-in. AA and smaller guns	2
Royal Oak .	,,	,,	,,	,,	,,		
Revenge .	1913	,,	,,	,,	,,		
Resolution .	,,	,,	,,	,,	,,		
Ramillies .	,,	,,	,,	,,	,,		
Queen Elizabeth type:							
Malaya .	1913	1916	31,100	75,000	25·0	8 15-in., 12 6-in., 4 4-in. AA and smaller guns	2
Valiant .	,,	,,	,,	,,	,,		
Barham .	,,	1915	,,	,,	,,		
Queen Elizabeth	,,	1912	,,	,,	,,		
Warspite .	,,	,,	,,	,,	,,		
			BATTLE-CRUISERS				
Hood type:							
Hood .	1916	1920	42,100	144,000	31·0	8 15-in., 12 5·5-in., 4 4-in. AA, 23 smaller guns	6
Renown type:							
Renown .	1915	1916	32,000	112,000	31·5	6 15-in., 15 4-in., 4 4-in. AA	2
Repulse .	,,	,,	,,	,,	,,		

Of the battleships enumerated above, three—the *Barham*, the *Queen Elizabeth* and the *Warspite*—are of pre-war design and have already exceeded the age-limit of twenty years laid down for battleships and battle-cruisers in the Washington Treaty. Moreover, of the total of fifteen capital ships, only eight were in full commission in April, 1936 (according to the May issue of the Navy List), when the situation in the Eastern Mediterranean was still full of tension. These eight ships were the battleships *Nelson* and *Rodney* and the battle-cruiser *Hood*, all serving with the Home Fleet; the battleships *Barham*, *Queen Elizabeth* and *Valiant*, and the battle-cruiser *Renown*, serving with the Mediterranean Fleet; and the battle-cruiser *Repulse*, then on its way to join the fleet in Mediterranean waters. Of the seven other capital ships in the British Navy, three— the battleships *Royal Oak*, *Warspite* and *Malaya*—were undergoing extensive refitting and would not be put into commission again until they had been specially protected with guns and armour against aircraft attack; and the remaining four vessels had been virtually laid up for lack of officers and crews, a large part of the available personnel having been detached to man mine-sweepers and destroyers against any emergency in the Mediterranean.

Of the total fleet strength at the beginning of 1936 only 2 battle-cruisers, 36 cruisers and about 65 destroyers and 40 submarines were of modern design. To a navy thus reduced in fighting efficiency was relegated the task of patrolling 80,000 miles of imperial communications, of guarding the China and the Red Seas, the North Sea and the Mediterranean, of protecting two thousand British merchant ships in all waters, and of safeguarding the daily delivery to British home ports of 50,000 tons of food supplies, of 110,000 tons of merchandise, and of 30,000 tons of oil.

[4]

Never before in modern history had the Battle Fleet dwindled to such meagre proportions. From a two-power it had become a one-power navy. Both in ships and in men the fleet was unprepared for an emergency. The Abyssinian crisis of 1935–1936, if it had resulted in war between England and Italy, might well have proved a minor if not a major disaster for British naval prestige.

Fortunately, however, the warning was heard and heeded. No British Naval Estimates since the Napoleonic Wars have encountered less determined opposition than those which were presented to Parliament in February, and subsequently increased by two further allocations for naval construction. The escalator clause of the Washington Treaty was invoked by the British Government to save about 40,000 tons of destroyers which were due to be scrapped before the end of the year. And energetic measures were taken to remedy the grave deficiencies in the Fleet. The complete building programme proposed for 1936 and immediately put into operation comprised fifty-four vessels and numerous small craft. It included :

2 capital ships.
7 cruisers—2 of the Southampton class and 5 smaller ones of 5000 tons each.
2 aircraft-carriers.
18 destroyers of the Tribal class of about 1500 tons each.
8 submarines.
6 sloops—3 minesweepers, 2 convoy escorts and 1 coastal sloop.
6 motor torpedo-boats, 1 river gunboat, 2 small surveying vessels, 2 special service vessels and various small craft.

The two new battleships will be between 33,000 and 34,000 tons or the same size as the *Nelson* class. They will carry a large number of 14-inch guns, a battery of 6-inch guns and between twelve and sixteen anti-aircraft guns. They will be heavily armoured against submarines and aircraft. Each vessel is expected to cost between £6,000,000 and £7,000,000.

The total estimated cost of the new naval construction for 1936 was £11,359,000, which brought the total expenditure on the Navy during the current financial year to £81,289,000—the highest figure since 1920. The normal and supplementary estimates provided for the re-equipment of the Fleet Air Arm with new types of aircraft and for the equipment of the existing ships in the Battle Fleet with additional anti-aircraft defences. Provisions were also made for the recruiting of 2063 men for the fleet, an addition which will bring the total strength of the Navy in officers and men to 101,154 by March, 1937. Finally the Admiralty has decided to create a new naval training establishment at Rosyth, to extend the dry-dock facilities for large ships at Plymouth and Gibraltar, to strengthen the anti-aircraft defences of Malta, to enlarge the docking accommodation at the naval base of Singapore, and to build new and adequate storage depôts for naval munitions and oil fuel.

Thus the crisis of 1936 initiated a new era of activity for the British naval arm. The failure of the Disarmament Conference, the rise of Hitler, the renaissance of Germany and Russia as great military powers, the formidable increase in the speed and range of military aircraft, had for some years encouraged professional as well as amateur strategists to under-estimate naval power in favour of the new and largely untried arm of the air. The tension in Anglo-Italian relations in the spring of 1936, and the re-emergence of the Mediterranean in its historic rôle of strategic centre and battlefield of empires, dramatically restored the balance in favour of the sea. Whatever part may be played by aircraft in the next European war, the issue of the conflict, between the rival Mediterranean powers at least, lies with the power whose warships hold the waters which divide Europe, Africa and Asia.

CHAPTER V

THE MEDITERRANEAN IN THE NEXT WAR

[1]

THE most important consequence of the Italian conquest of Abyssinia, so far as the British Empire is concerned, is the decision permanently to reinforce the British naval forces in the Mediterranean. The signature of the naval pact with Germany in 1935 permitted Great Britain later in the same year to withdraw a number of important units from the Home Fleet and to concentrate them in the Eastern Mediterranean. With the easing of the Anglo-Italian tension which followed the collapse of Abyssinian resistance, the majority of those reinforcements were withdrawn. The fleet in the Mediterranean, nevertheless, was left stronger than it had been for several years past, and in the near future the naval forces stationed at Malta and at Alexandria—destined to become an important British naval base in any Mediterranean war —will be considerably augmented. In the autumn of 1936 the fleet under the command of Admiral Sir Dudley Pound comprises over 100 vessels, and includes :

3 refitted battleships of the pre-war *Queen Elizabeth* class (31,100 tons each).
2 battle-cruisers : the *Hood* (42,100 tons) and the *Repulse* (32,000 tons).
4 8-inch heavy cruisers.
5 6-inch light cruisers.
2 anti-aircraft cruisers with new and powerful AA batteries.
1 aircraft-carrier, the *Glorious*, with over 50 seaplanes.
38 destroyers, including 8 of the powerful new " G " class.
8 submarines, all modern and 3 of them cruising at 22 knots.

10 anti-submarine trawlers.

19 minesweepers.

6 sloops and various other craft.

In addition to which it is expected that a large proportion of the new vessels building or authorised (details of which have been given in the preceding chapter) will be allotted to the Mediterranean station.

Such considerable reinforcements, together with the British Government's stated intention to strengthen the anti-aircraft defences of Malta, and the discussions proceeding in naval circles regarding the creation of a naval base at Cyprus, make it clear that Great Britain has no thought of abandoning her traditional strategy in the Mediterranean. Her existing command of the approaches to the Middle Sea, by virtue of her possession of Gibraltar and Aden, is to be supplemented by the strengthening of strategic British possessions or dependencies within the confines of the sea.

In the event of a Mediterranean war in which, as was the case during the Italo-Abyssinian dispute, both Britain and Spain found themselves ranged against an aggressor state condemned by the League of Nations, it is probable that the Balearic Islands and possibly Ceuta would also become important bases for British naval and aerial activities. In Paris, Rome and Madrid during the winter of 1935-1936 it was currently and confidently reported that the British Government, with the consent of the Spanish authorities, had already explored the strategic possibilities of the islands of Majorca and Minorca. The importance of Ceuta is that, like Tangier, it commands the Straits of Gibraltar and Bab el Mandeb. Tangier is in theory neutral and international, and could not, under international law, be utilised by one state member of the international commission which governs it against another member. But Ceuta, which is nominally under the suzerainty of the Sultan of Morocco and actually under the administration of the Spanish Government, could be legitimately placed by Spain, as a member of the League, at the disposal of states empowered by the League Council to conduct military operations against an aggressor.

[2]

The grounds of naval strategy in the Mediterranean have recently been profoundly altered by two events of historic importance. The first of them was the Abyssinian crisis, which drew attention to the vulnerability of Malta, and the novel fact that Italy, by its aerial domination of the passage between Europe and Africa at which the Mediterranean narrows to a width of less than a hundred miles, was in a position to sever the great trade routes between Great Britain and the East. The second event was the agreement reached at the Montreux Conference in July to sanction the remilitarisation of the Dardanelles, and to permit free ingress and egress for the Russian warships in the Black Sea.

The provisions of the revised Statute of the Dardanelles have been analysed in an earlier chapter, but their effect on the future history of the Mediterranean cannot yet be foreseen. It is not impossible that at the first threat of war in these waters the Montreux agreement will become a dead letter. The present alliance between Turkey and the U.S.S.R. is not based upon any profound interests or principles in common. The neutrality of Turkey in any future dispute, whether it directly concerns the League or not, cannot be predicted with any certainty. The freedom of movement of ships of war or commerce between the Black Sea and the Ægean will be decided largely by the relations which exist at the outbreak of war between Russia, Turkey and the naval power which dominates the Eastern Mediterranean. It happens that at no period in past history, save during the Napoleonic Wars, when the naval mastery of the Mediterranean was still in dispute, have the relations between those three powers been simultaneously friendly. There is thus no precedent for united action between the three states which severally and collectively determine the freedom of navigation in those waters.

[3]

The newly discovered vulnerability of Malta as a naval base may have more easily predictable influences on Mediterranean naval policy. The British Government has made it clear that it has no more intention of abandoning Malta than it has of withdrawing from Gibraltar. Mr. Ormsby-Gore, the Secretary for the Colonies, stated in a speech in June, 1936, that "Malta is and will remain a British possession, and an all-important naval fortress, vital to our imperial interests in the Mediterranean."

The disclosure of official plans to increase the island's security from air attack, as it has already been secured against attack by submarines, followed closely upon this ministerial statement. Nevertheless the utility of Malta as a naval depôt, and a base for the repair and refitment of warships, has been considerably diminished by the enormous increase in Italy's air forces. An island within eighty miles of Italian bombing bases in Sicily cannot be regarded as a safe refuge for the concentration of the British Fleet in the Mediterranean. And however its air defences may be defended, the civilian labourers employed in its dry docks and ship-repairing yards cannot be expected to maintain efficiency under the constant menace of air attack, whether successful or not.

It seems likely, therefore, that Malta in war-time may be superseded as a naval base by the prospective base at Alexandria, which may be fortified by the British and Egyptian Governments if the Anglo-Egyptian Treaty is ratified. Alexandria has the supreme merit of being established on friendly territory, of being at a distance of 400 miles from the nearest Italian aircraft and submarine bases in the Dodecanese, and of commanding the northern approaches to Egypt and the Suez Canal. The British island of Cyprus, the virtues of which have equally been considered, has the further advantage of being within 150 miles of the coast of Palestine and the terminal of the Irak oil pipe-line at Haifa, and also of being within 230 miles of Port Said. On the other hand it is within easy bombing range of the Italian squadrons on Rhodes, and its only two harbours, Limassol and Famagusta, would require very extensive and costly operations to prepare them to receive large ships of war.

[4]

The creation of naval bases at Cyprus or Alexandria, or both, does not of itself solve the problem created for Great Britain by recent events in the Mediterranean. Malta has hitherto proved a valuable half-way house on the 1900 miles of sea route between Gibraltar and Port Said. If its dangerous proximity to a potential aggressor in Europe is to weaken it permanently as a great naval base, can the great British trade routes of the Mediterranean continue to be adequately protected by naval forces operating in time of war from places of security at the eastern and western entrances to the Middle Sea, or forced by air or submarine perils to restrict their operations to those waters? In other words, can Britain assume that her naval power will exercise unchallenged supremacy over all the Mediterranean, or would she in certain circumstances, as for instance a war with Russia or Italy, or both, be obliged to withdraw to the western half of the sea, abandoning Palestine, Egypt and Cyprus until a turn in the tide of war enabled the British Fleet to provide for their security?

There are signs that such an alternative has been considered by British naval strategists during the past year. It has even appeared that the contingency of an ultimate withdrawal from the Mediterranean proper, and the diversion of British maritime commerce to the Cape route, has not been excluded from recent Admiralty discussions. A brilliant and well-informed British naval writer, Mr. Hector Bywater, has provoked much agitated controversy in naval and commercial quarters by an article in which he set forth the advantages of such a policy to Great Britain in the event of a war which rendered Malta untenable as a naval and air base, and made the security of our traffic through the vital passage between Sicily and Africa precarious if not out of the question.

Mr. Bywater pointed out that during the Great War the losses suffered by British merchant shipping in that sea, through which is transported one-fifth of the total of British imports, were exceptionally severe, and that the enemy submarine menace in the Mediterranean was never really overcome. He argued that the re-routeing of

British commerce *via* the Cape would only affect the 8·7 per cent of our imports which come from ports east of Suez—the rest of the Mediterranean-bound imports being chiefly cotton from Egypt and copper and other minerals from Spain—and that with adequate shipping resources the longer distance to be covered would not seriously affect our food-supplies. Moreover the withdrawal of naval forces from the protection of threatened shipping routes within bombing range of heavily-armed powers would set free a great number of ships for escort duty in the less dangerous waters of the Atlantic and the Indian Ocean.

The Mediterranean, in brief, would become a closed lake in war-time, with its eastern and western entrances closely guarded by Great Britain, and its mastery left to be disputed between the exclusively Mediterranean Powers. The suggestion is not new in the history of British imperial strategy. It has been put forward from time to time, sometimes in conjunction with the proposal to surrender Gibraltar, sometimes independently of that oft-repeated and stubbornly rejected proposal.

The real objections to the evacuation of the whole or part of the Mediterranean are not economic but political. It would leave Malta, Egypt and Cyprus at the mercy of an enemy power. It would expose the territory of our French allies in Northern Africa—the coveted possessions of Tunisia and Algeria—to the fulfilment of Italian ambitions. Worse still, it would leave uncovered the Middle East, the coast of Syria and Palestine, the terminal of the Irak pipeline at Haifa, and the air routes to India. It would imply the renunciation of half a century of British struggle in Egypt, and the temporary surrender of the Suez Canal. It would leave India at the mercy of an aggressor from the east, the north and the west, for both aerial communications between England and India and rapid sea communications depend upon British command of the Eastern Mediterranean.

The withdrawal from the Mediterranean is at best an expedient, and a dangerous expedient. It is a policy that could only be adopted at the eleventh hour, in an emergency in which Great Britain was fighting not for her empire but for her own national existence, an emergency in which the units of the empire had perforce to be abandoned to their own resources, or to a favourable outcome of the struggle, and every available war-plane, man and ship must be thrown into the European battle zone, in a conflict of life or death.

[5]

It seems probable that the policy of total evacuation, if it was ever seriously proposed to the British War Staffs, has already been rejected. Nevertheless its concomitant—the diversion of east and west-bound shipping from the Mediterranean to the Cape route—appears to have been favourably considered. Since 1934 the Committee of Imperial Defence has discussed the development of a second route to India by way of the Cape. During the past two years considerable stores of oil fuel for the Navy have been accumulated at Sierra Leone, and that West African colony, nearly midway between Gibraltar and Cape Town, seems destined to play an important rôle in the new imperial strategy of Great Britain. The port of Dakar, 400 miles to the north of Sierra Leone, and the capital of French Senegal, has similarly become a strong strategic centre of French air and naval communications in the South Atlantic. It is the African point of departure of the very successful weekly air service between France and South America, and the trade outlet of the vast French possessions in Western and Central Africa.

The key to the Cape route to India would be held, however, not on the west coast of Africa, but at the southern end of the continent. At the confluence of the Indian and Atlantic oceans, and 23 miles from Cape Town, is Simonstown, the headquarters of the African Squadron. Simonstown lies at too great a distance from the great European air powers to be threatened by long-range bombing. It is conveniently placed on the routes to the Pacific, and without very extensive modifications its harbour could accommodate a much greater concentration of naval force than that now comprised in the African Squadron. The Government of the Union of South Africa, which took an exceptionally vigorous attitude towards the Italian aggression against Abyssinia, which it doubly condemned not only as a violation of the League Covenant, but also as a violation of the integrity of an African State, has urged the Imperial

Government to increase its naval forces at Simonstown. The visit to London during July, 1936, of Mr. Oswald Pirow, the South African Minister of Defence, was made largely to press this policy upon Great Britain, in the interests of imperial security.

The proposal to divert all or part of the present Mediterranean traffic *via* the Cape has much in its favour. Without implying the weakening of British naval supremacy in the Mediterranean, or any surrender of the Suez Canal, it frees a considerable part of the fleet for convoy duty elsewhere, in waters rendered less perilous by mines, submarines or air attack. It leaves the Mediterranean force in greater strength to provide for the defence of certain strategic or political interests. And it enables it to pursue more offensive tactics in that sea.

[6]

There is a further argument for the adoption of a second sea-route to India, and for the strengthening of the British forces both in the Mediterranean and in the South Atlantic. The position of Great Britain in the Far East has notably changed since the last war. Then Japan was an ally. The Suez Canal route was not seriously challenged by an enemy power. The British Navy held both entrances to the Canal. And friendly shipping held its course unmolested by the enemy raiders, after the first six months of the war, between Australia, India, China and Suez.

Since 1918, however, the alliance between Great Britain and Japan has been denounced. Japan has repudiated, sooner or later, every agreement for the limitation of naval armaments to which she has affixed her signature. A new race in the building of heavy and light warships is now threatened. The dangerous tension between Russia and Japan in the Far East may at any moment end in war, and once again, as in the Russo-Japanese War of 1905–6, a Russian fleet will sail east.

In 1905 the Russian ships passed through the Suez Canal without challenge. In 1940 a similar attempt might be violently resisted by the Japanese, who, during the recent Montreux Conference on the re-militarisation of the Straits, bitterly opposed Russia's freedom of egress for her warships in the Black Sea. The security of the Canal is far from assured. If free passage for ships of war in war-time is guaranteed by the International Convention, there is nothing to prevent enemy ships from denying them access to the Canal.

Moreover the 100 miles' length of the Canal is easily attacked from the air. It can be completely and almost permanently obstructed in peace-time by the simple expedient of sinking a ship laden with cement at any point along its narrow course. The first act of an Oriental naval power secretly intent on war might well be, as a prelude to the declaration of hostilities with the West, to delay by such measures the arrival of any European reinforcements in an Eastern theatre of war.

Thus any imperial system of communications which is based on the invulnerability and perpetual freedom of the Suez Canal exposes its defenders to the risk of disillusionment and disaster. The only policy by which a great empire can adapt its defences in a world of rapid progress in armaments, aggressive nationalisms, unstable alliances, growing racial feuds and ceaseless economic rivalry is one of suppleness, imagination and constant vigilance. Recent history has forced Great Britain to overhaul a strategic system unvarying during the sixty-eight years since the Suez Canal was opened. The Mediterranean, which during that period has been an open sea, threatens to revert to its antique position as a closed lake, and once more to divide the Western world from the Eastern.

[7]

During the pre-war phase of modern naval rivalry the prospective battle area was not the Mediterranean but the North Sea. Neither France nor Italy, the two strongest powers in the Latin world, pretended either to naval rivalry with Great Britain or to equality with each other. In the years which followed the rise of Mussolini to absolute power in Italy the most dangerous threats to European peace seemed to spring from Franco-German hostility on the one hand and from Franco-Italian suspicion on the other. The one was allayed—as it seemed permanently—by the Rhineland Pact signed at Locarno. The other, which proved a stubborn obstacle in the path to agreement on naval limitation, and which created a diplomatic deadlock between the two countries only ended by the Mussolini-Laval agreement in January, 1935, was the original *raison d'être* of the often-discussed proposals for a Mediterranean Locarno.

As originally conceived in 1926, when the late Aristide Briand was Foreign Minister of France, and the late Philippe Berthelot was the permanent director of French foreign policy, the projected Mediterranean Pact was intended to embrace in a system of mutual guarantees and pledges of non-aggression the principal littoral states concerned : Spain, France, Italy, Jugoslavia, Greece, Turkey, and Roumania. The question of the inclusion of the U.S.S.R., which was not at that time a member of the League of Nations, was left in suspense, although France and Turkey were strongly in favour of admitting her. The security of the Mediterranean against the aggression of any power, whether a signatory of the Pact or not, was to be guaranteed by Great Britain, as the strongest naval power in these waters.

The project was never, however, officially discussed. It was allowed to lapse during the last years of Briand at the Quai d'Orsay. In 1930, on the eve of the London Naval Conference, when Briand had been succeeded by M. André Tardieu, the French Government revived the proposal in a memorandum submitted to the Conference and referred to elsewhere in this work. But before the memorandum could be discussed the collapse of the London negotiations, and the truculent departure of Italy from the Conference, effectively banged the door on any further hopes of Franco-Italian naval agreement.

During the five years which followed, the rise of Hitler and the secret and finally open re-armament of Germany removed the danger zone of European diplomacy from the shores of the Latin to those of the Northern Sea. At the beginning of 1935, when the sixteen years of controversy between France and Italy seemed to have been buried if not obliterated by the Pact of Rome, fresh hopes were entertained of a naval Pact between the Mediterranean powers, based on the fundamental equality in that sea of the French and Italian fleets. In the summer of 1935, however, that hope was discovered to be illusory. A new storm was rising over the Mediterranean, and this time Italy was ranged not only against France but against all the other Mediterranean powers. The danger of a sudden Italian attack on the fleets of the sanctionist states was countered a few months later by the negotiation of a mutual defence pact between Great Britain, France, Greece, Jugoslavia and Turkey—the states whose littoral or whose interests were most directly menaced in the event of war. After the Italian conquest of the Abyssinian capital and Mussolini's proclamation of the Italian Empire, France and later Greece and Turkey withdrew from the Pact, but for some weeks longer Great Britain continued her unilateral engagement to protect the Mediterranean states against Italian aggression until finally, at the end of July, the Foreign Secretary announced the withdrawal of Great Britain's pledges of assistance. Once the Abyssinian affair has been liquidated, the question of a comprehensive naval pact for the Mediterranean may again be approached without prejudice, and may prove the point of departure for a rehabilitation of the sadly-weakened League of Nations.

CHAPTER VI

THE CRADLE OF CIVILISATIONS—AND THEIR TOMB

[1]

WITH the rise of a second Roman Empire a phase of Mediterranean history which has lasted for nearly a century and a half—from Nelson's victory over the French at the Battle of the Nile to the Italian conquest of Abyssinia—comes to an end. A new era—and perhaps its most adventurous—opens in the history of the Latin world. The arming of the powers on the shores of the Pacific, which in the early post-war years seemed to prefigure the non-European character of the next great naval war, is now being repeated in the nearer and narrower waters of the sea which washes the coasts of Europe, Africa and Asia Minor. The Mediterranean basin, in which the Old World civilisation has grown to maturity, in which earlier civilisations have risen and flowered and fallen to decay from the earliest days of recorded time, seems likely to witness another great conflict of empires. While America, Russia and Japan struggle for power in distant Asia, the first blows have already been struck in the struggle of the European powers for dominance in nearer and less exploited Africa.

Of all the partially explored and partly exploited continents, Africa is the least calculable in its influence on the history of the white races. Its northern fringe has played a notable rôle in European politics since the rise of the earliest dynasties in Egypt and the empire of Carthage. But the future of its great interior, the dark forests and great rivers of Central Africa now being opened up for exploitation by French airmen, soldiers, explorers and scientists, is still unpredictable. The black races of Africa have already had their baptism of blood under the artillery fire, aerial bombardment and gas attacks of modern European warfare. During the Great War they were brought into Europe to bridge the gaps blown into exhausted white armies. During the Italo-Abyssinian conflict they realised the power and deadliness of the white man's weapons, perfected in eighteen years of European peace.

The lesson is not likely to have been lost. The Arab renaissance already in active progress in Syria, Palestine, Irak and Saudi Arabia, and now spreading to the French territories in Northern Africa, may be followed before a generation is out by a negro renaissance in Central Africa. The naval and aerial activity of the French at Dakar, the steady penetration of the principles of European commerce, power-politics and warfare into the French Sudan, Nigeria, the Congo and Senegal, the development of the alternative Cape route to India, and the recurring race conflicts in South Africa, all mark the significant stages in the emergence of Africa, the hitherto and still largely Unknown Continent, into the foreground of world politics.

Twice in two thousand years has Africa invaded Europe. Each time she advanced victoriously—Hannnibal with his elephants, the Moorish conqueror Tarek el Zaid with his Arab horses—bringing with her the military science, the culture and the splendour of civilisations already old when Central and Northern Europe were peopled with woad-painted barbarians. And each time the Mediterranean was the path of invasion. The whole history of the Mediterranean has been one of conflict, pillage, piracy and conquest from the days of Homer's heroes and their " wine-dark sea," the organised piracy of the Crusades, the long conflict betweeen Venice and Constantinople, the insolence of the corsairs under Barbarossa, the expeditions of Charles V and Don John of Austria against Algiers and Tunis, the lament of the galley-slave Cervantes, the naval wars of Louis XIV, Cromwell and Nelson, down to the Greek adventure of Byron, the Carlist conspiracies, the submarine-raiding, the gun-running in the Riff War, and the war of conquest against Ethiopia. There are no signs that the long and stormy chapter is yet at an end.

[2]

Since the sixteenth century the course of the sea-raiders
has been altered. The direction of the armies of conquest
is no longer from south to north, but from north to south.
During the remaining years of the present century, doubtless, that course will remain constant. A flourishing white
civilisation will establish itself upon the sunny and fertile
fringe of Northern Africa, upon the vestiges of ruined
civilisations, part African, part Asiatic, thousands of years
older. But what of the twenty-first century of the Christian
era, and of the twenty-second? Will Africa remain
quiescent, submerged, content to remain the recruiting-
ground for cheap labour and cheap cannon-fodder, the
home of the helots of our modern Greeks? Or will a
race-conscious and partly civilised Africa assert its power
against a divided, exhausted and decadent European race
and establish itself upon the southern shores of Europe,
as during the past three centuries Europeans have established
themselves on the northern shores of Africa?

The Mediterranean basin has one supreme lure for land-
hungry, power-hungry or sun-hungry races. It is one of
the few regions of the globe equally habitable by white
men, yellow men and blacks. Its coasts are warm, fertile
and on the whole sparsely inhabited. Its waters swarm
with edible fish. Its shores are almost entirely free from
venomous reptiles, or dangerous fevers. It is free from
fog, rain and snow, and therefore offers almost all the year
round ideal conditions for aircraft. Its harbours are deep
and frequent, its waters generally calm and almost tideless,
its natural refuges for seaplanes and submarines many.
The race which dominates Europe or Africa during the
centuries to come, whether it be black or white or yellow,
cannot fail to establish its centres of government and its
seats of power on the shores of this great inland sea.

At the moment all the signs seem to predict that the
dominant power will be white. It will not necessarily be
of Latin origin. Three thousand years ago the Mediterranean was invaded by migratory peoples from the North.
A second Nordic invasion is well within the bounds of
possibility. The Nazi masters of Germany have for the

first time in European history demanded power and sovereignty in terms of race. The rapid expansion of Hitler's Third Reich outside the political bounds of Germany indicates the nature and the scope of the peril. The effective diplomatic subjugation of Austria achieved in July, 1936, has already extended the racial domain of the Germans from the North Sea and the Baltic to the shores of the Adriatic. The economic penetration by Germany of the Balkan peninsula, described in earlier chapters of this work, threatens to bring the Nordic dream to fulfilment up to the very edges of the Eastern Mediterranean. During the next twenty years doubtless the German drive to the south and to the east will be halted by Fascist Italy, intent on the realisation of her own imperial ambitions in Europe and Africa. But there are a hundred millions of Germanic people in Europe, and barely 45 million Italians. The two races are equally prolific, but the Nordics have far too great a start. The advantages of industrial science, military power, material wealth and far-reaching and long-sighted ambition are with the Nazis rather than the Fascists, the Nordics than the Latins.

[3]

There is a further consideration. The Nordic peoples have reached racial maturity, national consciousness, political development and scientific advancement by a slow process extending over twenty centuries. They have emerged from their swamps and forests, rock-bound or marshy coasts and icy seas by great efforts and bitter struggles. They have conquered the advantages of material civilisation, have accumulated vast wealth—if incidentally they have not overcome material poverty. But they have not succeeded in conquering one harsh and inalienable enemy—the climate. They have failed to harness the sun.

Every great civilisation in the past, as it reaches the period of splendour which precedes its decay and ultimate decline, has manifested some form or other of sun-consciousness. It is apparent in the history of religions, manners and clothes. As the barbarian exchanged his skins and furs for woven or spun garments of wool or silk he grew sensitive to climatic conditions. The transition from the fortified castles and iron armour of mediæval times to the stone and stucco houses and silk brocades and satins of the Renaissance brought with it in Northern Europe a greater sensitiveness to cold and a greater appreciation of the sun. In modern Europe, as in modern America, the wealthy, leisured and powerful classes have fled from the factories and chills of their harsh industrial north to build great white pleasure cities in the warm south. In Europe the Germanic peoples in particular have responded with an almost neurotic eagerness to the solar attraction. The Kaiser led his subjects in the race to the south with a villa on Corfu. Before and after the war they filled the villas of the Italian and Adriatic coasts. The cult of nudism was an unmistakable post-war manifestation of the same urge. Since the advent of Hitler political or racial refugees from Nazism have established large colonies of sun-worshippers in Southern France, in Capri and Corfu, in the Balearics and on the Mediterranean coast of Spain. Social or political factors have doubtless encouraged this general North European migration to the south, but at the bottom there is a racial instinct deeper and stronger than any other : a race memory possibly of that ancient impulse which thirty centuries ago drove other Nordic peoples to found colonies in Greece and Macedon and to vanquish the Minoan dynasty in Crete.

The wheel may still come full circle. The Mediterranean may again be the scene of a great civilisation as powerful and as pervasive as the Egyptian, the Sumerian or the Aztec, the centre of the power, pleasure and learning of a white race which has subdued all the other white races in Europe, and which seeks to revive or to surpass the antique splendour of the cities of the sun. At the dawn of the industrial age the northern regions of Europe possessed advantages over the south which far outweighed their natural and climatic deficiencies. They had a practical monopoly of coal and iron. Iron meant wealth. Coal meant carrying power. The nation that possessed both in natural contiguity and in adequate quantities could assert political and economic hegemony over the other nations, and could achieve the mastery of the seas. The North was frozen, but in its frost-bound earth and under its chilly fogs lay the mineral wealth which created the Industrial Revolution and laid the foundations of the British Empire. For two centuries the North struggled with the South in a rivalry at once political and economic, at once spiritual and material. Then the Mediterranean empire of Charles V and Philip II and Philip III collapsed, and the supremacy in Europe passed to the North—to the Protestant and trading countries of England and Holland and Sweden. During the next two centuries the rising industrial power of England gave her the mastery of the world, and that mastery was not challenged until the second decade of the twentieth century, in a war which left her weakened but still triumphant.

[4]

But the age of coal and iron is over. The key to ocean power is no longer coal but oil. The key to economic power is no longer coal but electricity. In modern steel iron is but one of many components—most of which are derived from sources outside Northern Europe. In the production of electricity for industrial and motive power Southern Europe no longer depends upon Northern coal. It has successfully tapped the waters of the Alps and the Dolomites and drawn power from the bleakest mountain valley, the torrent and the avalanche. Spain, Italy, Switzerland, Southern France, Austria and the Balkans are now lighted and power-driven by great chains of hydro-electric plants. Industry as well as shipping in Southern Europe is becoming independent of the partly-exhausted coal deposits of the North.

Nevertheless the Super-State of the future pre-supposes the domination by one power equally of Northern and Southern Europe. The North would probably continue to contain the great industrial centres of Europe. The seats of power, the cities of pleasure, relaxation and games, the schools of science and learning, might be created under the mild and beneficent skies of the South. Future centuries are not likely to see maintained the present political or military objections to the administration of all Europe from a single city. The problem of swift transport has been solved by aviation. The problem of government and control, of the rapid communication of imperial decrees, has been solved by radio broadcasting and television. The masters of the Europe of A.D. 2500—white or black or yellow—may rule their great domain from shining towers on the Mediterranean coast as tranquilly as the Emperor Tiberius from his villa on Capri. And from their windows they will look out over the same ancient and dangerous sea.

THE END

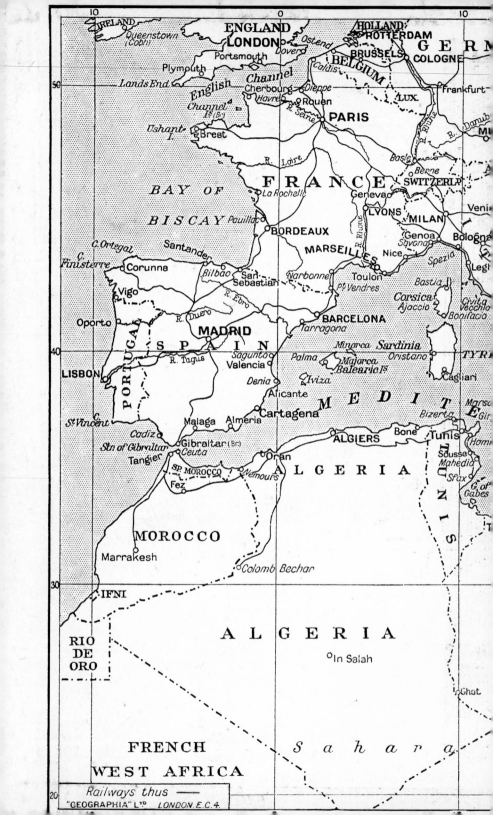